FOR YOU AND Y

D1390986

Speaking out for a better future

Doug

Epigraphs

…these youth workers are a great potential force for change…. (Bill Hickey, 1971, *The youth movement in Britain 1780-1971*)

…any solution which excludes political action is merely cosmetic. (David Marsland, 1979, *Coming of age*)

It did not include the exploration of ideas or skills that could liberate the young from their lowly stations in life. Such liberation, in our view, is virtually impossible within our political system. (Sidney Bunt and Ron Gargrave, 1980, *The politics of youth clubs*)

…they make unlawful Conventicles and Confederacies, they hold and exercise schools, they make and write books, and they do wickedly instruct and inform people, and as much as they may excite and stir them to sedition and insurrection. (*Statutes of the Realm*, 1401, an Act demanding the burning of heretics, in this case the Lollards, an early radical sect who believed in the power of enlightening ordinary people with the Bible translated for the first time into English)

You've had your anti communist fun, and you are pardoned for it – time to get serious again! (Slavoj Zizek, 2010, *First as tragedy, then as farce*)

We do not lack communication, on the contrary we have too much of it. We lack creation. We lack resistance to the present. (Gilles Deleuze and Felix Guattari, 2004, *A thousand plateaus, capitalism and schizophrenia*)

The market doth not serve to look on minds,
'Tis money makes the way with everything;
Coin alters natures in a thousand kinds,
And makes a beggar think himself a king,
The carter whistle and the cobbler sing:
Money, oh God, it carries such a grace
That it dare meet the devil in the face. (Nicholas Brecon,
1600, *Pasquil's madcap*)

Contents

List of abbreviations   x

Acknowledgements   xi

Introduction   1

Part I: Recognition

1   What youth workers do   11

Part II: Political/economic contexts

2   Youth workers and neoliberalism   47

Part III: Political realities

3   Youth workers as workers   87

4   Youth workers as professionals   103

5   Youth workers as trade unionists   111

6   Youth workers as socialists   121

7   Youth workers and the state   133

Part IV: Professional demands

8   Youth workers in defence of youth work   147

9   Youth workers as negative activists   157

10   Youth workers as reflective, analytical practitioners   169

11   Youth workers as leaders   177

Part V: Future considerations

12   Youth work and inequality   183

13   Youth in a suspect society   203

14   New youth workers and new youth work   215

References and further reading   237

Index   261

List of abbreviations

CCTV	closed circuit television
CHYPS	Confederation of Heads of Young People's Services
CWDC	Children's Workforce Development Council
CYWU	Community and Youth Workers' Union
DENI	Department of Education Northern Ireland
EU	European Union
GDP	gross domestic product
IYSS	Integrated Youth Support Services
JNC	Joint Negotiating Committee (for Youth and Community Workers)
LGA	Local Government Association
NAFTA	North Atlantic Free Trade Assocaition
NAYCEO	National Association of Youth and Community Education Officers
NCVYS	National Council for Voluntary Youth Services
NEET	not in education employment or training
NVQ	national vocational qualification
NYA	National Youth Agency
PYO	principal youth officer
TUC	Trades Union Congress
WLGA	Welsh Local Government Association

Acknowledgments

I am honoured that Shelley and her family were pleased that a book would be written in her memory. Shelley's words to me two days before she passed away were that it was a "lovely gesture". That was inspiration enough. In the Community and Youth Workers' Union (CYWU/Unite), my comrades' support has been, as usual, appreciated far more than I show. It is also a tremendous responsibility because I do cover some sensitive and controversial ground and do not want my great big boots to splash mud on others.

I am grateful to Kev Henman, one of Shelley's closest friends, comrades and colleagues and long-standing editor of *Rapport*, the national journal of CYWU/Unite, who commented with his customary insight. So too did two other great youth work practitioners from the South West and wonderful trade unionists Dave Ireland, a Cockney from Cornwall and Kevin Sweeney a Glaswegian from Wiltshire. Lucky they didn't dictate their comments, however. Graham Griffiths, with beard and pipe, of Bradford Community College, and Carolyn Lowry, with her 'wa wa' twang from Belfast, two of the greats of youth work, also generously made their critical contributions. I thank them for their frank and helpful comments and their swift attention to detail in a compressed timescale in the leave season.

Les Elliott, one of the greatest socialists I ever met, was an extremely mild mannered, unassuming and highly effective trades union official in the former Engineers' Union. To my knowledge, apart from his own regular reports on his work to his members, he only wrote one document. This was on the nature of communist leadership. I have adapted his highly profound short note on this in Chapter 11.

During the course of writing this book I have also been thinking about the advances in critical pedagogy made by a relatively small group of academic writers in Britain and North America. I can only hope that some of their work has rubbed off. I am thinking of Pat Ainley, Paula Allman, Henry Giroux, David Hill, Peter McLaren,

Glen Rikowsky and Ira Shore (see the References and further reading at the end of this book). With the exception of Pat Ainley, their knowledge of youth and community work in Britain is very limited, yet I believe that their theoretical work should be used to infuse a new, more transformative practice. The implications of their work have an impact far beyond the debate about teaching in the classroom.

Youth work training sways periodically between an emphasis on learning theory and sociology. Reactionaries have always criticised the leaning towards the latter. In recent times there has been a danger that youth work could stagnate in a hinterland between the two and take on a psychological emphasis as an alternative mode. This has led to a susceptibility to behaviour management and leisure activities devoid of social aspiration or awareness. Some contemporary sociologists and thinkers and a geographer could usefully find their way onto training course curricula to politicise things again. I am thinking particularly of Zygmunt Bauman, Danny Dorling, Alain Finkielkraut, Jurgen Habermas, Jacques Rancierre, Richard Sennett, Richard Wilkinson and Slavoj Zizec. I have found it useful to touch on their works here and very stimulating to read them over the period of writing this book. Their works, I believe, need further alignment in relation to the sociology of youth which has been best informed by those with youth work knowledge (see, in particular, Williamson and Williamson, 1981, 1995, 2004, 2008; Furlong and Cartmel, 2006; Furlong, 2009).

My son Paul is a terrific architect and designer (see www.pauldnicholls.com) and I thank him for introducing me to the beautiful sculptural creations of Sarah Sze (www.sarahsze.com) that influenced the way I thought about constructing this book, and I thank him also for creating the cover design from one of his own powerful images that captures for me the history of youth work. From a few lines of origin, to a flowering, to chaos and fragmentation, to a new order that I argue should now emerge.

I produced a paper for CYWU/Unite's Education and Training Committee called 'Reflective analytical practice' which was enriched by the debate of the committee of those attending on the day; thanks to Dave Ireland, Ian Richards, Pat Thornhill, Kerry Jenkins and Richard Harris. An expanded version of this paper appears as Chapter 10.

In relation to questions of power and democracy, I have been very inspired by recent visits to Venezuela and of course greatly moved by the animation of young people in their flagship youth work provision there in the El Sistema music programme. From this powerful youth work example some of the world's materially poorest children create some of the world's most spiritually uplifting and well performed music. They are one of the greatest inspirations. Youth work that aspires to higher things and excellence rather than remedial activity and leisure has always interested me most, and best attracts the description 'youth work'.

The period immediately preceding the writing of this book was associated with the inspiring work of Marie Taylor, CYWU vice chair, and Dave Mathieson, chair of the Local Government section in the union, to shape up a fighting back agenda on public services and with work by Paul Boskett, chair of the CYWU section, to hold an important sitting of the UK Youth Parliament, which I had the pleasure of attending, along with Andy Driver. Andy has been CYWU's youth work convenor and a lifelong champion of the work. Fittingly for a CYWU president, Paul Boskett makes everyone feel special. Andy is a descendant of Robert Kett, one of my heroes and leader of the great revolt of the peasantry that heralded in the modern epoch and crystallised many early socialist demands (Cornwall, 1977; Wood, 2007).

I am grateful most of all to those who put up with me as I disappeared again into cyberspace to try and open up real space for renewed critical dialogue and the assertion of this vitally important thing called youth work. The skill and commitment of youth workers never ceases to amaze me. I am grateful that the best have been so generous to me in allowing me to steal some of our free time for this project.

I am solely responsible for the final text and would not want anyone tarnished by my reputation for angry polemic against really pathetic ideas of which I am increasingly intolerant, in a nice youth-worky sort of way, of course.

Introduction

Shelley Giorgi was a great youth worker, a great trade unionist and a great socialist, and spent her working life in South West England, mainly in Taunton. Sadly she was taken from us far too soon, at the age of 55 on 21 February 2010. Her passing coincided with a period of intense and renewed debate about youth workers and youth work. Shelley was intellectually clear about many of the key ideas that she believed made youth work such a powerful force. She worked to assist youth workers in combining together to make them a group capable of significant social changes. She worked for a working-class, and therefore revolutionary, concept of workers and youth work.

It was evident to me in a period in February 2010, coinciding with Shelley's last days, and as the struggle for youth work hotted up again, that the perennial internal confusions that have bedevilled youth work had somehow been passed on to another generation. I am not sure what or who passed them on – lecturers, our general, undemocratic times, pressures of poverty and inequality? Some say it is the condition of being Thatcher's children, but in my view, this just serves to inflate one prime minister's influence and power.

The repetition of outdated ideas at this moment of danger to youth work means that history could repeat itself, but this time as an awful farce. This is epitomised by the current Coalition government's launch of a stream of what I see as incoherent policies under the banner 'Positive for Youth', at a time when things have never been so negative for young people. Today's generation of young people is the first, certainly since the Second World War, to be facing fewer positive prospects.

The individualism, fragmentation, selfishness and weakness flowing from certain ideas being repeated today will only assist the disintegration of youth work as an educational, emancipatory and democratic practice. Youth work jobs should not be sold for trivial redundancy packages. I therefore decided to write this book as a tribute to Shelley and all those like her, and to advocate that more youth workers should join us, as part of a necessary resistance.

We are able to do this in these times without fear of disembowelment, hanging or imprisonment, but this was not the case for distant ancestors who, in the 15th and 16th centuries, were killed because they believed that the Bible should be translated into English so that the 'merest ploughboy' would be able to understand the word of God and thereby be able to participate in the sublime (King, 2004). They held democratic meetings and Sunday schools to begin the long process of establishing 'a pedagogy of the oppressed' that existed in Britain long before Paulo Freire wrote about it (Kelly, 1992). We should make the best of this current period of relatively benign tolerance. The aggressive responses to young people's rebellions are indeed the signs of new, less tolerant times.

This book is therefore an attempt to bring together the stronger ideas that the majority of leading and organised youth workers have brought to bear on their fragile and vitally important work, although Shelley, of course, cannot be blamed for the polemical way in which I have presented these ideas. She was far more skilled and subtle than I am in presenting her commitment to the one great hypothesis of our time (Badiou, 2010).

The shocks that capitalism has dealt to the economy and previous political commitments to social inclusion and democracy are great, and I believe that we must find a new way forward (Klein, 2001, 2008; Zizek, 2010a). This will involve the normal process of continuity and change, recognising that youth work seriously underestimates its power in this new situation. Youth workers are indeed a powerful transformative force. In fact, they are just the kind of force that society now needs if it is to be genuinely 'big', or, more appropriately, a 'good society'.

Many ideas about youth work seem feeble beside the biggest ever cuts to youth services that are currently being made (in 2012). In the fight to protect youth work and youth services, youth workers must think anew. It is not just cuts that are being faced, but demolition and the loss of the universal right of young people to support and free

–

2

association. With this loss goes the erosion of democratic engagement in the public sphere, in a citizenship based on the needs of a class.

Something clearly new was stirring when the Conservative Party proclaimed in 2010 that it wanted to remove youth work from local authority provision because volunteers and the voluntary sector did it better, when the Children's Workforce Development Council (CWDC) tried to push through a youth professional status assessment scheme that would help destroy professional specialisms such as youth work, when several more cases of intense victimisation of youth workers for doing youth work occurred and when, thanks to the efforts of youth workers in the Community, Youth Workers and not-for-profit section of Unite, there was finally agreement with the other Joint Negotiating Committee (JNC) unions to a joint statement on the importance of youth work. By November 2010 a special inquiry – a first – into services for young people by the Parliamentary Education Select Committee had been announced, a special Westminster Hall Debate on the Youth Service had been held, and an Early Day Motion had been tabled. There was some real urgency in the air within a period of just six months.

This was sustained as the Choose Youth campaign developed in a great defence of youth work and youth services throughout 2011. The government was forced to backtrack on some elements of its worst proposals and some local authorities were forced to reduce cuts to youth services. In fact, the combined effect of public campaigning for youth services and parliamentary concerns meant that in 2011 youth services achieved their highest ever public profile, demonstrating a popularity with the public matched only by an unpopularity with Tory councillors and Members of Parliament (MPs).

Some three months after Shelley's death, the political landscape in Britain fundamentally changed. It was no longer business as usual. A new government emerged with a policy of wiping out what remained of public services and public service trade unionism. It declared an all-out offensive on pay, pensions, jobs, welfare and trade union legislation. By March 2011 it had generated the largest trade union demonstration in recent history, and by November 2011,

–

3

the largest strike action since 1926. From problems caused by New Labour with the integration of youth services, we moved rapidly to a new set of problems caused by the new Coalition government. This book has therefore been written in the midst of the struggle for youth work, with whole service closures and mass redundancies being announced more or less every week and the construction of complex legal challenges and broad coalitions of public resistance.

It was a very British form of Blitzkrieg that set upon youth workers with the May 2010 General Election. It was the kind of genteel shock doctrine that British capitalists have been so good at. We are, after all, the only country perhaps that could have three polite inquiries into the illegal war on Iraq and somehow manage to avoid any prison sentences. Only in Britain could you get an elected dictatorship of this sort ruling with absolutely no mandate to put in place, in only a matter of months, a complete onslaught on the vestiges of the welfare society. The Coalition government has even been able to make slightly whimsical popular heroes of some of their most lethal proponents of austerity and attacks on workers' and trade union rights. *Strictly Come Dancing* made Vincent Cable an almost debonair, suave sort of character. Yet his higher education reforms could seriously undermine the future of youth and community training courses as their funding allocations reduce beyond what youth workers consider reasonable.

The previous Thatcher government played it relatively cautiously: they introduced incremental anti-trade union laws that eventually culminated to nullify lawful trade union action. There was a planned attack on one main union at a time: first steel workers, then miners, then printers and then teachers. Heavy industry was laid to waste and then the utilities were sold off. Compared with Thatcher's sedate times, the barrage unleashed by the Coalition government on every single front is pulverising, resting for its success on the lack of class consciousness and organisation of workers. There is so much to fight against it is not been easy to know where to start to resist effectively.

When Chancellor George Osborne introduced his Emergency Budget in June 2010 he said it was not really about economics, but a way of changing the way in which Britain was 'governed for ever'. In essence this meant using the power of the state to roll back the beneficence of state services, to destroy local government and to transform the voluntary sector into a private sector conveniently placed to take handouts from 'philanthro-capitalists' keen to do tax fiddles by helping the 'deserving poor'. It quickly also became a plan to break up the National Health Service (NHS) and throw more of education to the market through school academies, while transforming higher education into the privilege of the rich anxious to study real subjects like law and engineering and to avoid the awkward questioning and social and cultural examination that goes on in the humanities. Universities were rapidly transformed from places of learning to businesses.

The Parliamentary Constituencies Bill was subsequently designed to make it near impossible for a non-Conservative Party to win a parliamentary majority. We have started to see the emergence of the very British equivalent of the thousand-year Reich.

This constitutes an ideological attack wrapped up in economic clothing, and its immediate effect has been to politicise the young in ways that endless organisational speeches and motions have not been able to do for 25 years. The sleeping giant has started to rouse, led by university and school students and many users of youth services. Some youth workers have been left behind, some were at the forefront, new faces have emerged, old faces have re-emerged. What has been heartening all round, from the unprecedented marches in far-off rural areas to defend youth work to the unprecedented occupation of the City of London and St Paul's Cathedral, has been the sudden and deep politicisation of a younger generation.

Against the mantra that the country was 'bust' and had to 'tighten its belt' until it nearly strangled itself to death, came new, eloquent voices demonstrating that better ways of doing things were possible and challenging the very root and branch of capitalist social organisation.

The foundations of the Youth Service were laid in the early 1960s when the national debt was much higher than today. Even in capitalist terms, a programme of spending to build and to create public services remained open. Chasing huge unpaid corporation taxes, taxing financial transactions and stopping madcap privatisations would make all the cuts unnecessary. In anticipation of this kind of alternative based on proper tax collection, the government caused huge disruption in the Inland Revenue by seeking to privatise it quickly.

It has rapidly become clear that the Youth Service is facing demolition, as is the post-war welfare society and social democratic consensus. And so scared has the Coalition government been of young peoples' anger, they have started to 'kettle' and punish students. A 12-year-old was pulled out of class without his parents' knowledge by Special Branch and questioned about forthcoming demonstrations that he was involved in against Youth Service cuts in David Cameron's constituency.

Despite the onslaught, at one well attended youth workers' conference in July 2010 the horror on the majority's faces when someone suggested that youth workers needed to get more politicised again created a memorable picture. By October 2010 the story was different. Community and Youth Workers in Unite (CYWU) Section Branches gathered in Eastbourne to express a new resolve to fight alongside the upsurge of activity from students and young people generally. In November the Federation of Detached Youth Workers conference intently debated Brian Belton's proposition that Che Guevara's work on guerrilla warfare was the most illuminating to describe youth work practice in Britain. Town halls were being occupied in protests against Youth Service cuts. By December 2010, when CYWU Section Branches met again in a crisis conference, the biggest ever coalition of forces to resist the youth cuts was being formed by the union. February 2011 was the chosen time for the largest ever representative rally on the Youth Service. It was a fitting anniversary to Shelley's passing. This was followed by the largest and most effective Youth Service lobby of parliament.

If you want to see your way across a track on Dartmoor in the middle of the night during a hurricane you would not light a candle.

Shelley, and those like her, who unionised and joined the long tradition of women workers from the voluntary sector building a union for youth workers, held much more effective and illuminating arc lights against the icy storms that surround us in these dark times.

This book is my account of some of the key features of the ideas that will best enable us to see a way ahead. They have been generated in a collective debate. It is a debate that most contemporary historians of modern Britain ignore. Even Andrew Marr only mentions teddy boys (but not skinheads), and doesn't once refer to youth or the Youth Service in his widely read book on British history (Marr, 2007). This book aspires to inform a general reader and academics from other disciplines a little more about the importance and history of youth work. The fact that a trade union has been so significant to this history is an interesting feature that few perhaps appreciate. It is a challenge to currents of thought that conceptualise unions as uselessly incorporated parts of the state and automatic forces of reaction. It challenges those who think that doing the work itself is more important than self-organisation and professional integrity and dignity at work, and it is a challenge to those who associate unions with something militant and inappropriate or outdated.

In very general terms, youth workers have not sufficiently seen themselves as workers, trade unionists or professionals, and I seek to challenge the ideas that have hindered the recognition of these vital areas of self-awareness and the action that follows from them.

In this book I try to set a new consciousness of these matters in the context of a history of youth workers' organisation and the new political economy and culture that we inhabit. I add an indication of the very acute problems of youth policy and the social condition of young people. I then consider some areas of professional practice that I believe must be sharpened up in order to meet the new challenges that also require a greater internationalist perspective.

We have built a profession that uniquely opposes elitism and despair, social injustices, inequality and exploitation, and all forms of oppression and discrimination. But we need to get better at opposing these things as the new demolition squad in parliament

–

sizes us up for a dose of Dr Smiles who believed that no welfare or public services were necessary because Heaven helped those who helped themselves.

I have listed a number of books in the 'References and further reading' section, which have sometimes been ignored, sometimes suppressed and sometimes are not widely known in youth and community spheres that I hope more youth workers will find useful.

Feedback is always welcome.

PART I
RECOGNITION

1

What youth workers do

Changing things through professional practice alone is insufficient; significant changes for youth work have arisen from youth workers' own self-organisation. In Ireland, Scotland and Wales, youth work has been recognised as an important aspect of education, but it is recognised less so in England, particularly since the creation of the new Integrated Youth Support Services (IYSS), where the social care, or even worse, reactionary, social pedagogy models have dominated. Paradoxically, however, in 2011 some improved recognition, in rhetorical terms at least, of youth work's educational value in England was asserted. In this chapter I look at some official governmental definitions and legal underpinnings of youth work in the UK and Ireland, and reflect on their origin and resonance and relevance. These government definitions and legal underpinnings represent another aspect of what youth workers have achieved: they have defined, campaigned for and managed to get governments to recognise their work.

Youth workers educate and support young people and amplify their voice. It is the combination of these three intended impacts that makes their work unique. The three threads cannot be unwoven; if they are, it is not youth work. Youth workers are on young people's side for the purpose of emancipating their minds and altering the social constraints on them.

There is a fourth element strongly implied by the notion of gaining a voice for young people, 'speaking truth to power' and debating power relationships, and that is, of course, that no educator can give someone a voice, they can only facilitate, encourage and nurture it in a freely chosen relationship. Youth workers are therefore informal educators in the traditions of social and cultural education outlined particularly at an international level by Paulo Freire and Antonio Gramsci, and domestically by a range of authors, from Josephine Macalister Brew to Janet Batsleer, Bernard Davis, Kate Sapin and Mark Smith.

You can educate in order to create acceptance of the status quo and the world as it is, or you can educate for change. Change is a neutral concept. Much can appear to happen, but not much may go on, or actually change. It is an automatic consequence of any educative process, but educational change is not necessarily structural change to the conditions that create ignorance and poverty in the first place. It is therefore the purpose of youth work to move from individual and group transformation through education to social change in action. This action must remove power from oppressive forces and attain it for the oppressed.

Education

Youth workers educate for change for a variety of reasons and personal and professional motivations. This book argues that the change they must educate for is a more profound form of emancipatory transformation than has previously been dominant in youth work so far. It has to become a more social, political and economic change that is sought in their practice and self-organisation. In raising aspirations they should never deride, underestimate or forget what has been achieved through various strands of youth work practice in the past. Youth workers must have an understanding of what went before in order to understand where they are going; foundations must be built on, not denigrated and demolished.

Youth workers have defined youth work, managed to campaign to get the state to adopt its key principles and purpose and to defend it when the state ignores its commitments. They have struggled hard to get the state to legislate and fund in its favour to get it to pursue progressive youth policies and to get the media to promote more positive images of young people. They even managed to get the newly elected Conservative chair of the Parliamentary Education Select Committee, amidst the most appalling budget in history, to recognise that his committee should consider 'informal education' and 'youth services' within its deliberations throughout 2010. His committee then went on in 2011, in a most unprecedented way, to strongly criticise the government when it failed to respond properly to many of their more progressive recommendations.

The state has been compelled in part to appreciate the power of youth work as being integral to education. This has been as a result of struggle and the articulate influence of youth workers. But state legislation has not guaranteed progress. In fact, progressive state legislation has been more honoured in the breach, and the rhetorical comfort given by having useful governmental approval and even firm legislation has often preceded neglect, cuts in services and distortions of the work. Perhaps the very positive Youth Work Act (2001) in the Republic of Ireland is the best example of good words followed by little action and hardly any money. In the history of the struggle for youth work the state has frequently used sympathetic rhetoric as a form of appeasement, then dashed hopes on the rocks of empty coffers.

It is useful to remind ourselves at the outset how youth work is officially seen. Official statements approved by governments and local government bodies should not be ignored as they do provide a substantial basis for a better recognition by society of what youth workers do. Such definitions should not be simply rejected as attempts at state appropriation or empty rhetoric, even if that is their apparent position and sometimes their historic effect. There are contradictions in everything. The impetus to create them was a positive one.

Wales and the idea of extending entitlement

As the Welsh Local Government Association (WLGA) says, 'Youth work involves a broad range of activities, concerned with education

---

13

in its widest sense. Youth work is concerned with the education and development, both social and personal, of young people aged between eleven and 25 years, particularly those aged 13 to 19 years' (WLGA, 2010). This, in turn, reflects the underpinning statement for youth work in Wales, *Extending entitlement* (National Assembly for Wales, 2001, p 5), which outlines the key tasks of youth work as follows:

> ... to enthuse young people to seize opportunities for learning:
>
> - by demonstrating that this will help them get jobs and progress in employment
> - ensuring that all the services on offer to young people are of high quality, matched to their interests and aptitudes, and
> - promoting equal opportunities in order to ensure that all young people are able to take advantage of all that is on offer.

Learning, of course, does not guarantee jobs, as thousands of graduates are now finding out, and the purpose of youth work is not to fuel the labour market. Nor are youth workers employed to convince young people that skills acquisition alone will secure happy employment for life. For the first youth workers, enthusing young girls to work in sweat shops for 16 hours a day was difficult, just as it is today, enthusing young workers to serve up fast food fries for a 10-hour shift. In the culture in which we now live there are many jobs requiring no education, and there is much education that does not lead to jobs, and many communities and groups of young people endure a kind of itinerant, casualised, joblessness within the prison of their own estates and alternative economies (Williamson, 2004).

We have other dilemmas, too – young people feel over-tested yet under-educated; they exit education often over-qualified but end up under-employed (Ainley and Allen, 2010). There are also great imbalances in the labour market (although five million citizens of working age are not employed). Graduates exit university to the dole, or perhaps soulless, low-paid jobs. And once in work there is a real problem of work–life balance, and young people's leisure time in which youth work is supposed to operate is often very limited, or saturated by the intrusion of individualised, frequently violent and competitive computer games and other distractions.

Youth work can give some respite and alternative to these dilemmas in the informal education sphere, but it cannot clinch jobs for tens of thousands of young people, let alone the more than a million unemployed. The Youth Service is not a careers service; it is not a direct employer of the young. It does improve employability, however. Communication skills and adaptability are not just required by a de-skilled flexible, capitalist labour market; they are aptitudes that are generally useful within critical thinking and useful labour in a socialist alternative future. If young people are unable to think critically and feel valued in useful labour, they are more likely to be manipulated and exploited in the labour market.

A socialist society needs workers with skills and enthusiasm for the application of technique and inventiveness in useful social labour as opposed to the useless toil of so many jobs within capitalism (Morris, 1986). Some argue that the health service merely benefits the demand of capitalism for relatively healthy workers, ignoring the fact that if you are a worker and break your leg it is quite nice to have it fixed so you can jump around with your friends as soon as possible outside of work, on the squash court perhaps. A job is a job for many purposes, and exists within a different context within capitalism and socialism. Seizing opportunities for learning is a fundamental right and should be asserted. It assists the liberation from the docile position that capitalism requires all workers to adopt.

Full employment is a basic right, whether within or outside of a capitalist system. Young people should not be unemployed and do not want to be, and youth workers should never reject the issue of unemployment, or the need to assist young people, where they are requested to do so, to get jobs and enjoy employment. It is not quite clear if governments see it this way. For example, *Extending entitlement* (National Assembly for Wales, 2001, p 5) is one of the most comprehensive governmental statements on young people and the role of youth work. It states:

> There are strong links between the health and social welfare of young people and their capacity to achieve, develop skills and contribute through work and as citizens and parents. To achieve the vision of a more prosperous and fairer Wales we need to do a better job in ensuring that all young people have access to the support they need to make a success of their lives.
>
> For most young people this support is provided mainly by home, family, friends and school. But where this support is lacking society has a responsibility to fill the gap – if it does not it will both fail the young person and lead to much higher costs on public services later. The model suggested by many who work with young people is that we should do more to strengthen the fences that prevent people from falling over the cliff – rather than providing more ambulances and police vans when they do. Young people who need extra support should not be stigmatised – many young people from stable families encounter problems and all young people need access to challenges and opportunities beyond their home and community. (p 5)

As discussed later in *Extending entitlement*, support for young people does not mean counselling and guidance services alone. It is closely linked with providing opportunities for achievement and is offered through a wide range of services including education and training, local authority youth work, the very diverse voluntary youth sector, arts, sports and leisure opportunities, and specialist provision for, for example, homeless young people or young offenders:

The contribution of the voluntary sector is recognised as a key partner in the network which already exists and which needs to be developed. The voluntary youth work sector in Wales, through both national organisations and local groups, has a long tradition of work with young people, based on strong commitment and values, together with great diversity and flexibility. It has often provided essential support to young people where no statutory services have been available. It is crucial to build on and support this tradition in developing and strengthening the wider response to the needs of young people in Wales. (National Assembly for Wales, 2001, p 6)

Having provided a socially aware context, the document can base itself firmly in a rights-based approach to the development of youth work. *Extending entitlement* says:

... young people want respect and understanding – and many feel stereotyped and demonised by adults

– young people want to be consulted and taken seriously – and often feel patronised or ignored by politicians and others in authority

– young people greatly value accessible and affordable places to meet each other and often feel unwelcome in commercial or community venues

– young people share the same aspirations as other people: to have a job, a home, a relationship and security

– young people share many of the same concerns as others in their community – eg for the viability of rural communities and for the safety and future prosperity of deprived urban areas. (National Assembly for Wales, 2001, p 28)

In exercising these rights young people have an entitlement to association with a youth service that is educational and striving to inspire them within the framework of lifelong learning and the notion of enjoyment and the pleasure of informal learning for its own sake. It recognises that youth work:

– supports other agencies in developing styles of work which are effective with young people

– enables young people to have a voice and influence in the services provided for them and in wider policy developments

– aims to provide a bridge between young people's priorities and the aspirations of public policy. (National Assembly for Wales, 2001, p 44)

It then goes on to appreciate what has already been achieved on a shoestring budget:

Youth services work with young people in many different ways to promote lifelong learning, employability, citizenship and healthy lifestyles. They engage with young people as individuals with the object of building their capacity to make choices and pursue constructive paths. A key principle is that young people choose to participate and are able to do so in ways that build on their interests.

One of the strengths of the youth work sector is its diversity of process, offering choice to young people to participate and achieve in different ways through provision with different styles. (National Assembly for Wales, 2001, p 44)

Such diversity of provision itself reflects the multiplicity of needs and rights that young people have, and youth work is especially important to any progressive education agenda because it expresses the overall rights of participation of young people:

… it respects young people and places them at the centre – it views them as individuals not as problems and creates opportunities for them to contribute to the management and delivery of services

– it is inclusive and preventative – it starts from the premise that all young people should be able to access the advice and support they need when they need it

– it offers support not in a stigmatising way but as part of a service geared to enjoyment, challenge and opportunity

– it values young people and encourages them to think of themselves as contributing individuals with rights and responsibilities to others. (National Assembly for Wales, 2001, p 45)

In other words, what youth workers do is express a right that society believes should be enacted for all young people so they can be purposefully engaged, educated and participating in that which does them and others good. This should not be derided as a liberal democratic and conformist development. As I seek to argue in this book, this is a contradictory phenomenon, but in the main, compared to where the powers of capital seem to want to take us today, it is a very important and progressive development, a collectivist, positive public service commitment. Without its utterance we would be further behind. Without our commitment to the rights of young people at a time when they are being abandoned, the situation would be much worse as rights are eroded and the condition of youth is made totally uncertain and disposable (Bauman, 2003b; Bunyan, 2009; Furlong, 2009).

Northern Ireland

The Department of Education Northern Ireland (DENI) unsurprisingly sees youth work as a vital part of education:

The Youth Service exists to support and encourage young people to mature and reach their potential as valued individuals and responsible citizens. It is educational in the sense that it provides a social education within the context of a broad spectrum of diverse activity. The policy aim of the Youth Service is:

to ensure the provision of opportunities for children, young people and young adults to gain for themselves knowledge, skills and experience to reach their full potential as valued individuals;

to encourage the development of mutual understanding and promote recognition of and respect for cultural diversity.

Participation by young people in the Youth Service is voluntary, and activities which are firmly rooted in a social education ethos, are generally out of school or work time and non formal. (DENI, 2005, p 1)

The work of youth workers in Northern Ireland through the most extraordinary of times rested on the first statutory underpinning of the Youth Service made in the Local Government Act 1972. This was consolidated and confirmed in the Education and Libraries (Northern Ireland) Order 1986 (No 594 [N13]), and a Youth Council was set up to support the service in the Youth Service (Northern Ireland) Order 1989 (No 2413 [N122]). Union campaigning in 2009 ensured that the service was not also fragmented into the district councils. The recognition of the role of youth workers in some of the most troubled communities was a testament to the role played by youth work practitioners from all parts of the community, and their work played a much underestimated role in the peace and reconciliation that gradually emerged in Northern Ireland.

Indeed, even a recent study (McAlister et al, 2009) showed the extreme popularity of youth work from both sides of the Northern Ireland community, and how young people consistently expressed the view that of those adults with whom they had regular contact, they felt most respected by youth workers. This simple social provision of respect and non-judgemental validation that is so skilfully expressed by the best youth workers is a much underestimated element of the youth work approach. As society fragments and individualises further (Bauman, 2001a, 2010; Sennett, 1999, 2006), youth work is increasingly key in a range of communities where young people's identities are turned from social and communal spheres to other more tribal and instinctive areas (Pitts, 2007a).

Personal and social development endorsed

Another piece of progressive youth work legislation was passed in the Republic of Ireland in 2001. The Youth Work Act straightforwardly defines youth work in this now universally accepted way: '"youth work" means a planned programme of education designed for the purpose of aiding and enhancing the personal and social development of young persons through their voluntary participation which is complementary to their formal, academic or vocational education and training' (Irish Statute Book, 2001, p 1).

This roots youth work in education and is based clearly on the voluntary principle of engagement and the recognition of the importance of personal and social development. How youth work is 'complementary' is not quite clear, but the point is made perhaps that it exists within a range of educational approaches and fulfils needs other than those addressed by formal, academic and vocational training. In other words, it must be informal, non-academic and non-vocational. The implication is that it is pleasurable in the terms defined by young people themselves and that is absolutely fine, surely? In fact that seems to be the nub of it. We have defined a service that young people enjoy and shape.

While moves to legislate in youth work's favour have been developing at a snail's pace and only emerged relatively recently in the history of the service, the state has also sought to take more of an interest in the mechanics of what workers do at work. In broad terms, attempts have been made to define the 'competences' that determine a particular job or profession. In some areas these have been welcome and novel and in others, reactionary and unwelcome. Youth workers were deeply critical of the original form of National Vocational Qualifications (NVQs) that unrepresentative bodies sought to foist on them (Norton, 1994). Having rejected the worst attempts to stifle the creativity of the work and redefine it in competence-based tick boxes, youth workers were eventually successful in getting a set of occupational standards in place which provide a good base for self-definition and protection of the work. These fit into any legislative utterances so far adopted by governments as well as relating to the progressive values developed by youth workers themselves (Lifelong Learning UK, 2009).

Community learning and development

In Scotland a comprehensive consultative process and analysis of youth work by the Scottish Executive led to the following perceptions and promotion:

> Youth work has a significant role to play in delivering our broad vision for Scotland's young people – that they are nurtured, safe, active, healthy, achieving, included, respected and responsible. Youth work opportunities can also support young people to live their lives as confident individuals, effective contributors, successful learners and responsible citizens.
>
> We believe that all young people can be like this. But we also recognise that young people are individuals with different needs, abilities and learning preferences. Youth work opportunities can enhance the life of any young person but, for some, youth work will have a more important or even critical role in enabling them to see and fulfil their true potential.
>
> Youth work has a major part to play in providing life-enhancing experiences for children and young people – and the learning and development opportunities

it offers must be seen and valued as an integral part of what society provides for young people across the board – children's services, school education, post-school education and training.

We recognise the value of youth work in contributing positively to young people's personal growth and to the growth of the communities they live in. We recognise the value of both:

a: open access youth work activities, open to any young person who wishes to attend, offered by local authorities and voluntary organisations; and

b: specialised targeted provision designed to meet the needs of young people who are particularly vulnerable or who have specific needs.

A vibrant youth work sector needs both. As well as enhancing the lives of young people from all backgrounds, universal youth work opportunities can have an early intervention and prevention role. It can engage in positive activities young people who might otherwise become involved in anti-social behaviour, alcohol or drug misuse, or who would leave school with few qualifications and skills, perhaps not progressing into education, employment or training (entering the 'NEET' group). Universal youth work opportunities can also offer vulnerable young people a non-stigmatising route into finding more specialist support where they might not be ready to go directly, eg to a project for young people with specific problems eg mental health issues.
(Scottish Executive, 2007)

This continued to embed the work in a strong tradition of community development and learning and to value its position as a force for collective improvement at neighbourhood level.

English issues

The National Occupational Standards (NOS), that were agreed following substantial consultation and ideological struggle throughout the profession in the UK, recognise youth work contributes to the broad educational spectrum of lifelong learning. The key purpose of youth work is identified within the NOS as follows: to

> 'Enable young people to develop holistically, working with them to facilitate their personal, social and educational development, to enable them to develop their voice, influence and place in society and to reach their full potential.'

> This statement refers to the holistic development of young people, recognising that personal, social and educational development can also include, for example, physical, political and spiritual development. (Lifelong Learning UK, 2009, p 5)

Most significantly these standards are underpinned by very strong values that are worth highlighting in full:

> These values also illustrate how youth work is involved in the holistic development of young people, and are as follows:

> - Young people choose to be involved, not least because they want to relax, meet friends, make new relationships, to have fun, and to find support,
> - The work starts from where young people are in relation to their own values, views and principles, as well as their own personal and social space,
> - It seeks to go beyond where young people start, to widen their horizons, promote participation and invite social commitment, in particular by encouraging them to be critical and creative in their responses to their experience and the world around them,

- It treats young people with respect, valuing each individual and their differences, and promoting the acceptance and understanding of others, whilst challenging oppressive behaviour and ideas,
- It respects and values individual differences by supporting and strengthening young people's belief in themselves, and their capacity to grow and to change through a supportive group environment,
- It is underpinned by the principles of equity, diversity and interdependence,
- It recognises, respects and is actively responsive to the wider networks of peers, communities, families and cultures which are important to young people, and through these networks seeks to help young people to achieve stronger relationships and collective identities, through the promotion of inclusivity,
- It works in partnership with young people and other agencies which contribute to young people's social, educational and personal development,
- It is concerned with how young people feel, and not just with what they know and can do,
- It is concerned with facilitating and empowering the voice of young people, encouraging and enabling them to influence the environment in which they live,
- It recognises the young person as a partner in a learning process, complementing formal education, promoting their access to learning opportunities which enable them to fulfil their potential,
- It safeguards the welfare of young people, and provides them with a safe environment in which to explore their values, beliefs, ideas and issues. (Lifelong Learning UK, 2009, p 7)

It is important to recognise that these progressive values and standards for the youth work profession throughout the UK have been forged in a democratic debate which itself was shaped by youth workers and on many occasions very substantially influenced by their trade union,

CYWU/Unite. I believe that youth workers have a tendency to see themselves as victims of elaborate conspiracies by an unloving state. This feeling belies the reality of themselves as active determinants of key changes in legislation, policy and professional practice. Youth workers do not just do youth work, they promote it, fight for it and get governments to recognise its importance.

This work to promote youth services has been integral to trade unionism in the sector and would be impossible through the agency of a professional association. Even the early professional associations registered themselves as trade unions (Nicholls, 2009). Youth work is based on a clear and strong set of professional values that substantially expresses a wider societal value, a unique one. In summary, the values upheld are that young people are important and should have a voice and their own social and educational space outside of formal systems. This is a powerful set of values that influences professional practice and political action by youth workers in their defence and application.

At a national conference in February 2010 which promoted the In Defence of Youth Work statement referred to below, CYWU/Unite moved a motion that called for the reinstatement of Youth Work Week, an important, long established week of activities which the National Youth Agency (NYA) had decided to abandon. Six weeks later, this week of events was reinstated, and in 2010 it was held under the banner 'Celebrating youth work'. Furthermore, the conference recognised that the long-standing work of the union to promote firmer statutory provision and resourcing for youth work in England in particular, where legislation is weakest, needed some further promotion. Six weeks later, the NYA circulated a reminder to all local authorities of their statutory duties for youth work (Blacke, 2010).

At a small scale this skirmish reflects the history of youth work. When organised workers have stood up and protested, progress has been made (Nicholls, 2009). This has consistently been the case and is key to understanding the history of youth work.

Legislative underpinning in England

The 2010 circular from the NYA on the Youth Service in England is worth recalling quite extensively as it reveals how the participatory practice of youth work and its role in youth development were managing, with many limitations, to influence legislation. As the NYA circular (Blacke, 2010) points out:

> The legislation also requires that the educational leisure-time activities and associated facilities to which access is to be secured must include sufficient educational leisure-time activities (and facilities for such activities) which are for the improvement of young people's personal and social development. This sub-set of 'educational leisure-time activity' relates to activities which are delivered using youth work methods and approaches (para 19).

> The consequences of failure to deliver the statutory duties under section 507B are set out in the guidance:

> Failure by a local authority to fulfil their statutory duties under section 507B (including their duty under section 507B(12) to have regard to this guidance) could result in intervention by the Secretary of State under sections 496, 497 or 497A of the Education Act 1996.

The circular goes on to highlight how the legislative guidance gives a strong statement of recognition of the role of high quality youth work:

> [T]he Government's view [is] that high quality youth work, delivered by third and statutory sectors, is central to delivering our ambition of increasing the number of young people on the path to success (para 5.52, p 2).

The NYA circular also quite rightly stresses how:

—

The legislation creates new requirements that place young people at the heart of decision making on the positive activity provision available to them (para 5). Supporting and facilitating the engagement of young people in decision making and ensuring their voices are heard and their influence felt is central to youth work approaches and methods.

The local authority will also need to ensure that young people are involved in determining what activities and facilities should be available to them. In particular, local authorities should ensure they ascertain and take into account the views of young people who face significant barriers to participation or are considered to be at risk of poor outcomes such as young people in care; young people from minority groups; and young people with disabilities (para 31).

The legislation specifies that the local authority must ascertain and take account of young people's views on current provisions, the need for new activities and facilities, and barriers to access. As well as dedicated youth provision, the local authority should seek young people's views on leisure centres, libraries and any other activities and facilities which are intended to be accessible to young people and/or the wider community (para 32, p 3).

The traditional role of youth work in social and personal development is then emphasised, with a stress, unsurprisingly, on personal development:

Personal and social development, a benefit of positive activities delivered by youth workers is central to Foundation Learning. This is recognised in the delivery plan: *Raising the participation age: Supporting local areas to deliver* (DCSF, 2009, p 4).

This somewhat weak legislative framework in England is embedded within the Education and Inspections Act 2006 that threw education in schools, including services for young people, onto the market. All services have become subject to contestability, that is, a process of tendering for services on the open market. It is unsurprising that the services in question are confined to a more cumbersome and easily marketable concept of 'positive activities'. The idea of transforming youth work into a provider of 'positive activities' stems from this market-related imperative that the New Labour and new Coalition government both shared. It moulds the shape of youth work into the shape of government neoliberal political priorities. The questioning of negative assumptions and the challenging of prejudice that can be so distinctive of good youth work is not always immediately a positive experience and can be difficult to cope with. The definitions for England give no leeway for ambiguity and complexity in practice. They focus on imposed outcomes. (I challenge this reduced notion of positive activities later in this book – Part IV, Chapter 9).

The legislation in England passed in 1996 and 2006 replaced the Education Act 1944 that required local authorities to provide adequate leisure time activities. Following CYWU's questioning of the adequacy of this legislation in the famous Warwickshire court case, work was done to improve the definition of 'adequate' and the need for sufficient youth service provision to be defined (CYWU, 1994). This was followed tortuously, but eventually, by *Transforming youth work: Resourcing excellent youth services* (DfES, 2002) that established some consensual, but non-statutory benchmarks for identifying levels of youth work provision and staffing and expenditure ratios.

Youth work is educational

The official standard setting agencies and the main local authority and governmental organisations have adopted, by and large, youth work's definition of itself as a part of education. The struggle, as always, however, is how to manage the tendency of the state to appropriate and dilute these values and how to maintain an emancipatory, rather than a conformist, professional and political role in practice. This also depends, of course, on whether the overall youth policy framework is benign or malign. Under its current capitalist form, the state will never legislate for education as a form of liberation. But what there is must not be diminished. Liberating ideas and practices are more likely to emerge from what we have than if we have to start completely from scratch.

There has been further recent consolidation of the values and core elements of youth work. The subject benchmark statement which underpins higher education qualification courses in youth and community work and summarises the most advanced thinking by governments, employers' organisations, trainers and practitioners about the characteristics of the work, concludes that: 'All the definitions and values statements (concerning youth and community work) refer to participation, inclusion, empowerment, partnership and learning as fundamental principles of practice' (QAA, 2009, p 2). This encapsulates the fact that youth work is part of a wider, socially purposive mission that involves a social responsibility to include young people, a concern to empower them and enable them to participate and a recognition that this must be done in equal partnership with them. The kind of education that is youth work is, conclusively, a democratically relevant one. No wonder that the success of the UK Youth Parliament as a democratic voice for young people has been very much a result of the empowering influence of participation-based youth workers throughout the country who have deployed great skills of motivation and facilitation.

There is general consensus, and has been since the 1940s, among the leading providers, trainers and practitioners in youth and community work, in the succinct phrase of the Youth Work Curriculum Statement for Wales, that youth work, 'through its voluntary relationship with young people, offers inclusive opportunities for learning that are educative, expressive, participative and empowering'. Youth work is a unique intervention which seeks to respect the current condition of the young people it engages with and to assist them voluntarily in moving from this condition to an improved one in which greater understanding, skill, awareness, knowledge, fun, emotional pleasure or intellectual, physical or experiential attainment are developed.

The whole human being

Youth work is not just a democratic practice; it is a transformative practice seeking to move beyond the limitations of an initial condition. Its unique privilege, rooted in its voluntary relationship, is the capacity to work with young people across the full complexity of their being. As Bill Barnett, former CYWU President, said in his address to the union's 1967 conference:

> We deal with the most precious commodity in existence – human life – and deal with it at such an impressionable stage in its development, and in such an informal manner, that makes our task therefore unique. (quoted in Barnett, 1967)

Young people as human beings are very complicated, and in their face-to-face exchanges with young people, youth workers have to deploy methods informed by learning and behavioural theory, art, physical development, culture, political and sociological theory. Part of the attack on this work comes from a reduced and limited notion that those working with children and young people should be aware simply of a common core of psychological, developmental characteristics. Attempts to introduce the notion of a common core qualification to the English IYSS are embarrassingly elementary and reactionary, and again they emanate from the lowest common denominator stable of the CWDC, which even the Coalition government recognised was better off dead when it announced its eventual demise in November 2010.

Youth workers do achieve a lot and tend not to advertise it widely. In reality, however, youth work throughout the UK and Ireland has provided pioneering and internationally renowned services within the broad provision of community development and learning. This work has been a partnership in the UK in particular, between local authority education departments and voluntary organisations, and has also been developed independently by the voluntary organisations that originally formed and still play an active part in the JNC, the committee that negotiates pay and conditions and sets standards and service delivery benchmarks. It was recognised that the special educational nature of this work and its importance required separate, free, collective bargaining arrangements linked, in origin, to teaching (Nicholls, 2009).

More youth workers needed

Youth workers work on the front line with young people and adults in every community and most neighbourhoods in the UK and Ireland. Their voluntary relationship with them enables them to have a greatly beneficial influence on their lives. As analysts have constantly shown, this is always the case at times of difficulty. Ravi Chandiramani summed up this reality in a recent Editorial for *Children & Young People Now* called 'Youth work should be in the limelight', in which he states '… it is in economically tough times like now, where many families are under increasing pressures that youth work is needed most' (Chandiramani, 2010, p 3). Any examination of the council leader survey of the impact of the economic downturn on local authorities demonstrates a greater need for youth work to involve and inspire young people (LGA, 2009a).

Local authority associations and voluntary organisations, health trusts and prisons, further education colleges, Ministry of Defence welfare services, charities and funding donors have all increasingly recognised that the skills of youth workers are needed now more than ever. In England, for example, the Local Government Association (LGA) has undertaken substantial focused work on the position of young people during the current economic recession. Its emphasis was on how to engage young people more effectively and how to release their hidden talents in creative ways. In conjunction with the

Centre for Social Justice, three substantial reports have been written. This priority work reflects the fact that '115 out of a total of 150 local area agreements include it [helping disengaged young people] as a priority, more than any other single area for action'.

Finding hidden talents

As this important work unfolded it became clear from the many case studies of successful interventions undertaken that the youth work method within a community development context was especially productive and beneficial. Indeed, there is a focus in the main findings on necessary policy initiatives that can only be fully achieved by the increased deployment and support of youth and community workers. Consider how the three main local principles espoused in *Hidden talents III* (LGA, 2009c) require for their fulfilment the community development and learning skills of youth workers:

> Firstly, a focus on what young people can do including caring, volunteering, community service and informal learning – all of which can act as a stepping stone to or complement to work, formal education and training.
>
> Secondly, it is the responsibility of the young person to undertake meaningful activity, and the responsibility of their family and local community to raise their aspirations, instil positive attitudes, help them access opportunities and encourage achievement.
>
> Thirdly, developing ways of increasing participation should be undertaken with young people, their families and local communities. (LGA, 2009c, p 7)

The same report goes on to recognise the central importance of work to engage young people through the techniques of youth work: 'Locally accredited programmes of informal learning and volunteering should be expanded and included within the definition of meaningful activity' (LGA, 2009c, p 10).

Furthermore, in the Sustainable Communities Act, the LGA recognises that:

> Local democracy, with strengthened powers and resources, is fundamental to building the resilience of local communities. There is a clear need to rebuild trust in democratic institutions and in this, the vital role of strengthened local democratic accountability, so people genuinely experience greater control over their own lives and surroundings, through democratic engagement.... One quarter of people say that they would like to be more involved in the decisions that their council makes which affect their local area. (LGA, 2009d, p 11)

Such civic engagement has long been the central terrain of youth workers.

The impact of youth work is now more widely recognised. As Ofsted said:

> Youth services have a vital role to play in the community. The best services recognise that youth workers are essential to engage young people, including those with more challenging attitudes and behaviour. (Hadley, 2007)

Rising standards of youth work

The standards of youth work are continuing to rise while other services have seen declining standards, crises and tragedies. In 2007 Ofsted revealed that a greater proportion of youth services were judged as good or better in 2005/06 than in previous years (Ofsted, 2006). By 2008 Ofsted was able to report that: 'The proportion of local authority youth services judged adequate or better has risen over the three year period 2005 to 2008.... An increased proportion of services were graded good for young people's achievement through youth work in 2007-8 compared with the previous two years' (Ofsted, 2008). This improvement in standards was matched by evident cost-effectiveness. In recent research undertaken by the NYA for Unite and Lifelong Learning UK, the cost-effectiveness of youth work was highlighted (McKee et al, 2010).

Aiming high for young people (HM Treasury, 2007), the current national policy framework in England, describes an offer for 'positive activities' including youth work for all young people. *The Children's Plan* went further to talk about this as an entitlement. It is estimated that for a mere £350 a year per young person, all young people could access this offer. More specifically, the Joseph Rowntree Foundation commissioned an exercise into the costs of detached youth work. This found that a project providing a full range of services and in contact with 125 young people a week would cost £75,000 a year, or £16 for each contact. It concluded that 'a systematic street-based youth service would cost a small fraction of the amount spent on other services targeted at this group', citing, in particular, the £450 million budget for the Connexions Service (JRF, 2004).

Other research has highlighted the relative costs of the criminal justice system and other forms of intervention, including youth work. The *Every child matters* Green Paper (DfES, 2003) stated that 'society as a whole benefits through reduced spending on problems that can be avoided through maximising the contribution to society of all citizens. For instance a child with a conduct disorder at age 10 will cost the public purse around £70,000 by age 28.' The Audit Commission report into the benefits of sport and leisure activities in preventing anti-social behaviour by young people estimates that a young person in the criminal justice system costs the taxpayer over £200,000 by the age of 16, but one who is given support to stay out costs less than £50,000 (Audit Commission, 2009).

Other comparative costings include: £1,300 per person for an electronically monitored curfew order (*Hansard*, 2008); around £35,000 per year to keep one young person in a young offender institution; an annual average of £3,800 for secondary education (*Hansard*, 2006); and around £9,000 for the average resettlement package per young person after custody (RESET, 2007).

Against these, £350 per year per young person is a small price to pay to unlock the rich benefit of community-based provision for all, and to provide extra opportunities for personal and social development for those young people, who, by virtue of life experience and circumstance, are so disadvantaged they cannot successfully make use of mainstream services.

Furthermore, about a third of the amount spent by local authorities on youth work is raised by youth workers through additional fund raising each year. It is quite clear that investment in youth workers and therefore youth work is a highly cost-effective option in times of austerity, and failing to undertake such investment would be irresponsible.

Compromised

Youth workers have adapted cooperatively and effectively to myriad organisational changes that have resulted from these kinds of governmental statements and legislative developments and as a result of negative forces seeking to organisationally and ideologically undermine their work. These have been significant changes of context and of working patterns. Most youth and community workers now work within multiagency teams, for example, and many new and additional duties and responsibilities have resulted from this. There has also been an increased emphasis on late night, on-call and weekend working, and increased expectations to deliver face-to-face sessions. What education can be achieved at these times of the day is questionable, however, and the role of youth work is potentially being compromised by some of these activities, which are simply that – activities.

The youth work method relies on long-term relationship building. It cannot be easily measured on short-term outcome measurements. Job security for youth and community workers is therefore essential so that they can sustain effective local community relations. This is one simple reason why youth workers must fight for job security and sufficient numbers of youth workers in post.

—

In defence of youth work

At a moment of danger for youth work, when integrated youth service developments have begun to be recognised for what they always would be, a form of disintegration of progressive occupational specialisms, youth workers formed a new campaign. This also has resonance in Wales where the aspirations of *Extending entitlement* looked as though they had been thwarted. The campaign, known as In Defence of Youth Work, produced a document entitled *What we stand for*, which stated:

> Youth Work aspires to a special relationship with young people. It wants to meet young women and men on their terms. It claims to be 'on their side' and to start from their concerns and interests.... Within the present period of political confusion and dismay we want to reaffirm our belief in an emancipatory and democratic Youth Work, whose cornerstones are:

- The sanctity of the voluntary principle; the freedom for young people to enter into and withdraw from Youth Work as they so wish.
- A commitment to conversations with young people which start from their concerns and within which both youth worker and young person are educated and out of which opportunities for new learning and experience can be created.
- The importance of association, of fostering supportive relationships, of encouraging the development of autonomous groups and 'the sharing of a common life'.
- A commitment to valuing and attending to the here-and-now of young people's experience rather than just focusing on 'transitions'.
- An insistence upon a democratic practice within which every effort is made to ensure that young people play the

fullest part in making decisions about anything affecting them.
- The continuing necessity of recognising that young people are not a homogenous group and that issues of class, gender, race, sexuality and disability remain central.
- The essential significance of the youth worker themselves, whose outlook, integrity and autonomy is at the heart of fashioning a serious yet humorous, improvisatory yet rehearsed educational practice with young people.

Our definition is at odds with much that passes for Youth Work today. Successive governments in the neo-liberal era have sought to introduce the norms and values of the market into our work. Attempts have been made to impose the very antithesis of the Youth Work process: predictable and prescribed outcomes. A range of policies push us ever nearer to becoming little more than an agency of behavioural modification. The top-down imposition of an integrated workforce will harm occupational specialisms like Youth Work and damage the responsiveness of services for young people. (IDYW, 2011)

This proved to be a powerful statement, a rallying point for those interested in not just the survival of youth work within a destroyed social democratic context, but in arguing for a new centrality for youth work in a wider transformative programme.

Valuing true youth work

Youth workers campaign to defend what they do and what they do has some significant recognition, far more so than at any other time in its history, but what do they actually do? It is relevant, perhaps, to look a little deeper into the unique educational process in which they are engaged. What happens when the voluntary relationship is

daily practice must always be articulated in a wider context – what does it symbolise and how does it compare with prevailing values and realities? It must be politicised if the benefits of youth work are to go beyond the utopia of a perfectly realised moment in a set of perfectly enjoyable interpersonal relationships. We have to make those principles of voluntary inter-human engagement more universally applicable and also the principles on which the economy is organised.

What links the immediate with the bigger society are the thoughts and beliefs of those who practice in the service of youth. This is why the focus of this book is on the minds of youth workers, looking at how youth workers think about themselves and the world they live in and what they do.

Youth workers have made an empowering profession; now let them empower themselves a little more in these new circumstances. The conservative motto 'Don't think, obey' was turned by some into 'Obey, but think.' Now it is time to move onto a real critical alternative, 'Don't obey, think, then act.' If the state was once forced to recognise young people, why is it now demolishing the Youth Service? The answer resides in the new phase of capitalism known as neoliberalism and its failure to plan for the future.

PART II
POLITICAL/ECONOMIC
CONTEXTS

2

Youth workers and neoliberalism

The term 'neoliberalism' is much used, but not necessarily widely understood. In this chapter I give an account of its main aspects and relate its key features to some general issues affecting youth workers and the nature of what I call 'emancipatory education'. I show how neoliberalism shapes our world, professionally and politically. This chapter provides a more political and economic account of neoliberalism while also considering the new forms of consciousness it has led to. (In the last two chapters of the book I put neoliberalism into a more cultural context.) A changed economy has changed the way people think and relate to each other. We must consider this if we are to assist young people. Neoliberalism creates a passive culture of selfhood within the illusion of immense democratic activity and this must be questioned. I consider some of the recent effects of neoliberalism in Britain and in particular the cuts to public spending, and I look at the role of the youth worker in this context.

Neoliberalism is a set of economic policies that have become widespread during the last 30 years or so, bringing misery to people and the environment as well as war and economic collapse, terrorism and a new form of gullible individualism. Consumerism has become so extensive that even electoral politics have become a matter of individual choice on the market. What is economic is deeply political – it is impossible to split the two. I maintain that neoliberalism is a purely political project to maximise profits, and it is not in the best interests of workers. It is a phase of capitalism in which speculative finance capital dominates the productive, real

—

economy and finance houses to achieve, in a new way, dominance over national governments.

Creating the monster

'Neoliberalism' means a 'new' kind of liberalism. So what was the old kind? The liberal school of economics became famous in Europe when Adam Smith, a Scottish economist, published a book in 1776 called *The wealth of nations* (Smith, 1776). He and others advocated the abolition of government intervention in economic matters. No restrictions on manufacturing, no barriers to commerce, no tariffs, Smith said; free trade was the best way for a nation's economy to develop. Such ideas were 'liberal' in the sense of not having any controls. The markets would regulate themselves in the general social interest; this, at least, was the dream. This application of individualism encouraged 'free enterprise', 'free' competition that came to mean free for the capitalists to make huge profits as they wished, without restraint. The virtue of selfishness, which glorifies and justifies naked individualistic greed in our own time, was praised to the rafters by Ayn Rand, an American author (Rand, 1964).

This form of 'liberal' capitalism dominated until, particularly in the post-Second World War period, workers challenged it, whole sections of the economy were nationalised, and significant public services and welfare provisions were established. In Britain, for example, sound pension schemes were fought for, which guaranteed workers some dignity in retirement. The emphasis of planning and investment took over from the random roll of the dice of the market. Utilities were under public control and manufacturing capital, that is, the accumulated wealth of capitalists earning profits from domestic industrial production, had the most power.

Some countries, notably the Soviet Union and China, took their whole economies out of the capitalist world market and introduced planning systems led by the state. This threatened the rate of profit that was being made globally and in individual nations – not only do capitalists want 'more more more', they want it 'now now now'.

Instant gratification is a feature of this culture. It also gave a political emphasis to social development in industrialised countries based on quasi-socialist concepts of the public good, community, not-for-profit organisations and democratic accountability. Social solidarity was the goal of government intervention. Some commentators have called this the welfare economy – there was at that time a concept of common, social welfare as being a major function of both government and the state.

The return of Frankenstein

These relatively progressive developments only inspired the corporate elite to revive economic liberalism. They had been pushed out, and wanted to come back. They were being marginalised and wanted to return to centre stage to marginalise workers. This is what makes it 'neo' or new. They methodically planned their return using academic economists, think tanks and regular networks and meetings of like-minded people. Eventually they found General Pinochet, Prime Minister Margaret Thatcher and President Ronald Reagan to champion their cause (Callinicos, 2010).

So I would say that neoliberalism is more like an attempted resurrection – it represents a seizing back of power in a generational tussle between capital and labour. Now, with the rapid globalisation of the capitalist economy, we see neoliberalism on a global scale. Put simply, neoliberalism seeks to turn everything into a marketplace, and to make profit from everything. In the process, former democratic structures designed previously to hold a publicly accountable set of public services and economic investments together are being replaced by a new authoritarianism guarding the rights of the market to rule supreme. Everything, from football clubs to youth clubs, has to be targeted for making private profit. Instead of stable, trade unionised jobs, this new economy brings us flexible and non-unionised workforces, redundancies, outsourcing jobs, exporting manufacturing, freelance and temporary employees (Sennett, 1999).

—

This insecurity and mobility has created a new mentality and culture (Bauman, 2001a; Sennett, 2006).

A new contract between government and the people has been silently drawn up – its role has become less and less to ensure public good and to solve collective and national problems, and more and more to open the doors to the global market to address the personal issues of its 'subjects'. The role of the state in economic and social policy has diminished, and there has been a corresponding intensification and extension of its role as an agency of surveillance, obedience and control. Traditional politics has evacuated its previous role in the public and social sphere; it is selling off the nation's assets and seeks to privatise the rest.

The changes this new system is bringing about are so profound we will continually have to reflect on them throughout this book. To begin with, here is a basic description of the main, more detailed, characteristics of the neoliberal project.

Anatomy of the vampires

First and foremost is the rule of the market. Neoliberalism seeks to bring all human action into the domain of the market (Harvey, 2005). There is a process of liberating 'free' enterprise or private enterprise from any bonds imposed by the government, no matter how much social damage this may cause. There is greater openness to international trade and investment, as in the North American Free Trade Agreement (NAFTA) or the European Union (EU). Restrictions on trade, whether trade union agreements or international tariff arrangements, are systematically broken down. The main cost to capitalists, wages, are reduced by de-unionising workers and eliminating workers' rights that have been fought for and won over many years of struggle. Pensions have been attacked, their value to workers reduced and the contributions employers have to pay lowered. Meanwhile, huge pension funds have been squandered on the finance markets in endless speculation. Price controls have been scrapped so capitalists are constantly able to increase the price of

—

essentials, food and energy in particular. Workers' share of the wealth of their countries as wages has fallen sharply over the last 30 years.

All in all, the rule of the market means total freedom of movement for capital, labour, goods and services. To convince people that this is good for them, it is said that an unregulated market is the best way to increase economic growth, which will ultimately benefit everyone. But this, in fact, creates huge inequality. And inequality becomes the cause of many new behavioural patterns; for example, the rise of youth-on-youth violence and mass youth unemployment are directly attributable to this.

Neoliberalism means cutting public expenditure and privatising services like education and healthcare. It means reducing and scrapping the welfare state and all provisions for those less well off. The social safety net has started to disappear. The government's role in social welfare and cohesion is continually reducing. Public utilities have been privatised alongside essential human services. We now have to pay more for less provision. Although neoliberals don't oppose government subsidies and tax benefits for business, they do very little about mass tax avoidance by the super-rich. Privatisation is linked to the erosion of the concepts of democracy and accountability, and consultants and freelancers thrive in this culture. Cuts to youth services and the belief that they should be run by unqualified volunteers is an example of this trend. Wage cuts to youth workers and the de-professionalisation of their role is central to this whole programme. Do it badly, do it on the cheap, do it unprofessionally – this is the neoliberal way.

As part of its freeing of all areas of human endeavour for the penetration of the market, this new economy must sweep aside any form of regulation that gets in its way. Incessant plans are made to reduce government regulation of everything that could diminish profits, including protecting the environment and health and safety at work. This explains the attack on youth workers' JNC terms and conditions for youth workers and attempts to race to the bottom in wages. It also explains the government and employers' rejection of a licence to practice for youth workers. They want a deregulated labour market in which anyone can call themselves a youth worker.

Zombie workplace

Deregulation of markets requires an enforced obedience in the workplace. New managerial techniques have been developed, seeking to break up trade union collectives, to monitor and control workers and to remove their professional autonomy. This explains the outcomes culture, the target-driven nature of business. While workers are closely monitored the financial houses and investment banks can do what they like, and a huge deregulation of the role of finance capital takes place.

Eliminating the concept of the public good and the idea of community naturally follows these trends (Bauman, 1998, 2001a; Sennett, 2003). Instead we get 'individual responsibility' or 'choice' or the personalisation of services, where individuals are given vouchers to spend on their own 'choice' of services – such as the now failed Connexions card. The new government obsession seems to be pressuring the poorest people in society to find solutions to their own lack of healthcare, education and social security, all by themselves, then blaming them, if they fail, for being 'lazy'. This is like the demonisation of young people and the attack generally on the value base of youth work and community work – in reality such work provides important bonds in the cohesion of community and collective responsibility within a democratic framework.

Youth work also provides meaningful face-to-face dialogue within groups and support for individuals in a communal context. Another feature of neoliberalism as it develops the communications technologies to an unimagined degree is that it creates a number of fantasies that we are made free and more able to act politically and become involved because we have access to infinite information and infinite, individualised forms of social and instant computer networking. In fact, our common practices of searching and linking, our communicative acts of discussing and disagreeing, performing and posing, intensify our dependence on the information networks crucial to financial and corporate dominance (Dean, 2009).

While all technology can be used to our organisational advantage, there are some widespread illusions that the explosion of social networking and the like can fundamentally improve the quality of democracy. No one would deny the power of WikiLeaks to unsettle the empire, nor the power of instant communications to mobilise students and to assist them in deftly avoiding some of the strong arm tactics of the police; however, the experience of social networking and many of the claims for it are exaggerated.

We are encouraged to believe that we can create alternative apparently political and democratic zones in cyberspace that create for us the illusion of participation and perhaps even power. But such dialogues remain ineffectual and disengaged from the decision-making processes that really affect us. Just as real wealth in the form of securities and investments and equities and bonds is 'freed' to the microsecond speculations of the investment banks, so our ideas and characters, our dreams and desires, are freed to almost limitless profusion by the same technology. The authentic transformations afforded by face-to-face conversation are replaced by false exchanges with the computer monitor.

As Dean puts it, messages are 'uncoupled from contexts of action and application'. In other words, our intense passions and concerns and challenges to real injustice are neutralised and blunted within the virtual world (Dean, 2009). Our contributions to cyberspace do not necessarily have to be received and understood; they merely enter the vast sphere of circulation, their use less important than the fact they are circulating in the endless space of opinion and babble. No one has to act on our contributions. We are free to make them, but society is totally freed from the responsibility of replying or doing anything about them. Fantasies develop that Twittering and blogging can change the world. Democracy has become wrongly associated with the idea of expressing an opinion in cyberspace and being able to access unlimited knowledge. The notion of democracy

—

is consumerised and related to freedom of expression and not communal benefits resulting from collective action.

As some commentators have shown, the digital revolution has created a completely new set of revenue streams for a new generation of 'punk capitalists' (Mason, 2008). Piracy in cyberspace has become a new business model, not an effective source of rebellion and alternative human relationships.

The illusion of meaningful engagement and participation promised by the new communicative technologies reflects the underlying profound change in the neoliberal economy of the role of the individual in society and therefore our sense of selfhood. In summary, people have become socialised to be more selfish than selfless. This has a considerable impact on the role of youth and community workers and is worth outlining in a number of ways.

Agents of humanity in history

Youth work has assumed that the young person, the subject, is the agent of change. This is both an optimistic and positive faith in progress, but it is also sentimentalised in current circumstances and is based on what I consider to be outdated concepts inherited from the welfare society period in which youth work was consolidated and nurtured. Let us consider a number of fairly schematic ways of viewing the nature of the self and the individual over historical periods (Taylor, 1992; Arrighi, 1994; Rifkin, 2010). Just as the Industrial Revolution originally transformed man's way of thinking about himself and society, so the political economy that neoliberalism has created has made some significant shifts of perception.

Each epoch of civilisation creates a general view of human nature that has original progressive purposes. These then die away into irrelevance and become reactionary. Once they have faded they can become dangerous or laughable as a basis for future actions. The lingering appeal of ancient systems of belief in completely different social formations is one of the great puzzles of ideology. The great

—

mock-heroic poem *Don Quixote* is a humorous account of the pathos of tackling new situations with old remedies.

General views on human nature in the modern period can perhaps be schematised as follows. When the large-scale liberal capitalist market first developed in the West its first proponents battled with the medieval Christian world view that saw human nature as fallen, depraved and imperfect. Humans, it suggested, could only find salvation in the next world, should God so grant it to them. This was a world of hierarchies and slow, minimal technological change. Agriculture was the dominant economic force and the creation of a surplus for the lord of the manor was the aim of the game. Land ownership was primary. Individual and social change was slow (Braudel, 1981).

The first main proponents of a liberal capitalism in Europe developed what became known as the Enlightenment in which thinkers like John Locke, Adam Smith, the Marquis de Codorcet, Voltaire and others fundamentally challenged the notion that man was born into original sin and was reliant on an external benefactor. They said instead that man was rational, detached and autonomous. All humans had a common link in their shared capacity to reason. Through education and its application to common human issues, man could improve the world and his condition. Progressive educational theory, unsurprisingly, originated in this period. But because these thinkers were influenced by the new capitalist economy, they also said that mankind was naturally acquisitive, competitive and utilitarian; they believed that individual salvation rested on unlimited material possession and progress on earth.

Alternative, socialist views began to be put more strongly at this time. These were based on egalitarian ideas that as all people were born equal, wealth could and should be more fairly distributed. Later a communist position also developed that recognised beyond this capitalist system it would be possible not just to redistribute the wealth of nations equitably, but to eliminate private property relations which caused social divisions in the first place. The communist view was the newest fundamentally different world view in history.

—

Young nations and human welfare

What was needed to protect the emerging capitalist system two centuries ago were nation-states. These were created to protect private property relations and to stimulate market forces, to act as the surrogate self-interest of the citizens of one domain on the international stage in the competition between nations for resources and geographical influence. Through bitter struggle over generations, the workers who produced the wealth of these nations gradually sought enfranchisement within the political system and achieved universal suffrage, a vote for everyone over the age of 18 in parliamentary elections. This meant that all people, not just the very wealthy landowners, could at least vote, however limited the choices of candidates. The full adult franchise was not finally achieved in Britain until 1929. There was an expansion of the voting franchise and popular democracy that culminated in the post-Second World War nationalisations and welfare state.

A form of people's power emerged. It gained expression in terms of creating social security and protections in the 1942 Beveridge Report. Beveridge was a Liberal and it is with something perhaps more tragic than irony that his Liberal successors in 2010 teamed up in government with the Conservatives to undo his kind of welfare state.

Not only were individuals autonomous agents of change, they were clearly able to shape and influence history. Although the majority were excluded from power, they created a stake and changed things. Being actively engaged and part of meaningful structures that altered society became an increasingly common experience as time went on. There was disciplined collective engagement. At an economic level this largely 20th-century period was typified by the works of John Maynard Keynes. He advocated various forms of state-led economic management and investment to sustain employment and to manage a tax-based, redistributive welfare system (Keynes, 2008).

—

Civil society

This engagement has been called many things by different writers and thinkers – the public sphere, civil society, or, in Slovaj Zizek's case, sometimes the 'symbolic' world (Zizek, 2009b). This is, in fact, quite a useful concept in relation to this book. If a nation-state seeks to be the coherent force of private property and international relations, and forms a defined political way of expressing this, and if the workers then within it seek to democratise and humanise it, the inevitable struggle of resistance and accommodation that results creates many institutions, many behavioural norms with a common language and purpose. Stakeholders establish their stake and do not get given it by a patronising benefactor.

People will be citizens, consumers, voters, political party members, trade unionists, reliant on welfare, reliant on local government services, interested in governance, able and willing to volunteer. In other words, there will be sets of interlocking, collectivised symbolic orders that groups and individuals can negotiate and manipulate. The system has its own 'symbolic efficiency' and mutually agreed language so that coherence and order can be maintained. As many people as possible were included in this social democratic process, and greater equality of income and wealth was generated.

What happens if the set of institutions underpinning this symbolic efficiency breaks down? What if the nation-state dissolves into politicised trading blocs like the EU, if local government becomes a privatised cipher of government with little autonomy, if the voluntary sector is marketised, if trade unions become weak, if extreme inequality develops, if welfare provision is reduced and political parties are more similar in their ideological persuasions? Other institutions, those that have a significant impact on the lives of the young, are also in flux – the nuclear family, school, neighbourhood, sport and recreation and entertainment. What if the high point of praiseworthy citizenship is the celebrity, or the sportsperson paid exorbitant amounts for their personally enhanced talents? What happens if more and more power over us is exercised by those we do not elect?

The chainsaw massacre

All this surely has a profound effect on the certainties and common currencies of a shared society, although the cataclysmic effect of this is not always recognised. Taken to its extreme, if society starts to relinquish responsibility for its citizens, particularly the weakest ones, it starts to develop various modifications of the Nazis' first programmes of enforced sterilisations and then euthanasia of those with disabilities. As I show in the final chapter of this book, I believe that the concept of disposability of marginalised groups, particularly the young, is our contemporary equivalent to this form of 'social cleansing'.

Michael Hardt and Antonio Negri have sought to chart the profound cultural and psychological effects of these changes in a resurgent neoliberal world (Hardt and Negri, 2000). They argue that the previous citizen-subject of an autonomous political sphere as created by the Enlightenment and then the welfare society can no longer be said to exist. As the marketisation and financialisation of all aspects of our lives takes place in a gigantic explosion of consumerism and communication technologies, so identities become less fixed and certain – belief is replaced by brand. Everyone seems to have an opinion, and they all seem just as good as each other. We are what we buy. Our activism becomes reduced to our savvy within the market, our fashion sense, our ability to search out a bargain, or to spot a good investment. Another sociologist describes these trends as a 'liquid society' or 'liquid modernity' (Bauman, 2000, 2007a). Eveything is unstable and in constant motion.

Not waving, but drowning

In the new capitalist world order we cannot quite predict what an institution will do or what it will mean – it may be here today and

---

gone tomorrow. The authority and power of governments break down in the dominance of the money markets that constantly create and demolish short-term undemocratic institutions. An institution like a local authority may reflect our wishes one day, and the next it may turn against us. This institutional merry-go-round has been very unsettling and confusing for young people, and the creation of IYSS has not resolved this. Will the adult the young person goes to see support or monitor them, tell them off, or empower them? Institutional motives are less likely to be those of the public good and more concerned with the temporary profit motive they have adopted.

A once more common social identity becomes fragmented into many sub-identities and individualities. Even the word 'community' changes from referring to a largely communal way of doing things to a description of various groups, interests or occupations. If individuals lose the bonds of engagement with former collectivised, disciplined and purposive institutions, the meeting places from which we can see ourselves in human relationship, then they start to imagine various forms of allegiance in a new, individualistic way. The symbolic sphere that brings us together is replaced by the infinite imagination, a force encouraged by the fantasies of eternal possibilities of communication technologies and pseudo-social networking in cyberspace. Society is not so much decentred in a prospective democracy, but fragmented into competing identities and perceptions that keep the overall profit-making imperative and structures firmly in place.

If the purpose is to marketise everything, the individual must be 'liberated' from the collective, and a new illusion of freedom must be created. This has always been a feature of the system ever since the introduction of markets (Bruster, 1992; Caudwell, 2008a, 2008b), but the saturation of the market mentality following the break-up of welfare society make it more acute. Individuals are encouraged to imagine themselves in a wide range of lifestyles with which they can experiment. All things are mutable – if you can persuade an individual to move through various lifestyle periods, you can make more out of them. As Dean rightly says:

—

The variety of available identities and the mutability which characterises contemporary subjects' relations to their identities, moreover, renders imaginary identity extremely vulnerable. The frames of reference that give it meaning and value shift and morph…. So neoliberal ideology does not produce its subjects by interpellating them into symbolically anchored identities (structured according to conventions of gender, race, work, and national citizenship). Instead, it enjoins subjects to develop our creative potential and cultivate our individuality…. Consumption provides the terrain within which my identity, my lifestyle, can be constructed, purchased, and made over. (Dean, 2009, p 27)

Naive consciousness

Several writers develop this theme to analyse the pervasive influence of the market on the formation of consciousness. This must be the concern of youth workers, to reject the classic false consciousness that entraps subordinate groups into accepting their reality in passive and fatalistic ways, leaving the power and privilege of the dominant forces and power elites unchallenged. Youth workers must also reject what Freire called a 'naive consciousness'. This refers to a partial empowerment of people that relates to the secondary symptoms of oppression, such as engaging only with single issues rather than the underlying causes of social injustice.

There are, then, very significant differences between the liberalism of the earlier capitalist period and this later neoliberal phase. At heart, neoliberalism relies on a completely different notion of the individual, or subject. Early liberals like John Locke and Thomas Hobbes made the idea of the free, rational individual the foundation stone of the state, grounding and limiting legitimate government power. Neoliberals do neither of these things. Within this philosophy the individual is neither the source of natural freedom, nor the controlling force on government. The individual acts and reacts

—

according to a variety of economic incentives and disincentives. Social and political life is restructured in terms of the idealised competition within markets. Consumer choice in all things, including political democracy, is the key demand. Consumption must be excessive, unregulated and extreme (Cohen, 2003).

Consumer satisfaction

In all our relationships and dealings we are encouraged to act as consumers, making rational choices about what benefits us individually the most. Our identities, instead of relating to the context of the human collective, become purely imaginary in relation to the false desires and lifestyle allures depicted in the consumer market. In this book my underlying argument is that youth work must find a new place in counteracting all aspects of the fantasies and terrors of neoliberalism, or it will perish. This is both a matter of cultural engagement and structural and institutional change. One thing it certainly is not is a matter of psychological casework with individuals. We must not allow young people to sleepwalk through the political marketplace, picking and choosing politicians for superficial immediate needs.

Election supermarket

In a recent influential study of the voting conceptions and allegiances of young people in the US, the effect of consumer mentality on the construction of political awareness was analysed (Cassino and Besen-Cassino, 2009). This was an important work of detailed quantitative, qualitative and experimental research that revealed a great deal about how young people between the ages of 18-24 viewed the 'political' landscape in the US. Only 17 per cent of this age range identified strongly with either of the main parties. Young people in the US and elsewhere are becoming increasingly dissatisfied with mainstream parties, and are seeking alternative forms of expression and organisation. Cassino and Besen-Cassino (2009) set out to ration of highly politicised young people in the 1960s and 1970s has changed into something less radical and visible today.

They examined why young people chose not to be involved in mainstream politics, destroying the myth that young people are apathetic. They remind us that apathy takes work to produce and is a form of conscious activity. More importantly, they also remind us that to the extent that young people see the political world as being impervious to any change, it may be rational for them to opt out of it entirely. If nothing you can do within the projected political system will make any difference, it can be a logical decision to do nothing within it and to find ways of changing things in other ways. Perhaps a starting point is to define politics as everyday lived experience.

Real empowerment

In order to be engaged, people must have the imagination that enables them to connect their everyday experiences with larger political events. In order to create meaning for themselves and an identity, people need to feel themselves to be active agents able to negotiate their daily activities with larger social structures. To be part of the picture people need to have extensive interaction with the wider world through reading, talking, learning, exchanging ideas and exploring. These processes also convey a sense of self-worth, identity and empowerment.

In a highly marketised and media-emblazoned culture, with increasingly mechanistic concepts of learning and mass youth unemployment, young people endure various forms of isolation and alienation that actively discourage democratic participation and the critical questioning that underpins political discourse. Consistent studies have shown that young people who are less likely to vote are also more economically alienated. Many commentators have demonstrated how young people are targeted as consumers and their sense of self and development is moulded by market brands and lifestyles. Children are socialised into being savvy consumers from an early age. Young people increasingly have to work to see themselves through school and university. Work and social networking and consumer-related efforts compete as never before for young people's time. 'Politics' becomes one choice among many.

Cassino and Besen-Cassino found that young people, if they were Republican-minded, distrusted political leaders, whereas Democrat-inclined young people were concerned more about the progress of issues that they saw as problematic within a distrustful political system. But, like non-aligned young people, even those who were partisan distrusted most sources of information about politics in the media. The most popular form of political education turned out to be *The Daily Show* with Jon Stewart, a blend of satire and journalism about current affairs that is extremely popular in the US among young people.

Political brands

Differences between parties are conceptualised widely among young people as differences between brands of commodities – there is a style or demeanour associated with the Democrats or Republicans, just as there is with McDonalds or Starbucks. As Cassino and Besen-Cassino say:

> For a generation that has grown up entirely in the world where parties, politicians, and policies have been sold like soap, opting out from politics is no more consequential a decision that one to avoid pop music or shop at The Gap.... Attachment to a party is superficial, saying no more about an individual than the clothes they wear. (Cassino and Besen-Cassino, 2009, p 7)

The commoditisation of politics has much to answer for. Youth workers have to get back to face-to-face dialogue with young people to highlight the profound ideological differences between plans for change proposed by the established political parties and newer, alternative ideas developed in the new struggles. In talking to young people they must find new ways of appreciating the strengths and legitimate rights and demands of young people. Asserting that their lives and aspirations are intensely political is a starting point for meaningful re-engagement with young people.

Criminals in government

Alongside this new construction of the personal identity that is less rooted in institutions and collectives and less used to meaningful political debate on causes and effects goes another phenomenon related to the concerns of youth work. Attitudes towards crime have changed. In a more consolidated welfare state period, criminals could be defined as deviants from 'normal' social expectations. Institutions were so concerned to bind people together in the collective interests that those who stepped outside the normal pattern were said to have 'deviated' from an accepted path.

Of course many working-class communities create their own public networks of communal rules and norms that dramatically raise the level of ethical behaviour and mutuality – the factory, mine or large workplace echoed its collective approaches in the home and neighbourhood. But as soon as the harmonious string of industry and labour was broken, discord followed. The classic example is what has happened to once proud mining communities now riddled with drug abuse or worse. Deviants from the welfare society were not necessarily abandoned; a penal reform system was originally designed to rehabilitate offenders.

This attitude changes remarkably within neoliberal societies. Now there is a dangerous sense of abandonment (Howker and Shiv, 2010). Ghettos abound and spill over into overcrowded prisons. Crime is viewed as routine, as endemic, and engrained in the social system. It is the norm. It can break out at any time. Criminals obey market incentives just as anyone else, and control huge swathes of the economy (Glenny, 2008). As crime can break out anywhere, anytime, even in the most august investment banks, society adopts the policy of pre-emptive action. The great tool of this is the CCTV camera. A state of constant fear has to be engendered to justify this approach. Furthermore, policy making shifts away from trying to understand and repeal the criminal, to seeking retribution for the victim. As Dean again perceptively comments:

> The more anxious and desperate economic conditions become, that is, the more false and fragile the fantasy of free trade is experienced as being, the more monstrous and deadly become those imagined as criminals in our midst and the more they will have to pay since no one else can. (Dean, 2009, p 17)

The single most consistently painted image of youth is one of an almost automatically criminal deviant. While this has been a long-standing cultural bias, it is without any question at its most extreme now, and the greatest victims of the destitution created by neoliberalism, young people, are also the most constant targets of its repressive, controlling tendencies. Whereas Victorian culture, for example, depicted young people as dangerous outcasts ready to commit crime and mayhem, it also produced the great novels of Dickens, where young people were portrayed more sympathetically as victims, and it produced the first real stirrings of an empathic youth work tuned to the needs of young people (Duckworth, 2002). Neoliberalism abandons both.

More crime in the suites than crime on the streets

While youth-on-youth violence is now far worse than it has ever been in British history, it forces us to recognise two other aspects of criminality within our system. First, criminality is perceived hypocritically and disproportionately, and second, criminal behaviour is actually becoming increasingly violent. Young people are demonised for violence in a culture which goes to war and kills thousands and uses torture more frequently than for many years.

The young throughout the world are the most tragic victims of the war in Iraq, Afghanistan, and the violence of poverty (Davis, 2006).

Losing the apparatus of informed rebellion against the source of their alienation and isolation and confusion, excluded young people find their own extreme forms of inclusion and togetherness in gangs, whose damage-making potential is infinitesimal in comparison with the destructive powers of corporate leaders, bankers and military men who wield enormous power. The hypocrisy of a system that censures anti-social behaviour and nuisance at the street level, yet delights in the superabundance of profits from the arms manufacturers who stimulate and perpetuate conflict for profit globally is all too evident (Paxman, 1990; Pilger, 2002; Sampson, 2004; Peston, 2008).

Such hypocrisies and relativities must become increasingly part of the consciousness-raising of the youth work method. As Zizek has shown, there is a great gulf between subjective and systemic violence (Zizek, 2009a). The casualties of systemic violence, the deaths of older people in winter because they cannot afford to pay high energy bills, the early deaths of those in poorer communities, the higher infant mortality rate in poorer countries and so on, are politely tolerated and largely ignored. The aberrant behaviours of the casualties of those made abnormal by the system are dwelt on in gruesome detail in the tabloid press.

As soon as the cohesive power of the collective fragments into a society of individuals with their different personal and private idiosyncrasies, we become unable to do anything about crime; all that is left is surveillance, intrusion, control and a new form of the 'Big Brother' society. We move from collective confidence in authority to authoritarianism that no one appears to notice. Our nature as constituents, as constituting something with others like ourselves, as being part of constituencies, is broken down and we are shattered, in a very alien way, into fragments alienated from the more innate needs for affection, solidarity and being a part of something. The psychological traumas that flow from this are considerable (Rutter, 1997).

—

As society becomes more authoritarian, particularly in its attitude towards young people, it assumes that responses to the neoliberal order are as a result of intolerance and a kind of bestial ignorance. While neoliberalism cannot tolerate resistance to its ways, it projects onto the landscape a view that all those who oppose it must be lacking in liberalism and therefore full of dogmatism and bigotry. Those who see the failings of the system as resulting from inequality, exploitation and injustice are asked to be more tolerant and not to seek emancipation from these conditions.

Politics of fear

The art of contemporary politics is to conceal these concerns and sources of deprivation and corruption. If politics can be made to dwell on cultural and personal matters, even psychological ones, then real structural injustice can be masked. The politics of fear, fear of your neighbour, fear of a new terrorist power, fear of utter destitution, these are the real political weapons of neoliberalism. We, alternatively, stand with Stendhal, who said, 'People only ever have the degree of freedom that their audacity wins from fear.'

With fear always go panic and irrational behaviour, brutal responses to confusing and brutal conditions. A study of the language and slang of young people, heavily influenced by the US-imported media war games and police television shows, indicates a depressing absorption of the culture of violence that is systemically useful to an acquisitive and imperialist system (Gilbert, 2006). A diminishing respect for others is clearly a feature of our culture that reflects the new economy (Sennett, 2004). We also get another strange cultural imbalance that infects the mind of the young – a society built on competitive violence, foreign military interventions, punitive penal regimes and a structural callousness leads to two cultural extremes. On the one hand, the passionate zealotry of minority groups of terrorists, on the other the bland mass, apathetic indifference of individuals to the political system as a whole. These are two sides of the same coin of fear.

Making war

Neoliberalism also creates these dilemmas at an international level. Countries that want to stay independent of the new global capitalist market are subject to sanctions, continual harassment and ultimately wars of aggression. They are treated like deviant youths. This has been true of Cuba, Vietnam, Yugoslavia, the former Soviet Union and Iraq, Iran, Palestine, Honduras, Venezuela, Bolivia and many others. The authoritarianism domestically is matched by consistent warmongering throughout the world. This renewed aggression is reflected in a culture based on competition and violence. It explains the targeting of the youth market by big corporations through fashion, computer gaming and diet (Giroux, 2001a; Mayo and Nairn, 2009). It also partly explains the recruitment to armed services in our communities and the obedience of Britain to the US in its war-making adventures.

Many commentators have begun to argue that the worst victims of neoliberalism are young people (Giroux, 2009). The consequences of the social decay it brings make all those who are non-productive disposable commodities. Free market fundamentalism sees young people as commodities, irrelevant or threats to social order. Services and jobs designed to foster collective action and a sense of the public good, like healthcare, youth and community work or teaching, are attacked in an attempt to break the professional autonomy and value base of the workers directly involved.

Join the resistance

The fact that neoliberalism is a total social philosophy, a politics and economics and culture of capitalism, individualism and greed should lead opponents of this system as critical educators to empower and equip themselves with more comprehensive intellectual tools of resistance. They need to build into their consciousness an understanding of how this total political agenda affects everything around them, from everyday events to the lives of young people, and how to find forms of action and solidarity that most effectively oppose it.

Youth workers have tended to bounce between the immediate highly personalised relationship issues with young people, to local neighbourhood community concerns, to the widely global awareness of environmentalism, famine and the like. These contrasting terrains of struggle form an uneasy mix and I argue implicitly here that we need a new balance and direction. These spheres are interconnected: youth workers can only have a significant impact on those they work with face to face, but that face-to-face dialogue has to be informed by ideas and a consciousness that the wider picture is unacceptable and alterable.

This is vitally important and emphasises the significance of youth work to countering the neoliberal endeavour. If youth workers are increasingly lost as identities subject to market seductions and increasingly worried about their neighbour and their competitive or violent threat, they have to find ways of counteracting this. Inevitably in this occupation area the forms of resistance will lie in the quality of the face-to-face relationship and the quality of the mind of the youth worker as educator. It will not see the leap from immediate exchange with a young person or a group of them as a leap into the stratosphere; it will recognise that from the particular, the universal springs. Change the individual and you start to change society. An insight into common humanity in universally applicable thought will arise from particular circumstances and become a thing for itself, a transformative recognition that will be the centre of a ripple effect.

Immediate to universal

There must be something in a well-conceived emancipatory discussion in the immediate youth work exchange that will transcend the immediate context and speak more widely. The encounter between youth worker and the young person, whether familiar or a stranger, is a profound one: it is symbolic of a more desired set of human relationships. But much better recording of such moments is needed. Youth workers must be rooted as always in the direct experience of community and educational exchange, but to this rootedness must now be added a deliberate sense of social and political purpose. As I argue in the final chapter of this book, good forms of working need new good contents.

Youth workers also have a struggle to understand better why youth work and the Youth Service are under such attack, and why previous legislative and policy definitions outlined in Chapter 1 are under threat. They have to understand something about how the new political economy that has developed has influenced their position as public sector educationalists. They cannot focus on their technique outside of its context and this context is increasingly about wider economic matters that youth workers have shied away from.

It's the economy, stupid

Peculiar things have happened in this new context. The Royal Bank of Scotland, a significant player in the financial collapse and a significant recipient of public funds, has now lent to the US-based Kraft conglomerate to assist them in taking over the British-based company Cadbury's. British money has been flagrantly used to run down British industry at a time of high unemployment and under-employment.

What was once owned and controlled more democratically by the national and local state has been sold cheaply into private, often overseas, hands. More wealth has been accumulated by grabbing back services that they had previously run so badly that the state had to take them over. The railways are a classic example. It is indeed, as Zizek says, as if history occurred first as a tragedy and then as a farce (Zizek, 2010a). The railway companies made a mess of it in the 1950s and 1960s, the nation took it over via various forms of public ownership, then they stole it back and made an even bigger mess of it than they did the first time. The private went public, then private again. But in a new way. The point is that history cannot exactly repeat itself, and we cannot rest on conceptualisations of what we do forged in a previous welfare society.

All areas of local and national government expenditure now have to be tendered on the European-wide market. The EU Constitution that now governs our political economy demands the 'liberalisation' of all public services and pensions. Education and the NHS are the next targets. Even our community and voluntary organisations, once vibrant sources of independence and democracy, have been forced to compete with each other in a competitive market for funding. Government money does not flow into the banks alone: it flows directly into the pockets of private companies to run services. This is frequently done very badly, and billions have been wasted on this bonanza (Craig, 2006, 2008).

The effect of years of this privatisation is profound. The public sector has become like privately run businesses, while the private sector dominates public decision making and has the biggest influence over Westminster and Brussels.

Yet six million people remain employed by government and local government. There are 23 million employed in the rest of the economy and three million or more unemployed and probably another two million under-employed. It is this public sector workforce that is being blamed for the current financial crisis. This can also play on mindless prejudices that somehow the six million workers within the public sector are feather-bedded and enjoying gold-plated terms and conditions. Tell this to any nurse or housing officer, or low-paid civil servant. Public sector workers have become the target of attempts by government to make workers throughout the economy pay for the catastrophic failings of the finance system. This is highly sinister, and we can think of menacing historical parallels where groups have been penalised as scapegoats for crises they did not create.

In class terms, the divisions between public and private sector workers are entirely false. All workers fought for and depend on public services, whether road maintenance, refuse collection or the health service. For every £1 spent on public services, nearly another £1 is generated in other supplies and services. Investment in public spending is self-evidently a boost to the whole economy. The NHS alone generated 35,000 new jobs in 2009. It follows that any reduction in public spending weakens the economy and the prospects for all workers.

Having bailed out the banks and created a massive national debt, the government, and opposition parties, are saying that public sector workers must receive below-inflation pay awards again, and that there must be huge spending cuts and redundancies. This is dangerous. But the moves do reflect the weakened state of the economy and, above all, the economic thinking within the workers' movement.

The abandoned manufacturing base in Britain

British capitalism has given up on the real wealth-creating base of the country, its manufacturing and agriculture. Since the removal of exchange controls on capital in 1979 the City of London and finance capitalists have become the dominant group. Not only have they seen profit opportunities in the former public sector, they have run down the real productive economy. They have made quick bucks, lots of them, through financial speculation and encouraging unsustainable debt, owed at interest to them, among the general population.

British gas and oil revenues, now running out, partly concealed the huge trade deficit as Britain failed to produce and had to import more, and the figures are staggering. The negative balance of trade in goods and services in 1978 was −£7 billion; by 2008 it had become −£38 billion. Over this period the revenues from financial and insurance services also increased four-fold. There is a very big bubble still to burst at this rate because you cannot run a country without making things. Money and bank accounts do not create wealth; only work can do that.

Another false distinction is being talked about when proposing public sector cuts. We are told that no front-line services will be affected. This assumes there is something vital on the front line and something less important behind it. Anyone working to provide services knows that there is always integrated team working, and without supportive administration, for example, there would be no successful front-line delivery.

Freelance-led destruction

Rarely criticised, however, are the armies of freelance consultants who have made costly mistakes by taking on lucrative tenders to deliver essential services, inventing some that suit their pockets but not the needs of the public. Often ill equipped and under-qualified, they have in some estimates plundered £70 billion from the public sector since 1997 in schemes of little value or use. Private finance initiatives (PFI) and the like have benefited private companies (*Rapport*, 2010). The employment of consultants across the public sector has also led to the draining of skills in public services and the break up and fragmentation of once highly effective and professional departments.

The proliferation of consultants, quangos (quasi-autonomous non-governmental organisation) and private bodies running welfare, education and other social services that people rely on has had a profound effect on democracy. This has been worsened by the venal corruption in civic and parliamentary leadership. As the restraints on capital have been released, so, as a consequence, we have seen the bonds of democratic accountability broken. Whitehall's devolved powers to the EU-inspired regional development agencies and government departments tendering for business to thousands of unaccountable companies. This includes a whole legion of them in children and young people's services.

Customers or family?

Many caring and universally beneficial services in the public sector have inappropriately adopted the language and culture of cut-throat commercial business. Service users have become 'customers'. It would be an interesting concept if the inmates of privatised jails

—

were referred to in this way. For example, crime does pay for the private security firms that benefit from misbehaviour, and the internal market and profit motive in higher education has led to waste and duplication and has not prevented the massive cuts to universities we now face. Students have a right to education, yet increasingly have to buy it from departments run like businesses that sell knowledge like bags of pick and mix. What do you get for the 'privilege' of studying to help the national economy through higher skills? A huge student loan debt at the end that, once again, benefits the investment banks who lent in the first place.

Outsourcing is a polite word for theft. Delivery of services becomes less available to meaningful public scrutiny when services are outsourced to private providers. Trusts and boards, cabinets and mayoral offices step further away from the people whose needs should be met in a collective, transparent way. At another level, even Cabinet and parliamentary government is jettisoned in favour of diktat and a slavish obedience to EU and US decrees. No wonder that New Labour MPs like Stephen Byers, Patricia Hewett and others ended up describing themselves as cabs for sale to prospective punters when interviewed in a television sting. They had already tried to sell the country to the highest bidders years ago. Prostituting their own meagre talents off at the end of their reign was a logical and seedy conclusion.

New managerialism

The anti-worker tactics of the 'new managerialism' corporate have accompanied the corporate takeover of the country (Monbiot, 2001) and its public bodies. A climate of fear and bullying pervades in this new target-driven culture. The pirates and their hangers-on have developed a new aggressiveness in the workplace, avoiding public examination and community consultation. Contract managers have replaced public servants. Community organisations that once channelled collective recognition of need are transformed into bodies forced to compete for funding contracts, and their ability to criticise poor or irrelevant plans is marginalised.

The composition of the workforce has been deliberately altered. Gone are skilled, stable teams. In have come outsourced fly-by-night organisations. In too have come zero hours contracts and casual labour. Thirty to forty per cent of the public sector workforce is now casual. Many are fearful of redundancy, and many in local government are still embroiled in the time-consuming battles of implementing single status pay and conditions agreement. Managers with little understanding of the service they are managing bark out orders and a relentless pursuit of outcomes that may or may not be publicly beneficial. In many areas the fight for public services is being led by the users and new coalitions of concerned community activists instead.

Inequality kills

Another direct consequence of the malign power of finance capital to destroy industry and now public services and the democracy they represent has been, as discussed above, the acute inequality that has subsequently developed. Britain has always been a country of extremes of wealth, but the reforming zeal of the trade union movement and others ensured that in the post-war period at least free health, education, nationalised utilities and key industries and a welfare state narrowed the wealth gap. New Labour tore this post-war consensus apart. In 1976 the richest 5 per cent owned 47 per cent of the marketable personal wealth. In 2012 they own 58 per cent. The poorest 50 per cent of the population owned 12 per cent in 1976; today it is less than 1 per cent. Inequality, as experts have shown, leads to all of the forms of social breakdown we see around us. Inequality really has broken Britain (Wilkinson, 2006b; Dorling, 2010). The richest 1,000 people in Britain have £222 billion between them (*The Sunday Times*, 2010).

We are told that public spending must be cut. It is not a question of whether it should be, but by how much and when. The reality is that we have to increase public spending and confidently argue that this is both necessary and possible.

Total government spending in 2007 was £582 billion. Its income from all sources was £548 billion. In 2008 the gross domestic product (GDP) was £1,448 billion. By the end of 2009 the national debt was £825 billion. Wealth held by private corporations and landowners, of course, massively outstrips government income. When the Somerset Youth Service faced an 80 per cent cut in late 2011, researchers calculated that if just about half of the taxes owed to the Exchequer by the giant corporations and super-rich were paid, this would fund the entire Youth Service in Somerset, for example, for the next 833,000 years.

Prior to the Thatcher period, governments invested about 5-6 per cent of GDP into the public sector. Thatcher reduced this to around 1 per cent. New Labour sought to restore this, but only achieved around 1.8 per cent a year, and much of this over the last two years went to the banks and private companies. Even in the boom public expenditure years of New Labour it never reached pre-1979 levels.

As private financiers pulled the plug on the productive economy in manufacturing, so, of course, unemployment has risen. And it is unemployment that results in the most significant loss in government income and increase in state payouts. As social problems arise as a result, this then leads to more expenditure on acute crisis management, as we have seen in some of the most tragic cases involving children and young people. It is an acute situation. We even become immune to youth-on-youth gun crime after a while. The mean streets seem both inevitable and permanent.

We urgently need government spending on significant infrastructure and other large projects. For every 1 per cent of government investment as a proportion of GDP, there is a 3 per cent rise in GDP itself. It is the job of government investment to create a multiplier effect, with a beneficial knock-on effect on government income. It is a virtuous cycle. Yet the very opposite is being done.

This is why the countries that planned new government investment to ward off the recession have pulled through. Germany invested 5 per cent of GDP and China gave a stimulus to its economy of 13.2 per cent of its GDP. Many countries refused to allow their banks to play on the risky casino of the highly speculative markets and so avoided much of the shock. Such investment has focused on the rebuilding of the wealth-generating industrial base that in turn generates greater revenues for improved welfare and public services. In China's case recent investments have delivered consistently around 8 per cent of growth in GDP each year. Compare this to Britain's 0.1 per cent rise in 2009, or the devastation in Ireland as a result of their government's foolhardy refusal to invest and to tie itself to the euro.

Blame the workers

Neither should we forget that workers were not to blame for the financial crisis. Far from it. The financial bubbles blew because of irresponsible speculation and a move away from investment in manufacturing and public services areas of activity that generate wealth and jobs (Elliott and Atkinson, 2008; Callinicos, 2010).

In October 2008 the global financial system came very near to meltdown and that has had dramatic impacts on the real economy. Some of the figures this created were staggering; there was a 45 per cent fall year on year in Japanese exports, and 16 per cent annualised fall in German GDP. These are the sorts of numbers that you do not get in a recession; these are the sorts of numbers you get in a full-blown depression. Some whole countries have almost stopped functioning, and events in Greece are a clear demonstration of this. They will only be allowed to function again if the money markets can take control of them and put them into permanent indebtedness.

There has been a determination to avoid the mistakes that were made between 1929 and 1932, so banks have not been allowed to fail, as they were then. Interest rates were cut very hard, from 5 to 0.5 per cent, a measure to try and get things moving again. Over £1 trillion was given to the banks. Government borrowing has gone through the roof, as they have spent more and have found their tax revenues go down because of increasing unemployment, and the

Bank of England and other central banks have started to create their own money in order to try and reflate the banking system and to get credit moving again. Money was given to the banks to reinvest in the economy; they siphoned off a lot to continue to award unimaginable bonuses to their leading lights. Some individual bonuses to bankers were bigger than the annual Youth Service expenditure in England – the £6 billion of bonuses to the top bankers in the City of London in January 2011 would sustain the entire Youth Service in England and Wales at its current level of expenditure for 22 years.

The bubble burst in 2008 and everyone knew that the financial crisis and the behaviour of the finance houses and banks was the cause of the problem. Very quickly a media frenzy and right-wing crusade developed to deflect attention away from blaming the rightful culprits to blaming public sector workers for all of the nation's problems. The public sector was to be crushed and cut to pieces in order to solve the national economic crisis. Suddenly workers had to take the pain while others got incredible gains. By mid-2010 the daylight robbery of the banks was back in fashion.

In June 2010 the largest bank recorded half-yearly profits of £7.2 billion, having shed 4,600 jobs in 2009. It generously set aside £1.5 billion for staff pay and bonuses for the top elite. Other banks that were bailed out with public money did the same. The estimated assets of three government-owned banks was £850 billion. Yet they were refusing to stimulate growth and in fact encouraging the catastrophic policy of cutting public spending.

Why the financial crisis?

The world economy has been transformed. The post-war system had financial controls on banks, there were credit controls and limits on what the banks could do. It was a mixed economy so there was a large public sector as well as a private sector. The state actually owned large parts of the economy and there were strong trade unions – 30 years ago there were double the number of trade union members than now. There were policies that ensured that the fruits of growth were shared between capital and labour, and essentially the aim of economic policy was to have full employment rather than low inflation. There was a sense that markets were not there to serve the people who ran the markets, but to serve the people who made the thing bought and sold on the markets in the first place.

There were laws like the Glass-Steagall Act 1933 in the US that separated investment banks from retail banks; welfare states grew to ensure that there was a safety net for poor people and workers generally if they got into trouble; there was progressive taxation to ensure that the rich did not actually gain all the cash; and there was nationalisation that took certain key industries into public control.

This was all broken up by neoliberal economists and their right-wing political associates. They said there was too much producer interest and that consumers really should be given their freedom through greater competition. There was the growth of bodies such as the World Trade Organization (WTO) and the European Commission dedicated to injecting more competition into markets, even if it was against the wishes of democratically elected national governments. It was to the credit of CYWU members in this period that through lively debate members concluded that these developments, especially as organised by the EU, were sinister. Youth workers opposed the euro and how right they have since been proved. Through the CYWU conference they also opposed the EU Constitution which has proved a nightmare across Europe.

Other processes have been at work. There has been, as touched on earlier, a communication revolution. The internet and high-speed telecommunications means that information can be transmitted around the world much more easily. That has been of particular benefit to the financial markets that are the most globalised of all the industries. There has been a move to make everything financial, a move away in large parts of the developed West from the manufacturing sector and a corresponding growth of the financial sector. In the UK, for example, the financial sector grew by around 7 per cent between 1996 and 2006, whereas manufacturing stagnated.

The myth of globalisation

It has been accepted that this is the way things should be because of the third big change, globalisation, the idea that we are all one big global market and that countries should specialise in the things they do best. The idea was that as Britain was best at financial services, we should therefore put all our eggs in that one basket. This has proved a fatal strategy. Our ability to produce across a balanced portfolio of manufactured goods was deliberately broken up, and as a result, some traditional communities, where work and communal life and community spirit had prevailed, were ruthlessly torn apart. In many cases jobs were exported overseas, and this threat of jobs being exported has acted as a disciplinary force on the labour movement generally.

The growth of the financial sector has meant enormous speculation. Instead of doing the thing for which they were originally designed, to lend money to businesses and consumers, banks started to speculate in the markets. This action became reckless because the banks knew the government would bail them out if they gambled too unsuccessfully. As a result, the whole political and economic system became volatile.

A global economy developed which was heavily unbalanced between those parts of the world that produced things (such as Germany, Japan and China) and those parts of the world that consumed things (such as the US, Spain and Ireland). These predominantly consuming countries ended up running big balance-of-payments deficits, while some of the producing countries developed balance-of-payments surpluses, enabling them to reinvest their capital in the markets of the West and their hot money flooding into the City of London and Wall Street. This surge pushed down interest rates and inflation and allowed speculation to carry on and for people to continue to live beyond their means in an ever more vicious cycle.

'Spivs' and speculators

In Britain an unbalanced economy developed. The City of London accounted for about half of all the growth in the economy between 2006 and 2007, and the housing market was going through one of its more wild periods of excess, by allowing people to borrow more money than they could really afford. The government took the tax receipts from the City, which were unsustainable, and took the tax receipts from the housing market, which were also unsustainable, and reinvested them in the public sector which was looking, in fact, more and more like a fragmented private sector.

The financial markets became increasingly out of any democratic control, or any real economic control. Finance houses borrowed money, for example, in Japanese yen and put it all into Icelandic banks where interest rates were high. What followed was history. What the banks were doing was borrowing and lending more than their own capital base. They would have more in circulation than they really owned, sometimes by as much as 30 times. This was highly dangerous. It was back to the rule of the casino pure and simple; lessons of previous catastrophes had not been learned. Even Adam Smith, a key proponent of the original liberalism, believed that markets should be based on ethics and principles. We were living beyond our means, the banks were speculating ultimately with our money and our wealth and things got out of hand.

Key indicators such as the savings rate (how much people save out of their post-tax income) revealed the dangerousness of the picture. Historically people in Britain have saved between about 5 per cent and 7 per cent, and in the mid-1990s, after the last crash, it was something like 5 per cent. By 2007 it was −9 per cent – people were actually borrowing more money than they had actually got. They were acting like the banks. Communities have become infested by loan sharks and credit cards.

One effect of this was that workers forgot to fight for pay rises. The bottom 20 per cent of workers in this country have seen their incomes not just stagnate but actually fall since the last general election; there are also more children now living in poverty than there were even two or three years ago.

So what part can youth workers play in getting us out of this current economic mess? Key elements of the way forward are clear. A number of myths have to be broken and youth workers can help in this in their work.

National debt

The myth that public sector cuts save jobs and help to reduce the national debt is the most important one to break. Public sector pay generally, especially in local government and youth and community work, has been subject to pay freezes in 2010 and 2011. Yet this has not stopped the government with going ahead with proposals to destroy 450,000 public sector jobs. A national debt is not quite like a bankrupt business or empty family bank account. Many prosperous countries have lived for years with huge national debts – Japan, for example, has had a national debt of 130-140 per cent of GDP for years. The Trades Union Congress (TUC) has shown that the national debt could be practically wiped out in one year if the unpaid taxes from the rich and the corporations were properly chased to gather in around £30 billion, and if there was a modest 0.15 per cent tax on financial transactions, this could bring in another £100 billion.

But pressing even these modest demands would be fiercely resisted by the City of London. And it is only a willingness to take on the power of the traitors in the finance sector that will effect real change for the whole economy. The gambling of public wealth on international markets is at a staggering scale, and despite the weakness of our manufacturing sector, vast amounts of profit made from production in Britain is speculated and invested overseas each year. In 1990 Britain had about US$229 billion worth of stock invested overseas. By 2007 it had become US$1,701 billion. In 1998 British companies invested £310 billion overseas; by 2008 it was £1,075 billion. A total of £6 billion a year goes into the black hole of the EU whose accounts no reasonable auditor will audit and

—

82

who have, in fact, refused to do so for the last 14 years. We could wipe out our national debt by reinvesting wealth created here back into manufacturing, research and development, energy supply and public services.

Patriotic duty to fight for pay

The public sector struggle for pay is going to be one of the most important battlegrounds in the period to come. A rise in public sector workers' pay would mean a stimulus to the public sector and save jobs; this in turn would mean investment in the wider economy and increased funds for government expenditure. New youth centres, new youth facilities, 4,000 more youth workers to meet the levels recommended in *Transforming youth work: Resourcing excellent youth services* (DfES, 2002) – these are some of the factors that would set the economy upright. A guaranteed job or training place for every young person and an end to the iniquitous student loan scheme would also assist, and youth workers should continue speaking out more loudly on these matters. We have a real part to play in reversing the politics and economics of the current madhouse. But we can't do that if we think of ourselves as ineffectual middle-class people with little economic power. We have to appreciate that we are all in the same boat. What boat is this? This is established in the next chapter.

Youth workers must recognise communities of interests, of themselves as workers, of young people, of democratic forces, of nationally significant struggles and of international solidarity that must be seen in a new way. They must recognise the tangible interconnectedness between what is perceived as local and the overwhelming forces of global capitalism. CYWU/Unite has made great steps in this regard, but new and improved thinking is needed to link face-to-face practice with movements of social transformation. Between these extremes of immediate face-to-face delivery and economic structural change lies the empowerment and self-organisation of youth workers themselves, and this remains, as always, a missing link in the equation that now requires urgent attention.

—

Many youth workers have taken solace in the assumed 'radicalism' of the work and of having sympathetic ideas about global suffering (Belton, 2010), but for many the result has been a form of paralysis. This can only be changed by collective self-organisation. For a profession committed to empowerment, youth work has frequently struggled to empower itself. Yet its empowerment is the key to progress for young people and society more generally.

There is a direct connection between the quality of youth workers' face-to-face educational relationship with young people and the building of a more humane and people-centred society. This relationship disappears entirely if youth workers do not value the nature of the work that they do and, as a result, do not value themselves enough to organise and collectivise. The first port of call must therefore be to consider how and why youth workers are collective beings and what class of beings they belong to. Changing the world therefore begins with a few changes in youth workers' perceptions about themselves.

PART III
POLITICAL REALITIES

Youth workers as workers

In this chapter I argue that youth workers are part of the working class and that this recognition of their objective position leads to greater prospects for the effectiveness of their work and an improved capacity to change the overwhelming forces of reaction that often appear to engulf them and make them fearful and cowered, without hope. I believe youth workers can only be bold and brave if they are conscious of their class.

What class do youth workers belong to? Do classes still exist? Haven't we done away with 'us and them'? Youth workers are part of the working class. This has consequences, and practically all that follows in this book flows from this reality. Being working class means that you are part of the vast majority of the population who depend for their survival on a wage. The working class do not own the factories, utilities, services and companies that enable their owners to live off the work of others, they do not work at the heart of the establishment. In order to live they have to work. This makes them workers.

Cool cats

However much youth workers like to behave like cats and remain impossible to herd or, like water, impossible to sculpt, they are part of a working class, and they are both a brilliantly organised and frustratingly disorganised part of it. As I go on to argue they are an exceptionally important part of it but with too little acknowledgement of their importance and too little recognition of their position within a working class.

—

This reality has puzzled many youth workers and they have sought to deny it as best they can. They have sought to escape the fact they are working class by saying and doing various things that would appear to deny this. Many tried to establish a professional association in the belief that they were middle class and superior. The National Association of Youth and Community Education Officers (NAYCEO) is one of the remaining exponents of this tradition, and having merged with the union Aspect, is now merged within the Association of Teachers and Lecturers. Workers join unions and many youth workers have said this is too working class for them. They have preferred individual isolation as the levels of trade union density over the years have proved.

Many, recognising that workers are proud of their skills as well as their organisation around those skills, have attempted to distance themselves from any concept of professionalism. This is usually associated with the idea of elitism and reactionary protectionism. Continuing this theme of unaccountability, some argue that youth workers should not be regulated or licensed to practice and should not elaborate their values and public accountability into a code of ethics. They seek elitist, individualistic separation instead.

It is the intellectual denial of youth workers' position as workers that chimes most readily with the agenda of the forces currently ranged against youth workers at the moment. The neoliberal agenda in fact strikes a chord with some of the most reactionary thinking within youth work itself. Neoliberalism, among many other things, creates a deregulated labour market and privatises public services. Instead of stable, skilled staff teams in publicly accountable local government and voluntary sector organisations, cheap labour is marshalled into place by legions of freelance consultants. Even policy is made up at hugely expensive conferences organised by private companies on key themes affecting the workforce, but which the workers cannot afford the time nor fee to attend. Watch who says what at a profession-related conference these days. Who are they actually representing?

—

Individualised, private opinions opposing collective organisation within the field come very often from those uprooted from a permanent place in accountable fieldwork practice and working in the shady economy of short-term, fly by night contracts.

Well off and hard done by

How is class defined? For most people, the common idea is that it is a state of mind. For some it is a question of what gradations of income and lifestyle people pursue. For others for a significant period in youth work history, class was not an important concept; the focus of attention was on various brands of identity politics, ethnic identity, gender, sexuality and so on defined a person's precise form of oppression within the system and it was the relief of these oppressions that was the imperative to action. This divided youth workers into a hierarchy of competing fragments of oppression. Each competed with the other to be the most hard done by and as a result not much was changed. Ironically, as we now see, white working-class boys ended the period of the 1980s and 1990s as the worst performers in school. People were dreaming as the economics and politics of neoliberalism that led to today's disasters were brewing up quite nicely.

Having had a tradition of snobbery and a tradition of multiculturalism, youth workers are entering this new period with something more worrying in their midst. This is simply the notion of individualism without any sense of class enemies and class allies. It is accompanied by fatalism about the existing social order and all its inequalities and a consequent refusal to deal with the alien economic forces at play and the violent terrors around us.

People have become so used to constructing the world around their own position as consumers and individual purchasers of culture and so unused to being part of collectives with mutual responsibilities in a process seeking change that they actually prefer not to see themselves as part of anything, let alone a class with a history, a morality, a movement, a set of organisations and principles. They see themselves acting as individuals for freedoms and individual rights against an all-powerful authoritarian state.

Youth work practice has always lent itself to an anarchistic or libertarian tradition of thinking in which any form of organisation is seen as being bourgeois, except, of course, the organisation of the little networks that give each other jobs and contracts in the training and development market. This thinking also reflects those few workers who have somehow avoided a hard life and have avoided therefore feeling the humility of accountability to others.

So, in recent youth work history, there have been three sources of confusion about class. They lack sophistication so I will name them as I see them: snobbery, identity politics, and now, selfish individualism. They are all elements of the cruel, 'loadsamoney', 'me me me' society. All deny class relationship and position. Snobs want to be part of something allegedly higher than they are. People who put their identity first put someone else's second. Selfish free-floating individuals enjoy the 'I'm alright Jack' culture created by the Tories and then New Labour. The snobs wants to consume more status, the fragmented identity group wants to claim more rights than their neighbours and the individuals wants nothing for anyone except themselves.

A tradition in youth work, paradoxically one that often thinks of itself as being radical, does all it can do to escape the clutches of being working class. It does this because, as I seek to show throughout this book, being working class brings with it certain responsibilities and very few rights.

How then do we really define class? And what is a youth worker's place within the class of which they are part?

Dismembering class

The sociological dismembering of class has penetrated deeply into the consciousness of youth workers. The creation of the subject or self is distinctively scarred and determined by false senses of class composition, and misconceptions of class are deliberately and inadvertently replicated in practice and theory. There is a wide market for the cultural discussion of the construction of social identity. Invariably different identities begin to proliferate and man is declined, as the memorable phrase from Alain Finkielkraut describes it, 'in the plural' (Finkielkraut, 1988, p 57). Differences proliferate against the commonality of human features.

In short, the dismembering of class identifies 'working class' as the description of various kinds of victim and lower states of being. Often it insultingly means those doing dirty jobs with their hands. Often it means the poor on council estates who need to be helped by 'middle-class' philanthropists, or the beneficent state. The working class is also calculated as declining in number, denying historical trends in Britain in the most stunning manner (Westergaard and Resler, 1975). This false calculation identifies working class with weakness. An exaggerated view of the number of classes says by implication that working class equals 'hand', and others equal 'brain', forgetting that it is impossible to do anything without a combination of both (Sohn-Rethel, 1978; Katz, 2009).

Missing the point somewhat, this view includes the idea that there are more than two classes in Britain. It creates a fiction of class. It divides rather than unites. Worst of all, it associates gaining an education with rising above working-class roots. It creates guilt in achievement. Some youth workers feel they are joining another foreign, higher class simply by going to get a JNC qualification.

Although we are probably the least feudal country in Europe, the dominant notions of class shared by left and right, by Labour and Tory, many socialists and Liberal Democrats are feudal in origin (Calvert, 1982; Cottrill, 1984; Wuthrow, 1989; Meister, 1990; Corfield, 1991, Fine et al, undated). In this conception class is understood as an endlessly subjective grid of definitions according to one's place in the productive process rather than a relation to the ownership of production generally. It creates a hierarchy of subservience almost endless in its gradations.

The Registrar General's census formulation (however frequently or infrequently it is revised) labels a whole range of 'classes' a–z. This is shared by the advertising industry keen on targeted niche markets,

—

because it is a tool for the reformist engineering of social democracy concerned about the distribution, not the creation, of wealth. Its primitive division according to labour market location is the most important, commonly held 'popular' myth and academic formulation. Dentist is somehow superior to dustman. We get superficial sociology and pop psychology as a result – class is determined by accent or the contents of a domestic rubbish bin, a bag from Waitrose or a bag from Asda. There are press features about social types, be they 'yuppies', new men, techno freaks, dinkies, dunkies, want it alls, got it alls, info nerds or flexicrats. Then the death of these types, who never existed, is announced, to make way for the next lot, who don't exist either (Lynam, 1999).

Linked to this fragmentation of class is the greatest myth, that we are divided into races. The second greatest myth must surely be that we are divided into lower, middle and upper classes. Are youth workers part of a non-existent middle class simply because they can earn reasonable wages and have qualifications? Or are they upper class because they educate those worse off than themselves?

Class in the bourgeois definition is like a modern day *Canterbury tales* with an infinite cast of eccentric characters. If you define class according to superficial characteristics concerning people's attitudes and lifestyles and other financial categories, you can stretch the definition as far as you want across the population. What appears to have happened today is that it has been stretched so thinly that every individual is in a little class of his or her own.

Status and class

Status, using the sociology of Weber and Durkheim (Giddens, 1973), is pervasively mistaken for class. An aspect of class inequality, so the theory goes, is the multiplication of pyramids of prestige, the rituals and protocols of interpersonal relationships, lifestyles and kaleidoscopic hierarchies of esteem (de Botton, 2005). But as Westergaard and Resler commented in 1975, 'Taken by themselves the gradations of social esteem tell one nothing about the concrete structure of inequality – the cleavages of economic position, power and associated chances in life – from which they derive, sometimes by complex and devious routes.' They concluded, '… the niceties of status gradation which often loom large in discussions of class are hardly important' (Westergaard and Resler, 1975).

In recent years the gradations of esteem have become elaborated into sophisticated racial or sexual formulations that have created an additional haze within the fog. For a while we witnessed the rise of the 'isms', all of which have been variants of biological, and therefore reactionary, determinism and behaviourist psychology. This trend has been brilliantly criticised by the French philosopher Alain Finkielkraut as representing a fundamental retreat from Enlightenment rationalism (Finkielkraut, 1988). The progress made in the Enlightenment period put the universality of human thought to the fore and led to a formulation, 'I think, therefore I am.' The various forms of biological determinism, whether the 'black perspective' or 'woman's view', sought to go back to a less enlightened, and more dogmatic formulation: 'I am therefore I am right.' You couldn't argue with someone who believed there was no shared humanity with you.

Oppression

The fascination with difference and the replacement of a notion of class exploitation with notions of multiple 'oppressions' encourages the insidious cult of the victim. This gives a shrunken and introverted focus of attention. Depicting ourselves as defeated victims of terrible forces divides and demoralises, and it was a demeanour taken up within youth work for many years. As Dean observes:

> Shrinking the scope of political claims to those of victims needing recognition and redress also traps claimants in a double bind: to speak at all they have to demonstrate how they are harmed and vulnerable, how they are weak, inadequate, or suffering. They must speak as those who have lost, those who are losers. One who

---

> feels the political impulse to struggle, who is ready for
> a fight against injustice, is not injured enough to speak.
> For many leftists, the attraction of the position of the
> victim is thus double: one is always morally correct – for
> who can deny the suffering of the victim? – and never
> politically responsible – for victims are too weak and
> injured to govern. (Dean, 2009, p 17)

There could be no disputing the perception of, for example, the black activist, for many years, because no one else could possibly share their perception of oppression. This drastically cut off key sections of the working class from involvement in the overall struggle, as Shukra has shown (1998). Similarly, the integral role that women actually play within the class struggle is somehow undermined and made unnecessarily difficult by the more radical feminist traditions. A reassertion of the primacy of class relations in determining women's issues has been a solid, but minority position for a long time (Vogel, 1983). The debt that youth work pays to women practitioners who were and are among the best theoreticians and strongest advocates and activists in the union is also an interestingly ignored element of the history of youth workers as a group.

Identity politics to individualism

Much of the separatist and divisive construction of identity politics has built a new mythology in direct inverse proportion to the increasing scientific understanding of human commonality and therefore the lunacy of various, so-called racial characteristics. But even this form of muddying the waters has been superseded in the new millennium by something blanker, more dangerous, more insidious. It is the notion that any discussion of class is old hat, a waste of time, irrelevant. Crudely speaking, former debates used to centre round whether a person was an activist for their interest group or for their class. Nowadays the subject of the debate, if there is one, is whether a person is someone free to do as they please, or not. The marketplace has seeped into the consciousness of class politics and diluted it. People no longer feel themselves part of much, let alone a class. We are defined more by our individualism than any sense of collectivism.

We have to think more deeply about this vexed matter of class. The working class is the creator of its own destiny, the source of all production in the most elaborate and complex technical processes and industries now developed. It is productive. It is conscious, and generates its own tragic divisive delusions as well as its own objective common sense. It is capable of the best and the worst. It is a supreme class. The phrase 'working class' is more a concept and description of a social force in relationship with the productive process overall than it is a label that can be applied according to a variety of secondary, largely lifestyle features.

Working-class value

The law of value also applies to the class and it is simpler than it sounds. It says the more social time spent on conveying and creating a skill, or providing an education to a person, the more value they have to the system. Someone untrained on the capitalist market is worth less than someone trained. Capitalism will want to pay the trained as if they were untrained, however, and many youth workers collude with this reality in their sphere. But generally speaking, the more society invests in creating something, whether it be a car, or a skilled worker, the more value that person, as a commodity, or that commodity, actually has.

It follows that it is a nonsense to say that all people are equal. Some actually have more value than others. This does not, of course, mean that those who have less value on the market are less worthy. I believe that everyone is born equal and worthy of achieving their fullest potential. But this cannot and never will mean that all people produce equal values for society.

It doesn't mean that a civil engineer is any less exploited than a shop floor engineer. To the contrary, the more surplus value a person is able to generate, the more exploited they are. Some produce more value for capitalism than others. This does not put them within another class; paradoxically it is more likely to put them at the leadership of the working class. Political organisation has tended to accompany skill, and youth workers are skilled workers. Many describe it as a craft. The intense sacrifices they make personally to get on training courses is not a privilege; it is a commitment to acquiring an advanced skill that is socially useful. Because it is more socially useful, youth workers should get paid more for it. The historic pay benchmark for youth workers is with teachers' salaries. Youth workers are after all educationalists.

People may be abused or oppressed because of some personal characteristic; you could, for example, be a worker with a disability, but you are exploited because you are a skilled worker. The more skilled you are the more surplus value you create for the employer. Exploitation is much more powerful and therefore much more difficult to get rid of than oppression. If you can't tackle it, you have less of a chance with subsidiary oppression. You have to be part of a class movement to get rid of it, not part of a campaigning group alone. You have to be part of the main defensive movement our class has built for its survival, the trade unions, and part of the socialist movement that we have built to go beyond survival within the system.

In the complex British working class there are both radio actors and radio repairers. We meet organised writers in their trade union, university lecturers, including youth work lecturers, in their union, and coal miners in theirs. In perhaps the class irony of ironies, for years, organised and disorganised workers were content to let the 'horny handed sons of toil' and the shock troops in unions like the National Union of Mineworkers and Amalgamated Engineering Union do the fighting. This was a kind of inverted class snobbery that even the miners used to take up with their sometimes exaggerated scorn for the 'white collar unions'. But it simply did not work and is not a model that workers can rely on today with the traditional vanguard troops flattened and the glaring need for every worker in every workplace to take more responsibility and not rely on others.

—

In a novel by William Ash called *Heroes in the evening mist* the hero Colin Frere reflects on the nature of his class allegiance:

> He regarded himself as working class in so far as he, like any other worker, lived by the sale of his labour power. But if the fact that what he marketed was a mental rather than a manual skill did not alter his relationship to the means of production, it did alter the form of his association with fellow workers. Never for him the socialisation of labour in factory, mine or mill; and meetings of the Union of Journalists, in which he played an active part whenever he was in England for any length of time, were probably not much like the meetings of the unions of engineers or miners – which he supposed would be much freer of individual competitiveness. (Ash, 1990, p 75)

In youth workers' definition of class a youth worker is part of the same class as the most vulnerable young person they work with.

Class identity

Youth workers work with young people within their class as a commitment to the liberation of their class as a whole. However much of this has been disguised over the years as including motivations for religious enlightenment, the relief of suffering, the advancement of learning and behavioural improvement, the indoctrination of some conformist cultural ideas, or generally just doing something worthy, the impetus of improvement within all forms of youth work has been for a more human social system. It has been an area of work, like any other, with contested ideological, political and theological leanings, but it has always imagined a society free from the injustices of overwork among the young, unemployment among the young and reduced opportunities for them. Emphasising the contested nature of different ideological strands of youth work at this juncture is not

—

helpful. More important is to look back at a movement that has contributed to building more progressive values and a better deal for the young by seeing youth as a precious time in its own right, with rights and responsibilities attached to its important status.

The journey to paid youth worker for most of those who take the journey is interesting. The remaining common pattern is that individuals experience a positive life as part of a youth group themselves. They may stay volunteering with this group for many years, or they may go on to other employment. Then, with the memory of youth work experiences in mind, they may seek part-time paid employment. This involves training. It is enjoyable, and then for some, a career beckons, full-time dedication to the work seems possible. Sacrifices are made by most youth work students to study for a JNC qualification. Most courses don't accept students they have proved that they are committed to this journey through voluntary activity.

Youth workers have skills to assist the social solidarity and learning of young people for a higher social purpose. These skills are filtered through many perspectives and contexts and are deployed in many organisations, some state-backed, some within the counter-culture, some within highly partisan organisations such as churches or uniformed groups.

Youth workers bring a moral purpose to their work that is full of values and ideas far superior to those of professional intervention, casework, rescue and reform. This, I believe to be as true of the Scouts as it is of the Woodcraft Folk. The values, purpose and opportunities afforded by a host of youth work organisations outweigh the ideological emphases within the provision.

Exploitation

In youth work and youth workers' passion to end the exploitation of and cruelty towards young people, they imagine a different society, a society in which democratic, human values and priorities will pervade above all others. Human beings are at the centre of the social

—

and economic project. Youth workers should also be the strongest critics of the social forces and relationship that make young people so alienated and confused that they can behave so badly in the first place.

Youth workers have a judgemental approach, they want better human relationships, yet do not seek to punish and humiliate young people. They seek emancipation from unfair social conditions and enlightenment from mind-forged manacles and the ideas that keep those social conditions in place. They seek class consciousness and the recognition that their class holds the key to an emancipated future.

The role of young people in this emancipation is primary. The capitalist models of dominance and subordination place the economically inactive like the young and older people in a particularly impoverished position. For a period, youth work sought to further subdivide the category of youth into competing categories using racial and gender-based concepts. Disability was widely ignored and so was the overarching influence of class and economic position. Progressive forces in the CYWU consistently challenged this divisive framework that did great damage in delivery. There was a quasi-religious view that somehow everyone was equal. There was a convenient amnesia about the causes of all oppression and this coincided with the growth of inequality.

Beneath the veneer of a commitment to social justice, so fervently expressed by many at this time, particularly in the early 1980s, lay the bleaker realities of a widening gulf between privilege and exclusion in a system increasingly built on subordination and constraint targeted at the public spaces that young people chose to enjoy. Indeed the proliferation of social justice concerns helped to mask the widening gulf as it became the chasm that it is today. Youth workers are not cold hearted about the socio-legal roles that young people have or are given. Essentially they relate to them as other human beings. Uniquely, as a paid profession, they seek to respect and amplify and direct their voices on the full scale of human emotions and concerns. But as yet there has been no adequate intellectual tool to link the personal, human concerns of youth workers with those of the young people they work with, and this will not happen until a greater class consciousness has been developed.

Humanity and the inhuman

It is this class-bound humanism that counteracts the dominant experience of the world as a set of inhuman interactions structured by monetary and contractual arrangements, or, as is increasingly the case, relationships of dependence and rejection, surveillance and authoritarianism. Creating the space and opportunity for interpersonal fun, pleasure, learning, exploration and generosity is an essential element in the struggle for a socialist society, and youth plays a distinctive role in this. It is the sense of a nurturing family extended beyond the home, of learning beyond the classroom, of understanding beyond knowledge that youth work provides and in all its forms with all its orientations it is overall a beneficial thing.

A capitalist system gives us the paradigms of contract and status and consumer in a vast array of interpersonal transactions. Youth work plays its part in restoring the bonds of friendship and solidarity at a highly impressionable age. This is not an insignificant role and must be sustained by a healthy infrastructure of volunteers and paid workers.

The clarity of Marx

If the contribution of Karl Marx can be simply reduced it would, I believe, be to this concept: capitalism creates only two classes, 'ours' must take over from 'theirs'. Many commentators themselves responsible for perpetuating illusions about class cite Marx as at best confused on this issue. I have always found the contrary to be the case. Take even the 1844 *Economic and philosophical manuscripts*: 'It goes without saying that political economy regards the proletarian, ie he who lives without capital and ground rent from labour alone, and from one-sided, abstract labour at that, as nothing more than a worker.' From the same year, in *Critical notes on 'The King of Prussia and social reform*', we find the formula: 'Only in socialism can a philosophical nation discover the praxis consonant with its nature and only in the proletariat can it discover the active agent of its emancipation.... But without revolution socialism cannot be made possible.'

Youth workers do not work manually to create physical objects for sale and consumption. They do not, like lorry drivers or shop assistants, for example, help circulate those objects for sale. They do not repair objects and do not help the process of exchange. They relate very indirectly to the whole production process dealing with the reproduction of workers, with the very sensitive and vital manufacturing of ideas and identities. But this does not make them less of a worker. They have the honour of working with young people, of shaping characters at a very influential time of character formation. Indeed, some would say that the period between the ages of 16 and 19 is absolutely critical in forming the ideological outlook and perspective of an individual.

Youth workers do not make a direct profit for anyone, although they indirectly assist what some describe as the reproduction of capital in that they assist in the creation of a fit and flexible working class. But as I have shown, this is a double-edged sword and much open to subversion, especially by educators. Youth workers influence the way in which people are able to think about the entire social system. They are a vital part of a welfare state that has run public services in the interests of people, they occupy a place within the education component of this, and express a very working-class commitment to improving the understanding and social position of young people and to enable their participation.

I believe a number of important points of clarification flow from youth workers' more comfortable recognition of themselves as workers. For a start they can become part of the workers' movement for change. Without being able to defend and change things at work, the key to that movement is likely to only partly open the door. Trade unionism is fundamental, and active membership and participation in a trade union is a requirement. Do as you would be done by. It would seem arrogant to advise young people on the world of work without mentioning the benefits of democratic participation and solidarity in trade union membership, for the many practical benefits they bring to young people. The responsibility to young people extends way beyond youth workers' face-to-face interaction with them into their own action as organised workers and into their ability to motivate young people to see through the unfairness of social relations of which they are part.

4

Youth workers as professionals

This chapter seeks to analyse how the word 'professional' has been understood within youth work and to define a more progressive way of using the word within the context of youth work and applying it to practice and the occupational and political assertion of youth work.

Dignity at work

It follows that if you are a worker that, despite the nature of your employer, or your manager, and their approach to your worth and value, you take pride in what you do and you want to do it well. This, in essence, is why workers are professionals. It is not a question of status. Youth workers, whatever their employment or volunteering situation, want to do a job well. Knowledge, skills and dedication, together with a clear recognition of capacities and boundaries, enable workers to do a job better and to feel in command of what they do.

The problem is that the words 'professional', 'professionalisation' and 'professionalism' have become associated with negative things in the minds of a small but vocal minority of youth work practitioners. Some have benefited from union rates of pay and pensions and stable jobs for many years, some have earned quite nicely within the freelance market and some have worked as volunteers within the voluntary sector and have devoted so much of their lives to unpaid or low-paid labour that they see any well-paid employment position as a bit of a cheek. Some more straightforwardly reflect employers' demands for a deregulated cheap labour market (Nicholls, 1997).

In return for all the expense of the blood, sweat and tears that went into the professional formation of youth work, as alluded to in the previous chapter, youth workers are still categorised in the official designation of occupational areas as a subprofession, or a para-professional occupation. And funding for youth and community work students is considerably less within higher education than it is for social work and trainee teachers. Unlike comparable occupation areas there is no regulatory body outside of the CYWU's Code of Professional Conduct for members.

The history of youth work has been self-defined in that they have done what they have done. But employers and the state have also defined it. The state officially defines youth work, as indicated previously, as a minor element of welfare provision; employers define it as a separate skilled specialism within the education sphere. So how in this context does the concept of 'professional' assist? In essence it asserts real value and social role of youth work.

Consider a phrase: 'They did a really professional job.' This could be referring to the plasterers fixing a front room wall, the mechanic fixing a car or an AA patrol person. It could refer to the care received in hospital or to the organisation of a child's parents' evening at school. The phrase 'doing a professional job' is synonymous with 'doing something well'. It conveys a sense that every angle was covered, that there was control and a skilled application of technique and organisation. Someone knew exactly what they were doing and why. And it also has a sense alongside it that things were done properly, a whole process, with recognition of boundaries, beginnings and endings.

Pride

Workers take pride in what they do. Manual workers, it has to be said those in skilled trades especially, whether it be printing or engineering, design or electronics, have always had a sense of doing a professional job. Many of the coal miners I met during the strike in 1984/85 referred to their pride in their professional coal mining skills. Nurses, obviously, refer to professional practice – the combination of compassion, understanding and the application of learned caring techniques and medical knowledge and human behaviour makes them proud of their deployment of their skill for the benefit of others. Some may say that nurses are only repairing bodies for return to the capitalist labour market and so are repeating the cycle of exploitation and the reproduction of capital. This, I think, is entirely cynical and destructive.

In Britain, the word 'professional' may also have a negative connotation of elitism and snobbery. 'I am a professional therefore I know best.' Certain professions, or areas of work, may shroud themselves in mystery and legislated conditions as if to protect their skill, or endeavour, and there is nothing wrong with protecting skills. Would you send your children to an amateur nurse or doctor for medical treatment? What about going to an unqualified dentist for root canal treatment?

If those who sell their labour power are workers, then 'professional' is a working-class term because what it does is consolidate the notion of what a job and what its related set of skills are, and defines them for the practitioners in relationship with their public partners. You need to have confidence that the doctor is registered and the dentist licensed. The labour market has to respond to the rates of pay and definitions of work that a group of professionals have set for themselves. Remember, however, that the more skilled you are the more you are exploited by the system; you may in some cases earn more so that you can live, when you have free time that is, in more material comfort with some of the superficial trappings of wealth, but this does not mean you have been elevated from the working class and entered the non-existent middle class for all eternity. The myth of the middle class is long dead.

The professions are usually associated with medicine, the law and education, and these are indeed worthy parts of working-class life. But being professional and being highly skilled and proud of what you do and seeking to control what you do goes right back to the organisation of the first trades and identifiable productive occupations. Stonemasons, millwrights, cobblers, printers, ditch diggers, tinkers, all those organised around their occupation to improve the mastery of technique, to ensure the price was right and to gain some recognition and status in a capitalist world. Employers do not give skill development; it is developed by the workers, and protection of that skill is something that only the skilled can do themselves. This is all part of the process of workers' control, maximising their identity and power within a system that seeks to exploit them. Encouraging self-respect among the young must be based on having sufficient respect for themselves as youth workers, and there is no greater expression of this than the collectivisation of shared interests.

A working-class profession

In his useful chapter 'Youth work as a profession', Howard Sercombe provides us with a lucid appreciation of how and why youth work must be defined as a profession (Sercombe, 2010). Sercombe's position rests considerably and helpfully on Koehn's argument that any profession is constituted by its ethical commitment to serve a vulnerable population and driven towards a certain form of improvement or transformation (Koehn, 1994). If this is an acceptable definition, and I believe it is, youth workers must have a clear idea of their target population, a real sense of the dimensions of their vulnerability and a vision and practical and theoretical understanding of the necessary forms of action and intervention that reduce this vulnerability.

There are also other ways of deepening this commitment. When the competence-based framework under the NVQ scheme was first mooted, the profession considered that a definition of the core elements of youth work needed to be analysed to demonstrate the complexity of the process and its unsuitability to fragmenting into NVQ competences. The working group that looked at this concluded:

The group felt the core to be less about separation out of all the functional strands, but rather their fusion together with the appropriate values, through and into action. The core focus of youth and community work training was seen as equipping workers to make such a synthesis. The core is distinctive because of its holistic nature and the degree of professional judgement and responsibility workers need to exercise in balancing sometimes conflicting forces. (NYA, 1993)

This holistic sense and understanding of the need to synthesise values, information and transformative practice is at the heart of recognising that youth work is a profession in youth workers' own sense of the word.

The craft of youth work

Many youth workers describe themselves as craftspeople – they have a craft that they are skilled in and proud of. As Sennett points out, the word originally used in Greek for a craftsperson was *demioergos*. It is a compound word of two parts, public (*demios*) and productive (*ergon*) (Sennett, 2008). Strangely, the very ethereal philosopher in the idealist tradition, Plato, traced the meaning of the word 'skill' back to a root *poiein*, meaning 'making'. Rarely do we make things for ourselves and our own pleasure and consumption and use. We depend on the products of others.

The Greeks thought that craftspeople civilised society by means of skilled production. Craftwork brought people out of isolation – craft and community were therefore linked from the start. That there is a craft of personal and social development undertaken through informal education methods is indeed a recent and real phenomena. Youth workers have craft consciousness. This also explains the perennial complaint that youth workers have that nobody really understands what they do. So few people are employed to mould and shape and support individual consciousness that it is difficult on occasions to explain the higher social purpose that underpins their work. Youth workers are craftspeople of ideas and feelings, of emotional and personal intelligence.

Respect in the public realm for the very public work they do is lacking in a world that disrespects the importance of the public sphere altogether. Think how we perhaps take the craftsman-like skill of computer programmers completely for granted. They are the modern smiths and wheelwrights. Or consider how the skills of nursing and bricklaying, or carpentry and counselling, are underestimated in a world that fawns over possibly untalented celebrities, or exceptional sportspeople. As the public sphere is broken up, so respect for youth work as a craft is reduced.

Sennett reminds us that craft is founded on skill developed to a high degree:

> At its higher reaches, technique is no longer a mechanical activity: people can feel fully and think deeply what they are doing once they do it well. It is at the level of mastery ... that ethical problems of craft appear. The emotional rewards craftsmanship holds out for attaining skill are twofold: people are anchored in tangible reality, and they can take pride in their work. (Sennett, 2008, p 16)

Craft means skill and skill means quality. It means direct engagement with the real concrete world, in the case of youth workers, the world of human social relations and individual perceptions and behaviour. Professional, skilled workers aspire to the excellent and the excellent can only be measured in human terms which is why youth workers require a high degree of emotional intelligence. The moral imperative in youth work urges youth workers to do something well for the community. This is both a vestige of a welfare society that has been traumatised and partly ruined, and, as I suggest in this book, a really potent seed of future transformation. It is a highly prized motivation. Real craftsmanship cannot be separated from social ethics, especially in a craft like that of youth work that fundamentally deals with ethics (Young, 2006).

Marx described craftsmanship as 'form-giving activity', creating order out of chaos and mutual human appreciation out of chance and formless nature. In the early works of Marx there is a great deal of appreciation of the dignity of labour coming naturally to people within a community. But what if the purpose of that labour, like youth work, is community? It has an exceptionally high social value.

Skill is trained practice, the opposite of inspiration and instinct. Those who repeat from generation to generation the mantra that the best youth workers they know are the untrained lack any social recognition of the needs for excellence for young people. As Sennett rightly says: 'We should be suspicious of claims for innate, untrained talent' (Sennett, 2008).

Like every other concept and word, 'profession' is a class-defined term. In working-class use it is a word used in recognition of concentrated skill, of a job well done, of something done because of the integrity of the performance, rather than grace and favour, or instinct, or the superficial incentive of temporary reward. It is a human thing, a bringing together of often highly organised intellectual, emotional and physical powers in an act of conscious transformation. Engineers, or mine workers, speak confidently of their control over technique.

Skill equals autonomy and respect

In class terms it is also a concept synonymous with the autonomy of collective self-definition of practitioners within a particular area of work. It has the connotation of dignity, of being in control over your work because you have learned from the collective and the practice over time. It is a combination of the technique involved in a job and the occupational, organisational and political culture that goes with it. This was put well in a political pamphlet on skill in the early 1990s:

> In practical realities of working life, there is a direct relation between the skill of the worker and the control that they exercise in the process of production.... The best organised and class conscious Unions have historically been those of the skilled workers – mining, printing, engineering. They are generally also more class conscious of their role as citizens....The higher the level of skill the greater the power of workers at the workplace and the stronger society becomes. (CPBML, 1995, p 3)

This politicised recognition of the nature of skill from British history and workers' experience complemented work at the time to categorise and define what professionalism meant in relation to various occupational groups. A definition by Richard Winter was influential in the youth work debate (Winter, 1991). He argued that over and above the particular skills and knowledge base of a particular occupation, seven other factors were required to determine its professionalism:

- commitment to professional values
- continuous professional learning
- interpersonal effectiveness
- effective communication
- executive effectiveness
- effective synthesis of a wide range of knowledge
- intellectual flexibility.

The choice for youth workers is a simple one, whether to consider themselves as being professional, skilled craftspeople, and to act like them, or demean themselves as amateurs. It is a question of whether youth workers want to transform the oppressive conditions of young people's existence, or entertain young people in a comfortable empathy in leisure-based activities. You can either do youth work or work with young people. You can be amateur and oppressed, or professional and liberated.

5

Youth workers as trade unionists

In this chapter I give a brief account of some of the features of trade unionism among youth workers, illustrating that it is the power of combination and solidarity offered by trade unionism that has been influential in the history of youth work.

A full account of the history of trade union organisation into the main union for youth and community workers, the CYWU, now a national section of Unite the union, can be found elsewhere (Nicholls, 2009). The purpose here is to emphasise some themes and aspects of this history relevant to this study of youth work. These elements appear to endure throughout the seven distinct periods of the union's organisational history identified in *Building rapport*, and may be summarised as: a combined strong commitment to public service, standards, self-worth, fighting inequality and defining the uniqueness and professional intervention of youth work. Such commitments lead to a determined, long-term approach to winning essential demands for the workforce.

There are three important examples of this that exemplify the vision, doggedness and ability to fight against all odds that have characterised the union's history to date.

Pay up

In 1945 the CYWU began to consider the position of youth workers' wages. At that time youth workers were all on different individualised scales throughout the country. In 1946 the union resolved to produce model terms and conditions and to make representation to the Board of Education to achieve proper recognition and national terms and conditions. This began what was to be a long struggle for national collective bargaining linked to qualifications and issues relating to the standards of youth work practice. The union persistently published details of the uneven and unfair terms and conditions of youth workers throughout the country, and lobbied government with its findings. In 1949 a government report known as the Jackson Report advocated that youth workers' terms and conditions should be made consistent and comparable to other professions.

'Cinderella' fights back

In 1951 a Conservative education minister described the Youth Service as a 'frill of education'. This led to the first significant battle to save what then existed of the Youth Service. The union combined with the voluntary sector not just to save and promote youth service provision, but also to establish national collective bargaining. In the jaws of potential demolition of the fledgling youth service, the union raised its aspirations. This would be a frequently repeated attitude within the union and it originates in a deep and abiding concern for quality provision for young people. It was in that same year that the Surrey Branch of the union negotiated the first set pay rates for youth workers, and these became a model for others to emulate and a further impetus to the argument that there should be national collective bargaining. However, in the pulse of aspiration and disappointment that accompanies the struggle for social justice, the union received a letter from the government indicating that it had rejected the recommendations of another important report, the Fletcher Report, which had argued that nationally determined pay rates for youth workers should be established.

Because of the good relationship established with the voluntary sector at that time (it was, after all, those organisations that had given rise to the union in the first place), the union was able to successfully argue with many authorities that its recommended pay rates should apply not only for anyone directly employed, but also for all those in the voluntary sector grant-aided organisations.

Although cuts to the service were biting, and although progress for the development of the profession was painfully slow in the1950s, the union became the source of absolute determination to improve the quality and length of training courses, to establish national terms and conditions and to achieve a recognised status for the work and state funding for the Youth Service. The union asserted what was to become a long-standing and in fact continuing lead role in approving proposals for training courses and establishing the criteria for the validation of those courses.

Each year the union produced research on the number of youth workers employed and their salaries. An important annual survey was undertaken in 1957, which revealed that there had been a 13 per cent decline since the previous year in the number of paid workers and that the service was down to only 706 in post. The post-holders were employed on massively varying terms and conditions. A third, however, were in local authorities where greater stability of employment and better conditions of service were found.

Successful campaigning

The consistent campaigning by the union on the value of the service and the consequent value that should be given to the workforce began to break the ice. In 1958 another education minister said that the expansion of the Youth Service should not be considered. This was a significant challenge and led to immense campaigning in conjunction with voluntary organisations that forced the government to establish the Albemarle Committee on which the union was represented. It was the report of the Albemarle Committee in 1960 that led to the recommendation to invest in Youth Service facilities and staff and to establish the JNC which sets appropriate terms and conditions and relates them to the required standards of qualification. National bargaining was achieved at last.

While the Youth Service was in decline and neglect, the union not only kept it alive but also forced the government to invest in it and improve members' terms and conditions. This determined approach was drawn on again later in the Thatcher years, where the conditions of young people and the fabric of the Youth Service were severely attacked and, of course, in the period that began with the result of the May 2010 General Election, a Coalition government. As we shall see later, campaigning for the very existence of a youth service and properly respected workforce have become central struggles.

The original JNC terms and conditions gave men higher salaries than women and did not include workers working part time. As a result the union immediately embarked on two vitally important equalities campaigns. The first was to get equal pay for all members, the second to incorporate part-time workers into the national agreement on a fully pro rata basis. The union was successful after years of struggle in achieving both.

Part-time workers

The struggle for part-time youth workers is worth considering as another example of the importance of the long-term, absolute determination that has been in the union's psyche. Again, this is discussed in detail elsewhere (Nicholls, 1995), but the outline of the work has current resonance here.

The union first admitted part-time workers into its ranks in the late 1940s. It sought to harmonise their terms and conditions and to improve the nature and quality of their training and professional managerial support. By 1973 insufficient progress had been made, and together with the officers' association, the National Association of Youth and Community Education Officers (NAYCEO), the union undertook a joint survey to expose the disparity in treatment of part-time workers. Just as their full-time colleagues had been once subject to different terms and conditions in different parts of the country, so part-time workers were employed on a vast array of different, usually poor conditions, of employment. The effect of this was to ensure that practice and delivery were uneven throughout the country and a postcode lottery of provision. It was also wildly unfair, with part-time workers, for example in Cornwall, getting for many decades far less than part-time workers in most parts of the country.

A Standing Committee on part-time workers was formed in the union in 1976. Among other things it proposed a sliding scale of union membership subscriptions that would ensure that the low paid contributed relatively less in subscriptions than the higher paid. It also ensured that, at last, part-time workers in union membership would receive exactly the same benefits, no matter how much they paid in subscriptions, as full-time workers. This made union membership for part-time workers more accessible and attractive. It led to more recruitment, with part-time workers getting organised nationally, and by 1979 the first major motion to the annual conference on the subject called for an urgent campaign to achieve full parity for part-time workers. This was accelerated by a special conference on the subject in 1981 and by the gradual election of more part-time workers onto the national negotiating team on the JNC.

Branches criticised the union for a lack of progress on part-time workers' issues in the early 1980s and a part-time workers' caucus was formed in 1985 at around the same time as major statements on training for part-time workers began to appear from within the profession. The first claim for part-time workers' parity was presented to the JNC in 1986 and promptly rejected. But the marker was down. An intense twin-pronged approach began that year, with the union calling on local branches to negotiate pro rata deals locally and the national negotiators to press the matter as hard as they could nationally.

This work led to the establishment of the first ever JNC Working Party on part-time workers; the ice was well and truly broken. And in 1987 the union launched its national campaign. By 1988 minimum terms and conditions for part-time workers were introduced into the JNC report. This was not a full parity agreement, however, and left part-time workers on lower terms and conditions with considerable local discretion. Campaigning by the union was intense in 1989, and the union forced the staff side unions on the JNC to begin to prepare an equalities case against the unequal treatment of part-time workers.

In 1990 the union signed a joint charter on part-time workers' parity with the NAYCEO, and forced JNC employers to concede a joint secretarial review of part-time workers' terms and conditions. Taking matters into their own hands, the union negotiated the first comprehensive equal treatment and parity agreement for part-time workers in Walsall. The ice was starting to melt. One local authority caved in. The union added a number of important tribunal cases to its challenge to unfair treatment and further JNC working parties were held. Additionally regional accreditation and moderation panels (RAMPs) began to be set up to bring coherence and national standardisation to the training of part-time workers. Importantly they also brought recognition and certification.

Such work led to the JNC agreement in 1991 which stated that all part-time workers working over six sessions a week would be entitled to full parity of treatment. This was not enough for the union, however, which said that all those working part time, even for just three hours a week should be entitled to holiday pay, sick pay, pensions, supervision and equal pay.

Unions were taking up the question of equality more generally, and in 1993 an assertive TUC policy was passed calling for general equal treatment. This led to pressures that forced the courts in 1994 to recognise that equality of treatment for part-time workers was required. This interestingly also coincided with the first year of issuing part-time workers' qualification certificates, through the RAMPs. And it coincided with the first stirrings of NVQs, which CYWU instantly opposed as a worsening of the opportunities and training for part-time workers and which was kept at bay for many years in the youth work sector.

The union pressed ahead and tabled a full parity for part-time workers' claim in 1994. This was eventually agreed in 1995. Without it part-time workers would have been a forgotten and exploited workforce. Just as holidays and pay levels are taken for granted by youth workers today, the reality is that every element of the JNC terms and conditions were fought for by a union that has been prepared, amidst the most intense attacks on workers generally, and on the productive economy, to take the long haul approach and to never give up. This is a frame of mind very much required today.

It took around 16 years of campaigning to establish national terms and conditions. The campaign was launched as the service was being cut to ribbons. It took around 16 years to win the demand for part-time workers' parity under JNC. The campaign was launched when the Tory government was beginning its onslaught on manufacturing, the unions and public services. Advances in the service have gone hand in hand with advances in terms and conditions for the workers.

Internationalism

One other element of youth workers' trade union history must be commented on briefly here. Within the union there is a very proud history of internationalism. This has taken different forms over the decades, but it has been consistently internationalist in an interesting way.

When the first union was formed in 1886, the Manchester Girls' Clubs Workers' Union, they almost immediately contacted their counterparts working with factory girls in the US to exchange news and views. Even in the critical years of the 1940s, when the union was involved in the creation of the identity of youth work, the investment in the first Youth Service and the formulation of pay and conditions, job descriptions and training courses, it was regularly in correspondence with embryonic youth services and professional associations from as far afield as Hungary and Canada.

In the immediate period of the aftermath of the Second World War, the union was approached to try and involve youth workers in important work to help create peace and reconciliation in Europe. Youth workers subsequently played no small part in bringing together young people from previously hostile countries to imagine a peaceful future. This established the work of the union's International Committee. This was pivotal and pioneering in ensuring that youth workers were funded and equipped to take young people overseas to widen their horizons and understanding. It was through such international exchanges that many young people, who would have had no chance at such things through schooling or work, achieved their first opportunities to visit overseas and to learn more about the world.

This work endured and expanded considerably until the 1980s, when a change of direction was agreed at a national conference. Instead of just facilitating youth exchanges and supporting youth workers in all ways to undertake youth work safely and productively, the union developed a very strong trade union sense of internationalism, giving support to workers in struggles in other countries, promoting understanding of conflict areas in the world, visiting socialist countries advocating peace and opposing war. In the late 1980s and 1990s, the union was very influential at TUC level in creating the first formal links with Cuban unions, it moved the main motion opposing the Iraq war and has been a consistent opponent of EU developments.

Union members were strong contributors to the anti-apartheid movement, and invited speakers from overseas from successful socialist countries or from countries undergoing serious problems. In 2010 the union's main full-time officer was Vice President of the Venezuela Solidarity Campaign and organiser of the first trade union visits and links with the Vietnamese trade unions since the Vietnam war.

Rapport, the union's magazine, features a regular column on international issues. Union speakers addressed youth workers' conferences throughout the world, and union leaders were invited to contribute to debates about professionalisation in many countries large and small, from the US to Luxembourg.

The union's central concerns for the quality of employment conditions goes hand in hand with its concerns and influence over the quality of professional delivery, the nature of youth policies and the need for proper state investment. Without organisation around these issues over the years, it is no exaggeration to say that youth work would not exist today. Many of the great theoreticians and proponents of youth work, from Josephine McAlister Brew in the 1940s to Janet Batsleer, Bernard Davies and Howard Williamson today, have been active union members. It has been an essential component of youth work. Key elements of the best of youth work practice, such as quality supervision of work, would not exist without the work of the union that at one stage even had a national standing committee on supervision. Quality supervision was to become one of the first victioms of subsequent austerity measures and this directly impacted on the nature and focus of the work.

6

Youth workers as socialists

This chapter reflects on youth work and its relationship to socialism and a general historical view of it . It seeks to understand how different youth work methodologies and theories, despite their different political persuasions, may in fact all amount to something very progressive and more essential now than previously.

Socialism is a new form of social organisation that grows within the womb of the old order, capitalism. Curiously, however, one of its parents does not want it to be born, and would prefer that it disappeared. It will make its coming into the world as difficult as possible. Capitalism depends on the existence of a working class that has nothing to sell but its labour power. And those who work for a living find their needs and fulfilment as human beings cannot be met by the system.

Capitalism is a relationship between classes. Ours is large, theirs small (Aaronovitch, 1961; Sampson, 2004; Hardt and Negri, 2005). The working class creates and produces everything, including the best and the worst ideas. To sustain yourself as a worker you need, food, shelter, healthcare, education, wages, civil administration and a capacity to organise together to defend your interests. You need to express yourself as a person and explore ideas without repression. You depend, in other words, on very collective, publicly supported things. You are part of a collective. The social relationships that you and your family depend on are collective ones.

Common wealth

The greater good flows from a sense of common wealth. Sharing and caring are the stronger values of a working-class world. In order to produce things that we need, whether food or clothing, it takes a collective organisation of the means of production. Yet these means of production are privately owned and therefore relationships within production are inherently unjust. We do the toil, they get the spoil.

The private nature of the ownership of production creates an overall structural injustice. Hence the continual resistance throughout the world by workers to attempts to privatise services, utilities and industries. Why should private wealth and ownership be amassed when its source is in the collective labour of the majority? Why should anyone profit from the natural resources that lead to water and energy supply? What is wrong with reapplying the notion of common wealth that originated when the first capitalists arose and which has been reasserted eloquently in our own time (Martin, 1989; Wood, 2007; Hardt and Negri 2009). Socialism, like capitalism, has many historic forms. In all previously class-divided societies there have been forms of socialism, although each previous form, in Britain especially, has been incapable of gaining a position of power because its understanding of social mechanisms and its aspirations have been limited.

Struggle

At the heart of society is a continual struggle between the ideas and organisations of collective aspirations and those that defend individual, private rights of ownership and control. If the private owners of production no longer want to produce because they can make quicker bucks elsewhere, or their rate of return is too low, they can shift and stop production at the click of a mouse, devastating communities that depend on employment in productive industries. It is the contradiction between workers' needs and those of the owners that drives history onwards and creates the civil war at the heart of our society. Youth workers are compelled to ask continually which side they are on in pursuing such and such a course of action.

Democratic practice

Alongside concepts of collectivity and social responsibility go important concepts of democracy and accountability. From a collectivist standpoint concepts of majority decision are better than minority decision. Concepts of discourse, dialogue, consultation and negotiation are better than concepts of imposition, order, monologue and diktat. You cannot be part of a collective unless you are in perpetual dialogue to test out ideas and agree courses of action in the interests of the majority. There must be a direct connection between the thought and the action and between those who decide it and those with the authority to carry it out in the collective interest.

Lifeworld

The concept of lifeworld and system, taken from the German philosopher Jürgen Habermas, is perhaps one that will have resonance with youth workers in regard to the debate about youth workers' contribution to socialism (Habermas, 1989; Finlayson, 2005). Habermas makes the distinction between regulated and less regulated spheres of existence. The lifeworld, or community as we may more commonly refer to it, is a description of the informal unmarketised domains of social life: family and household, culture, political life outside of organised parties, the mass media and voluntary organisations. It is an unregulated world of sociality where there are shared meanings and understandings and clear social boundaries for everyday encounters with other people. It is no less political than the 'politics' of the system itself, with its licensed parties and professional 'politicians'.

The lifeworld is the untheoretical world of everyday life. It is where communal activity and communication take place, as it were, naturally. People communicate constantly about their life and actions, what is happening, what could happen. It is the messy, gossipy, unplanned sphere of groups and networks within communities. It is a world that the market and dominant, establishment ideas find difficult to penetrate, although the mass media in recent years have been quite successful. It is a world that has a largely unwritten history and no significant media presence. Its life is stereotyped and transformed in soaps and reality shows. The media tend to project back an entirely false and dysfunctional image of the working class. Despite constant pressure and distortion, the working-class communal lifeworld is a place of mutuality and solidarity.

It is a world whose behaviour 'the Establishment' can never fully predict. It is a world that can exist within the best of highly organised workplace trade unionism, where workers have significant control over production and workplace decisions, and in the culture of the best trade unions that deliberately create a durable internal democracy and power base in opposition to that of the employers.

For this world to be successful, protective, creative and useful, it must have shared meanings and communal bonds. It must develop its own morality and ethics and develop continually through a renewed consensus. Superficially this may appear to make it subservient to the status quo. It is like creating oases of comfort in a world of wars. It may seem to tolerate and ignore the system by concentrating on an alternative that will never challenge wider systemic problems.

Unnecessary tensions

I, however, believe that this is not the case. The situation is far more complicated, and the community as a complex, alternative lifeworld in contradiction to the system is more dynamic than many recognise. It is, after all, the product of consciousness. It is the failure to appreciate that this alternative lifeworld has at the very least contradictory pulses within it which has led to many unnecessary tensions within youth and community work.

Workers agonise, often unnecessarily, about working in and against the state, for and against the status quo, by virtue of their employment position, compliant, by virtue of their professional action, defiant. Such debates have related fiercely to questions of assistance to young people in the labour market. Some say it is nothing to do with youth workers to encourage and assist young people in entering the world of work. This, they argue, merely recycles labour for capitalism and teaches them to be compliant workers satisfied with their exploitation. If entering the labour market as if grateful to have a job is the objective then there is something wrong. But youth workers want young people to have meaningful rewarding employment, to assert their rights, to be trade unionised at work and equipped to discipline employers who overstep the mark. Such work is an essential contribution to socialism.

The system

The system, on the other hand, as Habermas and youth workers may describe it, refers to established patterns and structures of action with an instrumental purpose linked to making profit. Its focus is on money and power. These are the mainstay of capitalism and its main coordinating mechanisms, and cut deeply into the fabric of social life, seeking to dominate community. All those who work for a company, from top to bottom, are driven by the profit motive – it is this that drives their actions. This motive was formed independently of the participants and in that sense is not the product of democratic consensus. Question the underlying motive of the company you work for and you diminish your chances of promotion. Questioning is discouraged. You have to be integrated into the 'system'.

Often the community is a release from the system, in either an escapist, conformist way, or in a challenging way. Affection and appreciation with friends and family and within community groups can be found that the system does not tolerate elsewhere. Elements of community life or a lifeworld are clear counter-cultural alternatives to the system. This in part explains much of the escapism inherent in some early socialist-oriented youth movements like the Woodcraft Folk, where the escape into healing nature and social solidarities and camaraderie was seen as being important (Davis, 2000). This was also a consistent theme taken up in the work and writings of the founder of the Woodcraft Folk, Leslie Paul, and may, in fact, be said to constitute a key element of youth work practice (Paul, 1980).

An alternative

In summary, much youth and community work has sought to build this alternative world, to add fun, challenge, exploration and utopian alternatives to the capitalist world. The politics of the excluded has been the driving force of history, and the politics of the great and the good has been a sequence of shadows and reflections, oppressions and suppressions (Harris, 2001).

In a communal lifeworld there are spheres of activity that are conducive to ideas of personal autonomy, meaning the pursuit of self-chosen ends, within a democratic framework in which actions are designed for the improvement of the collective. This is a sphere of democratic counter-culture. Its importance increases everyday as the incursions of the system become ever more intrusive. Money and power steer people towards ends that are not related to understanding and consensus. Alternatively, the collective sphere people work in seeks to steer participants to social goals and the process of achieving this requires understanding and consensus. It follows that for youth workers, the interrelationship between lifelong learning and community development and learning is vitally important.

It is the success of the lifeworld as an alternative place of refuge from the ravages of exploitation and alienation at work and the horrors depicted on the television of a world constantly in crisis that leads it to stick to its own, to satisfy itself with its little utopias of beneficial human relationships.

Habermas also shows how this more authentic world of human relationships is raided by the forces of money and power. This has great consequences for social cohesion and democracy. Community associations once able to negotiate with local authorities are unable to relate to the private contractors and transnational corporations that increasingly have power over planning and development in neighbourhoods. Strategic decisions that affect community life are left to the markets or to administrative 'experts' or private consultancies immune to public scrutiny.

Habermas shows how, as the sphere of community shrinks, the market moves into previously non-marketable areas with disastrous effects. As a result, shared meanings fragment and mutual understandings disintegrate. Highly territorialised mentalities and gangs may be an expression of this, racism another. Social bonds, often in communities intergenerational, begin to melt. Common caring and concern are replaced by indifference, a mercenary attitude and a blame culture. There is demoralisation and consequent unwillingness to take responsibility for actions and social developments. All this causes a breakdown in social order within the community. These obvious trends in social decay demand the restorative power of effective youth and community development in every neighbourhood.

The state of youth itself, especially, perhaps, the years between 13 and 19, are like a lifeworld, a community, a place that is difficult for the system to touch and destroy. The formation of ideas and self-perceptions during this period, the forging of identity within family and community, all make the condition of youth a site of competing battlegrounds. Every force, communal or sinister, wants to shape the ideas of the young in its own image, knowing that they will be difficult to reshape later as adults. This only stresses the importance to socialism of having workers with young people who will be seeking only to empower the young person to create themselves, their views, desires and actions within a democratically supportive environment. This is why youth work is so socialist.

Youth club utopia

Youth clubs have served in a very underestimated way as utopian commonwealths and mini democracies at their best, providing place and space for independent self-discovery and an appreciation of the value of free association. The difficulty of touching young people's minds directly has led neoliberalism to create an economy and culture that demonises the young, deliberately makes them unemployed, ejects them from expensive education and puts them under constant surveillance as if they were threats .Youth workers are a vital defence in preventing the system from polluting young minds further. Even rescue and reform have become revolutionary in their contrast with what is on offer now. Socialism would rescue and reform more young people from the ravages of poverty, unemployment, underemployment, brutal, low paid work and the corrupting chaos of a violent culture.

Some limited traditions of so-called radical community work, or radical youth work, have been nothing of the really radical kind. All they have tried to do is to introduce a challenge to the system from an inappropriate platform within the community. They see community as collusive with the state as tolerant of injustice and therefore part of the problem. Compared with neoliberalism's intentions now, vibrant neighbourhood development is a progressive thing. We could do with a few more neighbours running errands for each other and sharing facilities to combat the selfish culture that pervades. We could do with more community and youth workers creating dynamic connections between workplace struggles and those in the neighbourhood. Trade unions could usefully employ community and youth workers to develop a more inclusive culture internally and forge more links with the public externally.

Challenging

Challenging the status quo is a status quo concept. A challenge does not necessarily change things. It punches up against something and satisfies itself that it has done enough. All things constantly change, however. Capitalism itself is a dynamic system in constant change and flux, and its leading groups have, over the decades, been transformed and its methods of accumulation altered. It is based on robbery, but different kinds of robbery at different times. The financiers who recently pulled off the biggest heist in its history resulting in the current economic crisis did so in a more respectable manner than the armed thugs who first stole the land from the people after the Battle of Hastings (Beresford, 2007). The dependence of much profit on highly organised criminal gangs has been well charted (Glenny, 2008).

Just as workers working for a company can contribute to a corporate purpose contradictory to their needs and beyond their control, so youth workers over several generations have contributed to a purpose that some have not chosen and not necessarily been aware of. This has three interrelated aspects. First, they have assisted the consolidation, formation and reduplication of many community lifeworlds and advanced the social position of young people in society. Second, they have contributed to the creation of a culture of challenge to the system; and finally, they have made a significant contribution to the formation of the embryo of socialism within the existing capitalist order. The ideological motivations of the participants in these processes have been secondary to the overall beneficial effect, and strong ideological approaches have been subsumed in a general trend towards progress and enhancement.

Socialism

Socialist societies have put the care of children and the young at the heart of their social and economic programme and have involved a liberated youth in social and political change. The progressive practice of youth work in Britain has made a major contribution in this regard and created a unique public service on the side of young people. Youth workers can be proud to have been agents of a social control geared to other directions and proud, too, that within their traditions there is a rich seam of practice where youth workers have sought to be explicit agents of socialist control. Socialism is not an unreachable ideal beyond any individual action. It is expressed in the actions and gestures of fostering and nurture, mutual care and assistance and growth that so many youth and community practices contribute to.

An ultra-left approach to the contribution and position of youth workers will stress the ideological bias of the intervention and be particularly sceptical of the potential of any state-funded source of employment. It seeks to extract an abstract principle called youth work or radical community development from history and context and compare it as an absolute against practice that will always fall short. It condemns those traditions of community and youth work that are rich in the indoctrination of a particular religious or cultural bias as strongly as it condemns secular, state or voluntary sector-led interventions conducted under the illusion of neutrality.

Contemporary history throws these divisive debates into some sharp relief. Where would you prefer your children to go, to the Scouts, or join the local armed gang of drug dealers? In many communities the social breakdown is so extreme that the positive experience of supportive youth work is a tremendous relief regardless of its orientation. The youth work that starts where the young person is and develops their potential without seeking to indoctrinate into a theology or an establishment-related philosophy is obviously the kind of intervention that we require.

Within this other lifeworld, or community, adults run activities for young people and relate to young people outside of the family to enable them to have fun, harmless association and a fulfilling use of their leisure time. Voluntary youth organisations and youth workers spring from this positive motivation to be involved and to engage the young and pass on forms of communal solidarity and self-worth.

The value of voluntary activity led first to the recognition that positions for paid youth work needed to be created and to the recognition later that this work needed its own qualification system and then that it needed state funding. The problem is not that the state has sought to find its own alternatives to youth work, but that it has failed to take on and support youth work as a beneficial public service. This is arguably because youth work is so close to the community and so resistant to the world of the system. It is simply based on different values. Voluntary activity, as Beveridge himself observed and studied in his pioneering work to introduce the welfare state, was closely linked to social action (Beveridge, 1948).

Constituted and constituent power

The political philosopher Antonio Negri (1999) offers another useful distinction that helps describe the effective terrain of youth work's operations. Negri inverts the normal perception that the state is somehow primary and the ruled are secondary. He makes the distinction between constituted and constituent power. Constituent power is a community, the people, civil society, the lifeworld. It is socially creative, politically innovative and always in historical movement and dynamic change. Constituted power, on the other hand, is empty, all it does is try to contain constituent power. Constituent power animates the never-ending activity of resistance and organisation, rebellion, political dissent and opposition to formally constituted power. Constituent power relates to the democratic forces of social transformation, the means by which human beings make their own history.

The lifeworld of Habermas, or the oppressed, as Freire might describe it, or the excluded, as others put it, is not the domain of the permanently victimised and silenced. It is the living, breathing source of inspiration for a liberated future, a powerful wave of social transformation that has been responsible for the significant progressive changes in human history. It is the world of those who are excluded who do not want to be included in the existing social order of things.

The free play of thought on the circumstances of the lives we need to live in a powerful social transformation is a necessary precursor of collective action. This explains why the focus within youth work practice is on conversation; dialogue is the medium of learning for change in this occupation (Smith, 1994). But what is the topic of conversation? Content is equally as important as form. Youth workers have to start talking more about ending capitalist relations of production in order to exercise their professional role more effectively and have something really interesting to talk about.

7

Youth workers and the state

This chapter challenges some common preconceptions of the state that occur in the youth work debate, and explores how the practice of youth work itself filters an occupationally specific conception of the state. It argues that a new form of state must be imagined and built if young people are to prosper.

The state in a capitalist society ensures that society makes profit for the few, it protects private property relations, administers a capitalist economy and represses dissent. Youth workers help create beautiful things in young people. While the core purposes of the two are incompatible, in periods of active class struggle the state is forced to concede many beneficial public arrangements like healthcare, social protection, welfare and education. Through taxation it creates publicly available revenue that can then be fought over in terms of political priorities for expenditure. It is a paradoxical beast. The state stands over and above governments whose powers, especially under the Lisbon Treaty of the EU, are actually quite limited. And as we have seen recently, governments are also helpless in the face of the power of the financiers.

Youth workers experience the best and worst aspects of the state every day. It is both an organism over and above society, and an instrument of obvious forms of coercion and less obvious forms of consent making (Mandel, 1978; Negri, 1999). It has dominant coercive forms of management and integrative, ideological ones in which the range of ideas that benefit the rulers are promoted and reduplicated. Its integrative functions are achieved through instruction, education, culture and control over promotion into

---

133

leading civil service, military, media and administrative positions. At its pinnacle are a relatively small group of finance capitalists, media moguls, key state officials and armed service personnel (Aaronowitch, 1961; Paxman, 1990).

The elite

A relatively small but elaborate breeding ground of public schools and universities grow their own for the upper echelons of this state machine (Hartmann, 2007). In Britain's case the state functions according to a particularly strange set of unwritten constitutional conventions. These are somehow glued together by a peculiar compromise with a dysfunctional family that owns more land throughout the world than anyone else put together (Gray and Tomkins, 2005; Temple, 2008; Bogdanor, 2009). It arises from a closed circle of close acquaintants sharing similar outlooks. The state did not always exist in its current form, however, and exists as a testament to the incompatibility between the public and private spheres, the lifeworld and the system. Tribal communities do not have state structures, feudal societies have rudimentary forms within hierarchical structures, capitalist societies have complex state formations encompassing armed forces, prisons, tax systems, policing, parliamentary conventions, schooling, media control and the like.

For some youth workers, working for local government, or government, means working for an evil employer – the draconian state – and becoming tainted by its authoritarian patronage. It risks selling out. Some would argue that it means being paralysed at work, being unable to transmit an authentically emancipatory awareness and class consciousness among those with whom they work. This is like saying that the engineers who make tanks are war mongers. Regrettably, workers have to work for a living and cannot always politically choose their employer. The skills developed for an employer's benefit also benefit workers, and their class, if they want them to. Tanks could become tractors with the same engineering skills in a different set of social relationships. Similarly, youth workers could be employed as agents of coercion and control.

Two cheers for the bourgeois state

Contracts are one thing, job descriptions another. The state has countenanced thousands of progressive job descriptions in youth work. Its formal definition of youth work is contained in several places, as outlined in Chapter 1. The NOS retained by a sector skills council, Lifelong Learning UK, the validation guidelines held in the custody of the Education and Training Standards Committees of the four nations that choose to do so and sponsored and supported by all of their governments and the subject benchmarks agreed by the Quality Assurance Authority for Higher Education. It is worth considering these official definitions of youth work in detail to see how the state has been coerced in the interests of youth work. It is not all one-way traffic in this relationship.

All of these definitions have been foisted on state bodies by practitioners. They have literally come about because of wide consultation with the field, from practitioners, lecturers, managers, employers and volunteers. Youth workers have colonised the state to the extent that it has agreed with the underlying values and competencies they say go to make up their work and the training that is needed to prepare for it. Someone is a youth worker first and foremost – this is what marks the person out; a youth worker is not defined by who he or she works for. Employers are lucky to have skilled youth workers who deploy their skills where they can have the most impact and enjoy the best conditions of employment.

The first starting point in a discussion about the state is a heresy in some circles – the state isn't all that bad. If it was, it wouldn't have agreed to the self-definitions outlined in Chapter 1. Many of the aspects of the contemporary world of 'freedoms' and liberal democracy, the trade unions, collective bargaining, the universal vote for all those over the age of 18, widespread more or less free education and health provision, a certain 'freedom' of the press, all were won through long years of struggle and sacrifice.

It would be a grave mistake to condemn these gains as having been appropriated and neutralised to the extent that they themselves have become part of the state machinery. None of the developments were the natural consequences of capitalism; they were forced on it. The state changes and continually concedes and retreats, regroups, reforms, changes, goes on to the offensive.

Unincorporated

At one point in history industrial capitalists and the first workers' organisations saw the development of the state as a threat because it threatened free trade. Radicals opposed it because they saw it as an instrument of oppression against the poor and as rebellious. As organised and centralised local and national state functions became more necessary to sustain the physical requirements of an advanced society – sewerage systems, transport, schools, taxation etc – it became more acceptable to allow state services to enter a range of personal and social areas of life. There was a mixed set of imperatives causing this new expansion – capitalist self-interest was there, but so was charitable humanism and militant trade union demands and socialist and communist-led reforms. This made state formations and administrative systems a mix of positive and negative impulses from the start.

The great boost to forms of contradictory state intervention came after the Second World War when industries were nationalised, key utilities were brought under public control and the welfare state was created with its great pinnacle, the National Health Service. Personal security was socialised. Redistributive democracy became a social consensus, equality and high levels of employment were high, often cross-party aspirations. As a result the state and its government gained credibility as meaningful decision-making bodies. This growth for three decades after the Second World War was abruptly halted when capitalism got fed up with it and sought revenge. The new nationalised welfare state had made whole areas of the economy no go areas for profit.

One so-called international crisis followed another. The manufacturing base of industrialised countries like Britain was pulled apart, the traditional source of profit making in producing things through science and technology and manufacture was replaced by other ways of accumulating capital. It forced the sale of council housing and the mass marketisation of domestic properties and the expansion of unaffordable mortgage markets. It made the credit card and the idea of living permanently in debt and not fighting for wages a culture of individualism.

Meaningful trade union action was made illegal or so difficult as to be near impossible to organise legally. The deliberate collapse of industry meant mass youth unemployment and the serious demonisation of the young who rebelled against it. Today, as conditions generally worsen, and despairing individual acts of terrorism in the name of religion and a return to superstitious ideologies menace our streets, so the state becomes more and more authoritarian, seeking in effect to punish the world for the poverty, wars, alienation and despair that it itself was creating. In its drift to authoritarianism the state, outside of its main military and repressive components, dissipates its own authority in a range of unaccountable bodies and a mass privatisation of its welfare functions. The cult of the consultant and contractor takes over. No one is accountable and elected any more, it seems to me.

The community and not-for-profit sector become the so-called 'third sector', and the previous role of voluntary organisations in keeping an independent campaigning check on the incursions and gaps in the state's provision gets watered down as charities are forced to compete with each other like private businesses for a share of the market. The state becomes more and more a tool of the neoliberal culture and marketplace and less interested directly in the personal and social development of its citizens and their well-being. Personal welfare is a matter for personal, customised consumption. Prisons even, once public places for public reform, become huge privatised punishment blocks.

In this the role of youth work and its long-standing affinity to movements of social justice and civil rights becomes more, not less, vital. As the state changes and abandons its people, they become more necessary than ever as critics of the deterioration and collapse of liberal democracy. The issue is that history does not repeat itself, and the material conditions that gave rise to liberal conditions cannot be resurrected. So how can we think and act in a new way? Perhaps we are seeking to achieve what has never been achieved, the abolition of private property relations that cause the problems in the first place.

An evil state

I believe that the state is the oppressor of young people, the exploiter of youth workers and the great collective defender of the accumulation of capital. Its promotion of fear and authoritarianism, its dissipation of powers into huge conglomerates such as the EU or small and multiple consultancies and quangos, are also key problems of the historical moment. This is all part of draining power more and more away from the people.

The general understanding of the state within youth and community work is as ambiguous as the nature of the state itself. Some see it as universally bad, some as worse than bad, some do not think about it at all, some believe they are constantly at war against it, while others are secretly happy to keep quiet order to gain promotion and awards within it. There may have been plenty of self-definition in youth work, but in the absence of self-organisation in trade union terms, the understanding of the state is bound to be diffuse, contradictory and varied within the sector.

On the one hand, there is a general recognition that the condition of young people is worsened by the poverty created by capitalism and the distorted personal relationships that arise from the marketplace and the persistence of acute inequalities of opportunity and income. There is an accompanying awareness that these conditions are policed by forces and systems that seek to punish and oppress rather than nurture and liberate. There is an understanding, particularly among those who remember the miner's strike, that the state will physically attack and seek to destroy those who most oppose its purpose in regulating capital accumulation and the association of labourers.

There is a sometimes subconscious recognition that the state has a consistency beyond the ephemeral comings and goings of political parties and politicians in parliament. It is sometimes called 'the Establishment', a sinister set of conventions, manners and networks handed down from one generation of rulers to another. Their rituals demand obedience and conformity. But the workings of the Establishment are kept at arm's-length from the mind occupied with local neighbourhood improvements and face-to-face exchanges.

The role of the state and the relationship of youth workers to it is, then, as problematic as it is problematised. The main experience youth workers have of state employees from the other end of the interaction spectrum to them are with police officers. Crudely, police officers seek punishment and information leading to the prevention of or penalty for criminal behaviour. Youth workers seek to prevent anti-social behaviour and recognise that the circumstances that lead to crime, the social structures of division and decay, are more criminal often than the actions of young people in response to them.

The thought police

Strict professional boundaries are often drawn at neighbourhood level to keep the peace, and there are clear job demarcation lines between policing and youth work. The police, in obeying the law, primarily service goods and private property; youth workers serve young people. Community, preventative policing has always been a secondary function of policing, but who do you call if a young person on drugs threatens you and your child with a loaded gun? A police officer on the beat desperately saddened by the plight of young people on their patch is not exactly acting for the state, but how will that police officer act if called on to police your picket line when you are calling for more pay? To say that anything is inherently bad is to ignore the contradictory nature of all phenomenon. You do not always need a force of coercion to tell you what not to do; most of the time you make your own choices. We police our own thoughts.

The state is experienced all too often by youth workers in their work to support young people in the criminal justice system. It is not always conceptualised as a more complex social formation that has an impact on many elements of their lives including, of course, the punitive anti-worker and anti-trade union legislation on the statute books. It seems to me that the state appears to punish young people for the crimes that it has committed against them. The legal system seems to run on statute books that oppose workers and their unions and young people and their desperation. It sides with notions of respectability and order that cause the communal disrespect and chaos that provoke anti-social behaviours in the first place.

Youth workers, such as the oppressed Shylock in the *Merchant of Venice* (Shakespeare), who is classified as a non-citizen, watch the everyday operation and profitability of the law proceed happily despite the mounting inequalities and instances of social exclusion which turn out to be quite justified and entirely legal.

The law greases the wheels of commerce and authoritarian power and the unaccountability of the large, tax-avoiding corporations while latent injustices in the community remain unresolved. Social life collapses, the rule of law prospers. What seems like chronic social meltdown tearing into the lives of rejected, neglected, abused, unwanted, criminalised, sick young people in the eyes of youth workers, in the eyes of those closer to the repressive elements of the state, is seen as a temporary nuisance. The cynical indifference of the law to endemic, systemic social corruption and injustice is itself indicative of a sort of social breakdown.

However unreachable the upper pinnacles of the state may be to those primarily working within tightly confined neighbourhoods, the interlocking pyramids that make up the state are various and contradictory and within reach. Important distinctions need to be made between these elements so that youth workers can gain a better bearing as to where they are really placed in relation to them.

'Having a good chat'

Youth workers have to begin at ground level. They work in the medium of conversation, and conversation is composed of words. They often work with those most excluded from social participation and most feared by the state, with those generally speaking too young to have a vote or often too disinterested to exercise their vote. Among young people it is often the language of carnivalesque satire and exuberance, of inventive slang and humour, of irreverence and great sensitivity that creates a potent form of politics.

Meaning is often replaced by style. In young people's languages apparently normal connotations and sense are inverted; through them the world is turned upside down. Dialects and musical and lyrical forms emerge creatively from the street. Youth workers revel in the poetry of the genuinely authentic human perception, revelation or insight. They bless the relaxed and shun the formal.

The state pretends that it functions according to the rule of law. And law is conducted in particular through dialogue and the precise use of words. Both language and the law are communicative actions that bring us into relationship and community by externalising private experience and making it open to public judgement and response. Speech is a form of action and the silencing of dissenting voices is a key role for the law and the state. The illusion of free speech and free association does not necessarily apply to a group of trade unionists who have just successfully voted for strike action, or to a group of homeless young people who squat an empty but still owned property, or the group of unemployed young people who stand at a workplace entrance and demand employment there.

Youth work exists alongside the transforming energy of conversation in vibrant languages that express the constantly changing perceptions of young people in their lively, internal questioning of everything they see and feel. It is fluid dialogue with an unknown start point and an unknown destination. The conversation is full of uncertainty and disruptive unpredictability. Anything could happen. You never quite know where the journey will lead. The state's new managerial philosophy does not like this at all and wants every youth worker to target and accredit their interventions. It requires an accredited containment of inspiration and action and involvement. Opposition to this approach is effective opposition to de-skilling and managerial control over youth work. Youth workers are expected to speak the language of the employer, not of the streets, where the real power lies.

This domain of conversation contrasts dramatically with the nature of the youth justice system, the social work system, the police, imprisonment, classroom teaching and the more proscribed areas of intervention such as educational welfare, careers advice, probation, medical treatment and health education.

In my view youth work constantly makes a mistake by identifying the styles required within those other professional practices with stultifying state domination. In other words, the formal working practices of other state employees are disregarded by an ultra-leftist trend within youth work, as a form of coercion and repression. Youth work animates the often formless chaos inside young people. Other services seek to inject form into them. But this does not mean they are automatically reactionary and repressive. The cistern contains and the fountain overflows, as the poet William Blake said. Exuberance appears to be beauty in youth work and on the other hand, containment and confinement seem to be enforced elsewhere to create repression and ugliness. But it is not quite this simple.

In and against the state

This apparent contrast may lead youth workers to consider that their approach is the only viable one and the one that will most fully liberate young people from the clutches of an obedience-loving state. The compliance of other professions is challenged by the defiance of youth workers in action, and this results in ever greater tensions in the multiagency teams of integrated youth services. One thing is evident and that is that good youth workers side with young people and their rights more readily and passionately than many other occupations. As the state abandons young people, so this activity becomes increasingly against the state, intensifying the contradictions of working in and for yet against the state (Cockburn, 1977).

The state is the employer and, in part, the designer of all of these different approaches to young people. The debate is not really whether these other interventions with young people are good or bad or indifferent – ultimately they are all to some extent or another needed in dealing with different aspects of young people's lives, especially when they are broken by capitalism – but what is the overall balance, the emphasis? Should we be investing in punishment or prevention? Should policy emphasise education and development or casework and leisure? The precise nature of the state's intentions is revealed at any given time in an analysis of these factors.

This book argues that the balance is currently heavily tipped in the favour of negative approaches to young people. It is no longer the case that young people are seen as a threat in social policy terms, nor as a reserve army of potential labour. They are seen much more insidiously as a disposable, unwanted commodity. And this is exactly why youth workers and youth work are more needed than ever. We have moved beyond the state seeking to coerce and ideologically smother the young, to a situation in a war economy, in which the young and non-productive are seen as totally disposable.

Soft subversion

The state finds complex ways to accommodate and appropriate subversive and potentially disruptive activity. It has done this in the fields of religion, culture and workers' organisation ever since it was created. Like any other sphere of progressive activity, youth work can itself become subverted and constrained by the dominant order that maintains, and is indeed legitimised through, the pretence of 'making space' for what is, in fact, a wholly tamed and supervised 'subversion'.

But with its extremely positive commitments to the power of young people, its firm humanist confidence in the perfectability of all individuals, and its unfailing alliance with young people, youth work can take inspiration from itself that it is far more constructive in its relationship with the state than it may sometimes give itself credit for.

Some strands of thinking within the sector like to see youth work itself as the aberrant teenager, the jester revealing the structural hypocrisies of the system, the subversive graffiti artist brazenly daubing a gesture of opposition on a wall. I have always thought these are weak strands of thinking. Youth work does not ask simply how conventional politics can be subverted; it questions how they are established and maintained, it constantly brings to our attention the permanent state of crisis and collapse, contradiction and injustice within the system, a system that cannot guarantee a stable present for young people and therefore a prosperous social future.

This is a far stronger role than radical subversion. Its approach along with progressive education, play work, community work and adult education is key to the transformation and building of a new kind of education system within a new state. Humour must be one of its weapons, it must mock and make the natural seem abnormal. Unless it has serious objectives, it will lack humour. Its main objective is to be part of the creation of a new democratic state run in our interests as a class. None of us ever voted for the state that now rules over us, happy and glorious. Youth workers' starting point should always be a rejection of the state of things as they are, the state as it currently is and the ideas that hold it together.

PART IV
PROFESSIONAL DEMANDS

8

Youth workers in defence of youth work

What makes up youth work? It is not an abstract idea, or a set of methods linked to a vocation. It has a real presence, with real structures and organisations to promote and defend it. The battles to create and defend youth work over the years have been many, and key to their success have been organised workers campaigning in conjunction with progressive educationalists and the voluntary sector. There is a long legacy, as old as youth work itself, to this tradition, and the history of changes caused by the collective action of youth workers has only just started to be written. In this chapter I look at some of the important pieces of work that have developed in the struggle for youth work since the Education and Inspections Act of 2006 began the demise of youth work.

To cement youth work into place, youth workers' predecessors said that there must be a clear set of professional values and methods of working, that these must be transparent and recognised and should form the basis of all training for youth workers. They said that youth work should be located within a publicly funded youth service working in partnership with the voluntary sector. They believed that the voluntary sector should be politically independent and able to promote the needs of young people. And, if there was a recognised qualification and professional values, they naturally thought there must be national terms and conditions.

Youth work cannot be properly valued if every employer pays identically committed, skilled and trained youth workers differently and is not required to employ people with the right value base. This puts the market in charge of the value of the work and not the other way around. The Youth Service must be fully funded. It must be recognised that youth work provides space for young people and seeks to enlighten, educate, develop and emancipate. All activities are tools to this end. Therefore workers must be professionally autonomous; their relationship building must be measured by the quality of their work experienced by young people. Professionally autonomous workers, publicly accountable, must also account for each other and support each other. Anything that defends these positions contributes to the defence of youth work. We must look at recent events with this in mind.

There has been nothing spontaneous about the creation and growth of youth work. It hasn't arisen as if by magic. It has been created by generations of committed informal educators fighting for a better social, political and economic situation for young people. Over recent years youth workers have been forced to defend the organisation, funding, infrastructure, values and professionalism of youth work. The situation is now critical, and to go forward youth workers must take stock and realise where their platforms of defence are. The response to the attacks on services for young people is going to have to be deeper, more comprehensive and more combative.

Act and action

The Education and Inspection Act 2006 was interpreted as giving a firmer statutory position for youth work. 'Positive activities' for young people were interpreted as including social and political education and development, protecting the voluntary relationship with young people. However, this assurance was only given by a Labour minister in a House of Lords debate – youth work hangs by a thin thread indeed.

The Act was also based on the report by the accountancy firm PricewaterhouseCoopers that there was a £6 billion a year 'market' in children and young people's services, so all services to children and young people should be tested on the market and open to tender by any private company wanting to run them. Second, it led to a process whereby services to children and young people were integrated prior to commissioning out or privatising.

CYWU and the T&G (Transport and General Workers' Union), in a special conference at the time, won an assurance from the minister Beverley Hughes MP that this did not mean the disintegration of professional specialisms or funding. Yet this is exactly what this did mean. IYSS, as predicted, soon faced huge funding cuts, and even in the first year of IYSS in England it was clear in the CYWU research that youth work was being put into the blender and whizzed up into a brown mush both of mish-mashed services and multidisciplinary teams.

Soup or salad

The CWDC became the main vehicle for this blending. A number of private companies became the arm's-length ideological mechanisms whereby this blending was secured. These processes then hit the mounting economic crisis. Banks across the world nearly went bust and in Britain, as in other countries, the government had a bright idea that workers would bail them out with their tax revenues and as a 'reward', all public services and public sector pay would be cut.

CYWU/Unite opposed the privatisation of services and held a conference. They called again for discrete public investment in a statutory youth service. They also got commitments from ministers throughout the UK that that in integrated youth services professional specialisms would be protected and valued. This became a theme more honoured in the breach of the new Children's and Young People's Workforce Development Partnership on which the union was represented.

Professional meltdown became a reality in many reorganised local services, with more and more workers working in multidisciplinary teams, more and more becoming single disciplinary teams with workers taking on a range of duties that might be described as social caseworking, working with young people. This continual erosion of distinct professional interventions has become a key battleground with the CWDC in particular. CWDC significantly muddied the waters, causing many training organisations and employers to talk about working with young people and not youth work. Youth work, as an educational practice, rightly belongs within the footprint of Lifelong Learning UK, the sector skills council that covers community learning and development. However, this, too, has been abolished by the destructive new Coalition government.

An important debate rages that confuses integrated service delivery with integrated professional formation and management. At the centre of this debate is a universally unwanted initiative backed up with several contracts to consultants to make it happen, called the youth professional status. This was simply a proposal to introduce an assessment scheme to judge any worker within the new integrated services and to somehow award them youth professional status. No pay reward was going to accompany this, however, there was no incentive to qualify this way, and the assessment scheme, based on NVQ assessment models, provided an ideal 'little earner' not just for those who dreamt it up or plagiarised it but for those freelance consultants lining up to become assessors.

There has always been the danger in youth work of 'assessination', that is, too many people assessing the work and not enough doing it. Of course, the wasteful investment that is being thrown into it is indicative of the CWDC desire to erode professional specialisms. In the context of cuts and a depleted labour market, attacks on youth work and its emancipatory practice with young people, the introduction of a mystical designation of youth professional status threatened to become a convenient replacement of established professional qualification routes and a national pay and conditions schemes. It was an ideal neoliberal tool, but fortunately one that did not gain legs.

Integration to disintegration

IYSS developed, and battles raged about the funding, position and recognition of youth work within them. Many of the sturdiest defenders of youth work within these new services were sacked or forced to leave. The principal youth officer (PYO) became a thing of the past. Although youth work had invented integrated working and had called for it for years, it became one of the first victims of the disintegration.

A focal point of the new development was the protection of JNC terms and conditions. These symbolised the organisation of the workforce on better terms and conditions, and protected the link to the youth work value base by virtue of the link with the professional validation standards. An attempt to remove them in Wakefield and Lancashire was defeated. It was therefore vital at this time that these all important validation criteria were renewed, and a wide-ranging consultative process was conducted by the NYA to ensure that they were fit for purpose. They came out strong, and various attempts to highjack them into sectarian directions were stopped.

In general the integration of services meant that the PYO post was under real pressure, specialist youth work middle managers took on wider remits and many youth workers had job descriptions altered to become quasi-social workers. Youth workers took on other roles. The voluntary relationship with young people through youth work was misunderstood and challenged, and a profusion of casework issues appeared as managers without a youth work background were put in charge of youth workers.

Some youth services disappeared into other departments and were lost without trace. CYWU fought the contracting out of some services completely, most notably in Northamptonshire. The union held some of the biggest recent public demonstrations in various towns and cities where the service was under threat.

Private companies took over the running of services on the cheap. Terms and conditions were threatened in a race to the bottom. Targets, targets, targets. Child protection, in an ever-increasing spiral of decline caused by inequality, took over from development and prevention. Youth services were bought and sold.

Having advised the government to marketise all services PricewaterhouseCoopers advised some local authorities to cut their youth services altogether – this led to the Coventry industrial action´ commented on elsewhere and an important national rally about this in June 2010.

The economic crisis worsened. Pressures were put on voluntary sector providers. The national JNC employers sought wage cuts. Local employers sought savings and cuts. CYWU/Unite resisted to the best of its ability with the usual spate of victories and defeats. Then the national infrastructure came under attack. The NYA tightened its belt and experienced youth work colleagues left. Staff posts were lost – 40 posts at the agency were reduced by the end of the year, to about 16. Only one new NYA board member was from a youth work background.

During all the turmoil there were countless acts of quality work to defend youth work. Union members refusing to have their professional intervention changed and diluted contributed most. Senior managers and principal officers in membership fighting each day to ensure that budgets were protected and that youth work qualifications were applied also played significant roles.

Colleagues in the training agencies successfully agreed a set of academic benchmarks to protect the values of youth and community work at the point of professional formation in the universities (QAA, 2009). The union played its part in this.

Competence and values

Lifelong Learning UK embarked on a process of reviewing youth work competences. This was a lively and democratic and in part controversial process. Progressive youth work is defended within them and the value base on which they rest protects the voluntary, young person–centred, developmental relationship (see Chapter 1).

In 2007 Wales TUC adopted a motion from Unite on defending youth services and Unite developed a manifesto for the defence of youth work in Wales. In 2009 Wales adopted a comprehensive policy for workforce development, as did Scotland and Northern Ireland. An attempt to move Northern Ireland's Youth Service to the districts was defeated.

In 2009 the union instigated the largest workforce development manifesto work with Lifelong Learning UK that there has ever been. It was warmly welcomed in Ireland, Wales and Scotland, but traditional forces of inertia in England, then the National Council for Voluntary Youth Services (NCVYS) and the Confederation of Heads of Young People's Services (CHYPS), took until late 2010 to support it. They did so just at the time that the government refused to renew Lifelong Learning UK's license.

Youth work in the armed forces welfare services was also defended. A clear distinction there between individual casework assistance and educational youth and community work was retained. The difference between personal and community services is important, and the blurring of the two together accounts for the attraction of some to the largely social work bias of social pedagogy imported from Germany and other EU countries, where emancipatory youth work practice has been less well defined.

The Education and Training Standards Committees (ETS) throughout the UK developed their work and presented an account of their robust procedures to the JNC in 2008 and 2009. The All Ireland ETS was approved. The Wales ETS cemented a stronger position following the demise of the Wales Youth Agency. Importantly it relates all of the interrelated informal education practices together – community, play and youth work.

Further attacks on the JNC were resisted, and there was more joint union working. This culminated in a successful joint union rally on 5 June 2010. Training and qualifications for youth support workers was brought within the JNC ambit. A whole range of agencies recognised the value of youth work practice in their delivery.

These included prisons and health trusts, housing associations and environmental agencies.

For the first time a major children and young people's workforce development unit was established by the government. The union was invited into this to speak up for youth work. As certain local authorities such as Wakefield, Coventry, Oxford, Staffordshire, Lancashire, West Sussex and others proposed decline for youth work, they were met by strong CYWU/Unite opposition from union branches. The union is leading the campaign to ensure that youth work is respected as an occupation. The title 'youth worker' must be protected in regulation to ensure its practitioners are licensed in a system that they control and which unites the contribution of volunteers and senior managers.

Where other services received gloomy inspection reports youth work received positive ones. The standards of youth, work despite horrendous difficulties, continued to rise, and Ofsted reported repeatedly on youth workers' consistent improvements in practice (Ofsted, 2006, 2008).

New threats emerged. There was not enough funding for youth work on Fridays and weekends in the evenings so various forms of low-level activity-based leisure opportunities emerged, and confusing requests came for youth workers to be involved, effectively, in anti-drinking and crime diversion work at these times. Some youth workers took on semi-social work roles, and some refused. Some were forced into target-driven assessment and achievement work that did not appreciate the softer skills of relationship building and so on. Some refused to do this.

The number of youth work students trebled between 2005 and 2010 even though some notable courses such as Westhill closed. Some new courses have opened. Some lecturers are determined to retain youth work values; some are not. Although universities have effectively become businesses, facing 30 per cent cuts to their funding, youth work became a graduate profession as of September 2010. This completes a 70 year-long battle to significantly raise the status of youth work training.

There is not an overt recruitment and retention crisis in youth work on the basis of the current numbers of jobs, but there is a real crisis in terms of the numbers needed – 4,000 more nationally qualified youth workers were needed in 2010 to meet the generally agreed target of one full-time worker for every 400 young people.

Academic reports have been produced demonstrating the unique development of youth-on-youth violence in the context of worsening social inequalities. Other reports have shown how the youth work approach of engagement and support was having the best effects.

So the defence of youth work has had many layers, many battlegrounds, but what is key to them all? It is very much the trade union organisation of the majority of youth workers. Professional unity is now more essential than ever before. Only a strong union can defend individual members in their defence of youth work. When a youth worker refuses to do something not in their job description or when they are wrongly disciplined, as many are for doing youth work, they need a union that has the defence of youth work at its heart.

It was the union that again sought to establish the widest and deepest coalition of organisations to battle against what by the autumn of 2010 had in effect become the obliteration of the Youth Service. Thanks to the union an Early Day motion on the Youth Service was tabled, the Education Select Committee agreed to undertake an inquiry into young people's services, and opposition to the Tory-led demolition of the Youth Service in many parts of the country, particularly Oxfordshire, was mounted. Also a higher press profile for youth work was achieved, and probably the strongest ever parliamentary debate was held on 23 November 2010 as a Westminster Hall Debate. Services to young people became a real Achilles heel for the government alongside student tuition fees and the abolition of Education Maintenance Allowances.

This ignited a major national campaign, with young people and youth workers achieving unprecedented support throughout the country for their efforts to save the Youth Service. The work and the Service became, in its fight for survival, a major political priority. The normal popular cry to defend the NHS became very often and in campaigning publications and common parlance, a call to defend 'the NHS and the Youth Service' as two public services dearest to people's hearts.

9

Youth workers as negative activists

Legislation and government policy refer to the concept of 'positive activities' for young people. This is different from youth work. It is a concept that can lend itself to a merely leisure-based approach to young people and in doing so denies the role of education and development. It can also lend itself to consumerist and enforced activities. This chapter critically examines this concept and why youth work has been susceptible to its introduction, and advocates the importance of negative activities.

The confusion that has always existed in society between working with young people and youth work is clearly one that penetrates the minds of even the most influential policy makers. There is a muddle about the precise nature of youth work intervention. This has been quite deliberate and ideological, and flows from the definitions of the Education and Inspections Act 2006 that began the ideological attack on youth work and paved the way for whole-scale privatisation of youth work.

In this Act, local authorities are required to secure 'positive activities' for young people – not to provide them directly, but to secure them through a process of tendering services on the market. In one section there is a clear expression of the epitome of the overall neoliberal agenda – on the one hand, services are thrown onto the market fragmented and privatised. This begins a race to the bottom in respect of terms and conditions. It also lowers quality and introduces layers of bureaucracy to commission contracts and manage them.

New authoritarianism

In taking things out of direct control it adds to the culture of authoritarianism in two ways. First, it removes services from democratically accountable control and second, it tends to associate services with highly monitored crime prevention-type provision. Young people become the problem to be sorted. In this process it changes the nature of the work, transforming youth work into an activity, an event that is positive and lacking the negative, but always enlightening. Activities lend themselves to concepts of physical activity and diversion away from problematic negative activities through recreation. Youth work is associated again with leisure activity and crime prevention. 'Keep them off the streets' becomes the repeated cliché.

This, in fact, also reflects a long-held subterranean Tory Party view once expressed by a junior shadow education minister, Rhodes Boyson, when he said that 'young people only go to youth clubs to play games and establish friendship patterns' (quoted in Bunt and Gargrave, 1980). The conceptual limitation of the work to a form of leisure activity devoid of thought and intellectual challenge or social reform is an often recurring and reactionary one.

In new IYSS in England the bringing together of social work departments and educational services has, by and large, put the former in charge, both ideologically and financially, and the 'care' agenda has consequently outpaced the developmental agenda. The idea of targeting the vulnerable has replaced the notion of a right to a universal service. For many, putting young people first means coping with increasing crises among the most damaged. This creates in the worsening economic situation a vicious circle of decline. The decline is masked by the 'spurious' concept of 'targeting' provision to the most needy.

Target shooting

Positive outcomes lend themselves to those dreaded aspects of the new environment, accreditation and targets. Unite, the Union, was proud to sponsor and introduce amidst this confusion one of the best antidotes to obsession with measurement and targets, the publication of Jeremy Brent's *Searching for community*, in which he asserts the immeasurable quality of the best youth work practice (Brent, 2009). It is the mentality of the market that assumes that processes designed to foster human relationships can be quantified and weighed on the grocer's scales. The earlier reliance of youth workers on a self-confident recognition that it was process not product (Ord, 2007) has given way to a concentration on product that has made youth workers defend process again at the expense of a renewed sense of purpose in the product.

The government's guidance on positive activities focuses exclusively on delivering sports, arts and cultural activities (DCSF, 2010). Improving social conditions and enhancing learning have been integral to the traditions of youth work, however. The promotion in statute and policy of positive activities is a new development. It seeks to neutralise both the power of improving social circumstances and of promoting learning. One simply cannot imagine the CWDC approving of youth workers who, as previous generations did, created libraries of classical literature in youth centres. This would fire the imagination and knowledge of the young in their leisure time far too powerfully.

Measuring the imagination

Measurement and targeting take the control of the experience away from young people and the workers themselves and give this to the target setters and managers. The face-to-face exchange between the youth worker and young person is intruded on and interrupted by objectives that have nothing to do with those set by the young people themselves.

While there have always been currents of thinking in youth work that have opposed the most elementary forms of political education such as, for example, the experience of democratic self-government in youth clubs, or the politicisation of the curriculum, there has been a long-standing discussion about the relationship between the work of reclamation and rescue and engagement in work to prevent the need for rescue in the first place. In 1972 the then director of the National Youth Bureau, John Ewen, criticised youth workers for their trivial and timid adherence to a recreational, political and desensitised agenda:

> ... it is perhaps inevitable that the youth service which they [youth workers] offer should be about conformity, a kindly device to contain the young until they have had the 'good sense' to recognise the value of that which is. It must therefore be largely about play, like the bread and circuses of ancient Rome. It must above all avoid such issues as 'politics', as 'race', as 'poverty', for as long as the young are happy with their five-a-side and their discotheques, they are nice young people: not like those hairy students breathing revolution around every cloister corner. So we devise a youth service which reflects the beer and bingo conformity of safe society. Even when the kids are unemployed (as so many of them are now), we offer the day time opening of the youth club, so that they can play snooker and ping pong, in case they get into mischief or very their anger at the lamp post. (Ewen, 1972)

We are also reminded here of the classic criticism Saul Alinsky levelled at the metamorphosis of community intervention from social action to social passivity:

> You cannot, you dare not, come to a people who are in the gutter of despair and offer them not security but

> supervised recreation, handicraft classes and character
> building. But that is what we do, come to them with
> bats and balls. (Alinsky, 1969)

The educative engagement is one that inspires enduring, positive curiosity rather than activity. It is a habit of mind that needs to develop. In the pursuit of happiness, well-being and a meaningful moral life, curiosity plays a pivotal role. It demands a continual unease with what is given, a continual desire to see below the surface to inquire as to causes, to explore. Shor reminds us that we have to continually question answers and not just answer questions (Shor, 1993). It is this element that is so vital in youth work if it is to successfully fire the imagination. As Kashdan points out:

> Resisting our opposing craving for certainty, we
> discover that the greatest rewards come when we
> question authority, question the status quo, question our
> beliefs and question everything.... Rather than being
> encouraged to learn about ourselves and our interests,
> we are more often taught how to make decisions about
> what to do with our lives as early as possible so we won't
> waste time achieving our goals.... Curiosity serves as
> a gateway to what we value and cherish most. We can
> reclaim the lost pleasures of uncertainty, discovery, and
> play.... (Kashdan, 2009, p 79)

Discovering the unfamiliar in the familiar, playing with ideas to alter perceptions, exploring in order to grow, these are all dimensions of positive activity induced only through relationships and social interactions. Expanding one's sense of self is achieved most powerfully by entering into relationships. Having someone to assist and support in this process is one of life's greatest demands. It is a very human trait to cooperate in this way. This is why the dynamics of group work is such a vital part of youth work and so often misunderstood by some other professions.

The dynamic power of critical pedagogy has been to liberate minds from the activities forced on them in the present. It teaches defiance, and perpetual curiosity. The resistance of youth work to the Tory's previous attempts to introduce a curriculum has somehow lowered its guard to the illusion of positive activities and endless accreditation.

But there is a dilemma within youth work itself that makes it vulnerable to this attack. In summary terms this is a failure to relate youth work processes and outcomes to social and economic considerations. At a deeper level this arises because of an unchallenged consensus about the nature of thought and action, or put another way, about the nature of thinking and its relationship to the real world of activities and history.

Ideas and reality

In an ancient philosophical tradition that is still prevalent and recurrent in everyday patterns of thought, there is the belief that the idea, or the thought, is primary, and that consciousness is somehow separate from the physical world. This tradition is called idealism. In the socialist tradition, developed prior to Marx but systematised by him, what is called a materialist tradition prevails. This does not mean people are greedy to possess lots of objects; it means that ideas are related to their origin in the real world. The real world has a history and is based on the material production of the means of existence and the different relationships people enter into to produce those material needs in relationship with the natural world and the development of science and technology. Marx (1969 [1873]) writes:

> For Hegel, the process of thinking which he even transforms into an independent subject, under the name of 'the idea', is the creator of the real world, and the real world is only the external appearance of the idea. With me the reverse is true: the ideal is nothing but the material world reflected in the mind of man, and translated into forms of thought.

The consequence of this for anyone seeking social change within and as a result of their work is that material circumstances have to always be taken into account: social relationships and social production and relationships between the two always have to be dealt with. This demands an ever expanding curiosity, an inclination to relate and discover. It requires that people become more and more conscious of the world they live in, and this means that youth workers need social provision of lifelong and community-based learning.

Ideology

No individual can be conscious of the whole of reality and the truth. How the real world gets reflected in our minds is through an extraordinarily involved filtering process combined with our own creative imposition of our own vision of what is and should be. We all see reality to varying degrees in fragmented and incomplete ways. This is what Marx means by ideology. An ideology, rather than being a system of beliefs, which it is in other contexts, is, in fact, a partial interpretation of the world as it is. Cultural forces seek to create ideologies that avoid or neglect the painful truths about the causes and implementation of exploitation and injustice in the capitalist relationship.

The word 'ideology' is inflated sometimes to mean a totally false consciousness of reality. Scholars spend their lives filling libraries with interpretations of ideology, so a comprehensive definition would expand the References and further reading section of this book almost to infinity, but the aspect of Marx's use of the idea as meaning partial awareness is relevant to this discussion.

By ideology Marx refers to a mode of thinking which is partial or fragmented and therefore which produces a distorted understanding of the real world. An ideological consciousness is not necessarily false in the way that we might usually understand that word; it is distorted like a reflection in a funfair mirror. You don't get the whole picture presented to you. It's too fat, too wobbly, too thin, or too small. Sometimes you get everything completely upside down in ideological reflections. Marx's classic illustration of this is in his discussion of how people completely misunderstand what a commodity is.

A commodity is a thing made by people for other people. It has a use value. Some might say that a Mars Bar chocolate, for example, is a delight to eat. Generally we think it is nice because of the caramel, chocolate sweetness. We may even get a 'craving' or 'fetish' for Mars Bars. We are absorbed by commodities because we associate their value with something intrinsic within them. A bicycle is a bicycle because it is not a camel. The commodity simply appears to be what it is, yet it only has value when it is exchanged for cash.

This is strange. What we constantly forget is that every commodity is made by other people. We forget the social relations behind things and see only relations between things. A Mars Bar might have a good use value, but it has, within the capitalist relations of production, mainly got an exchange value. Under existing arrangements it is only made because it can be exchanged for money, not because it satisfies a lust for caramel. It only exists to make profit. The experience of the Mars Bar has nothing to do with its value. Like every other commodity, it has a multiple personality. They are, to use Marx's apt phrase, 'crystals of this social substance' made by labour and exchanged on markets (Harvey, 2010b).

Another ideological misconception is that money creates wealth. But how many times have bankers pleaded for bailouts because they consider themselves the creators of all wealth? Money is merely an exchange mechanism, and wealth is the creation of labour. Ideological perceptions can get the world completely upside down, mistaking causes for effects and vice versa.

Wealth in relationships

If ideas and consciousness are grounded in the real world and the particular form of social relations and material production that exist at any time, then it follows that to analyse the way in which people think and act you must seek to understand relationships, not just between people, but between ideas and the world, between the ways in which things are produced and the way people work and their concepts about the world.

The key word in this approach is 'relationships'. Relationships mean interconnections, complexity, change, movement, motion, fluidity, complexity. For a bland concept like 'positive activities', ask the questions, what is positive about them, who are they with, and what is the purpose of the activities?

Change

Things are not exactly straightforward – they are never permanent and they are always changing. Having a fixed idea, perhaps of 'sweets', is far less interesting than the prospect of many different kinds of sweets, milk gums, liquorice and so on, dispensed in various ways, in pick and mix, in vending machines, in sweet shops, as presents, as surprises, as treats, as sugary or spicy. Who eats sweets, and why? All these manifestations of sweets are more interesting than the fixed and stale concept of 'sweets'.

Contradictions

If you accept that all things exist in relationship to other things, and that things shift in meaning and context in their never-ending growth and development, you notice another reality – you can see most things two ways, as containing contradictions. A sweet is lovely, you want more, the more you have, the bigger the dentist's bill. If you accept that nothing can have a really fixed and permanent identity, then all things are in a state of growth and death, flux and entropy. Nothing, unfortunately, lasts forever. Even the most stable looking mountain is moving, shrinking, being worn by the weather. In everything there is literally a positive and a negative. For every positive reaction there is a negative reaction.

The negativity of the positive

How does this apply to youth work and the discussion of positive activities? First, every educationalist knows that positive learning can come out of negative experiences. Second, the purpose of youth work is not necessarily perceived as a positive activity. It is more about the internalisation of feelings and thoughts that are enlightening. For many years there were attempts to put youth services into leisure departments. This was resisted and the educational basis of the work was maintained. Education replaces the positive benefit of ignorance with the negative power of knowledge.

But the main reason why I believe that the notion of positive activities is flawed is that it is an idealist concept that fits with the consumerist, individualistic agenda. Youth work will allegedly provide young people with an activity that they can 'buy into', that they consider to be positive. This fundamentally forgets that the youth work relationship is voluntary and that the dialogue within youth work can seek to negate the weaknesses within a young person's life. Youth work can lead to negative thoughts that can lead to positive reformulations of self-identity and contribution.

Joined-up thinking

Habits of thought have developed that categorise things separately and do not see them in relationship. Youth workers may fix on the nature of their voluntary relationship with young people, but forget the relationship of that relationship to wider social relationships and purposes. As I seek to show later in Chapter 14, youth work has become transfixed by formal categories. It has stopped thinking about relations and change, and rested on what I consider to be lazy formal categories. Categorisation has a positive role (imagine horticulture or zoology without it), but it can have a devastating effect in other realms of endeavour. Some categorisations of young people, gang members, the dreaded NEETs, drug users, trouble makers and so on effectively impale them like specimens on the pin of an ideal concept that they may never escape from. Negative categorisation has a positive result for those who want to administer to the young rather than minister with them for social change.

Youth work thinking has ghettoised itself by forgetting its own relationship with other social activities. A pseudo-identification with the word 'praxis' has developed. This is supposed to inherit the Freirean and Gramscian notions of combining theory and practice in social action for change. But it does not. It has neutralised the concept as a matter of pure technique. Praxis, as Peter McLaren reminds us frequently, must take into account the totality of social relations. When this is done we can restore the powerful elements of Freire in which liberation is understood as being something that moves away from the liberal humanist notion of 'traditional democratic freedom' to that 'of freeing oneself and others from the relation of the dialectical contradiction'. Freire's work has been abstracted from its revolutionary and transformative intent. He has been reduced to a proponent of a neutral kind of consciousness raising by some, and distorted as a simple technician of the relationship between progressive teacher and potentially progressive student. The point is that this relationship is geared towards transforming capitalist social relationships generally (see, for example, McLaren, 1980).

A positive activity is like a sphere, a perfectly realised and enclosed shape, finished, final, complete, unchanging. But life simply isn't like that. How long will the buzz of the positive activity last? Why will it fade? In real life what is positive for a young drug dealer is not so positive for the young addict. A youth worker will seek to negate both negative behaviours. One young person finds them positive and one finds them temporarily positive, perhaps. Nevertheless, they are both negative.

At the other end of the spectrum a positive activity with a young person displaying no socially constructed deficiencies whatsoever may be to shatter their illusion of contentment as they realise that they can achieve much more, and that perhaps their complacency and positive attitude was a product of ideological influences that sought to mask their reality.

The notion of positive activity abstracts an idea and seeks to impose it on reality that is a bit messier than this. It suggests that it can create a nice space in untidy reality and create this *for* young people, not necessarily *with* them. They presumably have no choice in the matter. Youth work copies this same habit of thought by making much of its relationship-building capacities of doing things with young people, but little of challenging the context in which they exist and what causes the alienation and disenfranchisement of the young in the first place. It is not positive activities that will destroy youth work, but the pattern of thought that lies behind the idea and gets repeated in the formulation of youth work as technique devoid of purpose.

The big idea of positive activities does not fit reality. Trampolining is positive for many high flyers. But it is not youth work. We shouldn't be bounced into it. What are needed are truly inspiring negative activities that negate the causes of so many negative experiences that young people have.

10

Youth workers as reflective, analytical practitioners

In this chapter I argue that to deal with the current extent of
the attack on youth work practice and professionalism, a more
sophisticated and socially enriched form of critical reflection by
youth workers is needed. This is particularly so if youth workers are
to give meaningful leadership.

Informal education methods with children, young people and adults
have been enriched by the concept of 'reflective practice'. This has
originated within learning theory applied to school teaching and
from a branch of behavioural psychology in the US and Germany.
It has never fitted easily with youth work, play work, community
work or adult education in Britain in which more socially aware
traditions of education technique have developed. Nevertheless it
has been a useful tool in deepening critical, often peer-assessed ways
of working. It has also been of assistance in developing progressive
supervision and teaching techniques and it has been important in
providing self-defined terms of assessment and supervision.

Simple reflective practice has also had a positive role as being
the possession of the professional practitioner, a mark of their
professionally self-determined skills and autonomy. It has therefore
provided a useful foil against the array of what I consider neoliberal,
managerial weapons, such as targets, monitoring, evaluation and
job evaluation. It represents a mode of thought that only the
skilled practitioner can apply. I believe that youth workers have
to go through so many forms of external assessments that they

feel 'assessinated'. Reflection, coupled with analysis and enriching practice, is about taking back control.

Creation

In manual trades the concept is as old as the pyramids, if not older. The idea that in any process of construction or development the creator constantly reflects on the nature and form and functionality of their product is essential. It provides a constant check against faults and puts the creators more in charge of the process of creation.

However, it has had a purely empirical side to it. Reflecting theoretically on practice in social education processes often limits reflection to the immediacy of the practice itself, or to the immediate impact of that practice on the groups and individuals concerned. If social and political education is the purpose of youth work, then don't youth workers need a more developed idea about how to reflect on the very social nature of their practice? Don't they also need a keener sense of the economic and hidden political factors that impact on their work and method?

In essence, reflective practice is the intellectual process of subjecting work events, performance, interventions or longer-term involvement or experiences to critical thought and discussion with peers. The detail of work is placed under the scrutiny of thought. The power of considering how you have done is exercised. The effect of that context on the work, or the work on that thought, together with an assessment of the strengths and weaknesses of the performance of the work itself, are considered and recorded. The consideration is undertaken with a view to improving performance in the future and developing the child, young person or adult with whom you are working. It is not therefore a selfish, elitist activity; it is designed for social and educational good, for the improvement of technique. It seeks to build a more effective relationship in which a thirst for aspiration and achievement will be nurtured. In itself it is a good thing, but what is its scope? Does it sufficiently stretch the mind?

Traditional devices within informal education for structured reflection are the diary, the case study, portfolio, report, team meeting, supervision discussion and sometimes the anonymous influence of non-managerial supervision. These techniques, however, are no substitute for the attitude of mind that continually inspires workers to reflect on their practice, and this is a product of skill and the adoption of professional values. Skill and professionalism assert power. It is often the formation and operation of these values that is not sufficiently reflected on, but nevertheless this attitude generates a virtuous cycle of theory, practice and theory. This is described by Kolb (1984) in his model of the adult learning process which moves from concrete experience, to reflective observation, to abstract conceptualising, to active experimentation and back to concrete experience.

Stuck in the concrete

There is always a return to concrete experience and the process is abstracted from content and values. But is this always possible in an area of work that is looking for a collective social aspiration, seeking a state of experience that does not yet exist? The real world and the status quo become substitutes for what should be. Aren't we concerned to analyse the ability of the social educator to inculcate the values and organising techniques of change from what is now to something better? Surely change is needed.

Honey and Mumford (1984) built on Kolb's model to distinguish the preferences of learners as activists, reflectors, theorists or pragmatists, each with an inclination for one part of the Kolb cycle. We can also create distinctions between styles of thinking rather than forms of knowledge within the cycle. This helps to establish the recognition of more sophisticated concepts of emotional and multiple intelligences, and consequently demands that reflection be more complex and multidimensional. Such refinements of the Kolb cycle have been helpful in informal education professions that are so rooted in practice, dialogue, relationships and face-to-face exchanges. Our point of reference still remains within the paradigm of learning.

What if the main purpose of a learning method is social action? Are we perhaps dealing with the difficulty of applying concepts from formal learning processes to those of the informal?

Ripple model

A more developed approach to learning theory is found in Phil Race's work (2010). Here he introduces a ripple model. The pebble that causes the ripple is the need, or the want to learn. Concentric circles then ripple out from this: doing, digesting, feedback, teaching, feedback, assessing, understanding. Whatever the learning theorists' models, the notion of reflection on professional action has become one with educational technique and, using the familiar Freirean distinction, has attached itself more to the banking model than the social education model.

Although a counter to new managerialism, with all the pressures on staff time, the drift towards competency approaches, measurable instant outcomes and accreditation, there has been a tendency for reflective practice to become limited in its scope and in fact little more than practice described. There has been insufficient theory and time to lift it beyond this in a vicious circle created by the increasing rate of exploitation of workers. Reflective practice has become dominated by practice rather than critical reflection. The reflective mind has been dimmed in the darkness of immediate circumstances and lacking in any vision for the future.

Wood or trees?

It has become a version of very typically English empiricism. This is a pattern of thought that sees no wood, only trees; it is a way of thinking that deals with immediate solutions to immediate problems. It forgets to question the causes of problems and longer-term prevention of their recurrence. It is an approach that always gravitates towards the punitive solution to youth crime issues, for example, rather than prevention, or to the over-dramatisation of one-sided preventative strategies. It fails to include the collective.

Empirical thinking sees issues or events in straight rows, with each row and component seen separately from the other. It is one at a time thinking. Forget the wood, just count the trees! It involves thinking about what is in front of your nose, but not what is behind it.

The progressive idea of reflecting on practice alone has, perhaps, operated in the gaps between rows of dominoes, for example. It fails to look around or above and to see the row as a whole. What is above and beyond the immediate neighbour is forgotten. People simply love their neighbours without questioning the impossibility of this in isolation.

Under circumstantial pressures forced by the commodification of education and the fragmentation of its delivery mechanisms and straightforward manic speed up and increased pressures on workers, reflection has lost its power to instigate change. Schon (1991) and Kolb's concrete experience has become so concrete that practitioners are stuck in it. Pragmatism has replaced principles.

Workers' control

In order to reinvigorate professional interventions linked to higher education and social aspirations the concept of reflective analytical practice should be considered. This has been usefully outlined in such works as *Evolutionary playwork and reflective analytic practice*, by Bob Hughes (2001). It is something also engrained within the self-assessment framework *First claim*, developed by Play Wales (2001). In their work first claim play work practitioners seized their own ground and defined what assessment techniques were appropriate and what values and processes were suitable for assessment. This helped reclaim their control.

Under the broader light of reflective analytical practice, as I propose it for discussion here, the historic, social and economic elements that relate to the practice have to be incorporated in the reflection to give a more rigorous test to the validity of the practice. Hughes encourages a form of reflection that is not simply theorised, but analysed within an occupational culture and with awareness of all of the limitations, possibilities, traditions and techniques of that form of intervention and its demonstrable impacts. I argue that this needs to be widened further, and the historic and social horizons need to be considered within the scope of meaningful reflection.

To be effectively analytical practitioners need both a keen sense of the boundaries of their professional impact and its contribution to a much broader, social, political and human endeavour. Abstract conceptualisation therefore has no fixed position in the process. There is nothing fixed or formulaic about genuine analysis. It is not looking at practice, it is not a version of practice itself – it is integral to practice and practice is seen in a wide sense of the interlinked impacts and influences on the human condition with which practitioners are engaging.

By demanding an additional layer of thought beyond reflection on practice youth workers are encouraged to assess their effectiveness against a more demanding range of criteria, and also to locate of benefit or otherwise within a broader spectrum of factors. This helps enhance their status. It also helps them to deal more effectively with the dilemma of whether they are working in or against the state and the status quo. Are they 'gilding the ghetto', as the 1970s community development projects put it?

Collective vision

Where reflective practice tends to individualise and narrow the aperture of professional attention to the immediate performance, reflective analytical practice seeks to open a wider, more collective vision. It expands horizons as the best informal education practice itself does.

A form of analysis beyond reflection on practice is not just a play on words. Nor is it practice described in more sophisticated ways to enable the outcome gatherers to evidence yet more from limited practice in under-resourced services. It should be seen as a tool for enhancing professional autonomy and the value of work undertaken. It should lead to greater protection of that work and greater immunity from the structural and other changes that come and go with changes in government and the civil service. It assists to locate the work in its social and historical direction.

Reflecting on practice does not encourage youth workers to improve their skill; it encourages them to improve their practice. Skill is a deeper more meaningful concept. It requires a collective identity and a tradition and is generated by a context and transformative of that with which it engages.

In reflective analytical practice the question is not just how have you done, but why? How will you learn from the intelligence and predicament of those you have sought to educate? An equally important question related to the current need for a licence to practice and code of ethics is, what will you do to replenish and maintain the profession of which you are a part? This leads to the most difficult question: how will you help yourself to improve? Surely those you work with, if you analyse their situation, have more to teach?

It is time for the informal education professions in Britain to return to some of the progressive aspirations from which their work originated. The changes that the work and communities require do not yet have a concrete existence to reflect on. This is why reflection must be analytical and socially informed; it must include a vision of the future and test practice against that. It is a form of perpetual disobedience and discontent.

11

Youth workers as leaders

When the Youth Service was originally called 'In the Service of Youth', youth workers were called 'youth leaders'. This conveyed a sense of moral authority and reputable role modelling, reflecting, in turn, the reforming zeal of many of the early philanthropists who developed youth work as part of a wider social reforming movement. It is still used in other countries, but often in a religious context. I believe that it is a worthy phrase – youth workers cannot avoid giving leadership, although they also act as signposts and enjoyable friends, perhaps, rather than solely instructors or bosses. This chapter therefore seeks to define a new concept of leadership as crucial to both educational and social change.

The notion of youth 'leadership' has slipped away as the wider profession has defined itself as working much more closely alongside young people themselves, being seen as their professional friends, allies, surrogate voices, enablers and/or advocates. Leadership is a privilege, earned and granted, and it requires a level of self-organisation and discipline. It is a direct line of thought into others, fellow professionals, and young people. But it must also be a direct line back from the group being worked with to enrich future work and to change the circumstances limiting the immediate group's opportunities and knowledge. It is not a filtering of ideas to suit prejudice, or personal pride, and it is impossible if a subjective rather than an objective approach is taken. Youth workers must be non-judgemental in order to lead, you must, at the same time, make sound judgements.

Being unpopular

Leadership is honesty, not popularity, it is challenge, not agreement, it is respect earned with actions, not just words. Leaders are sometimes elected, but elections do not always make leaders, only honesty over time does this. Young people do not meaningfully choose their first interaction with youth workers – youth workers are appointed by others.

Providing leadership means having the courage to see things as they are, and to act accordingly. It is earning the privilege to walk in a direction, which may often be difficult, and to know that others will follow, as thinking beings who recognise the value of collective thought and action.

Leadership in the workplace often comes with skill and experience, but always with the recognition of integrity and a certain level of risk. It can never be adventurist, going too far to achieve change. It is often lonely, but never isolated. 'Leading by example' is a good phrase.

Self-discipline, not self-deception, is needed to lead. The discipline of collective leadership with the young people youth workers work with is something that sets them apart. While others may base leadership on ego, or the temporary attractiveness of an idea, youth workers base leadership on those who show their root in their class and those they educate by their actions and understanding of changing circumstances.

Within the profession, leadership is as great a responsibility and privilege as it is within groups of young people; indeed, the two should be inseparable. In my opinion there is no room in leadership for ego or self-delusion – self-delusion leads to errors that may harm others. There is also no scope for selfishness. Leadership is given in trust and must not be taken lightly.

What is a youth worker? To be a youth worker is to be a leader. To be a leader of young people is to have power, and to use that power to serve those young people within the working class is imperative. Youth workers will often be alone in a position of leadership and will have to be prepared to work alone – good leaders will not be persuaded by any doctrine. Intellectually they are therefore very alone, particularly in the new setup of integrated working and multidisciplinary teams.

The constant questions that must be asked are why are we leading and where are we seeking to lead others? There can be no personal foible in leadership and in answering this question. Leadership can only be collective.

PART V
FUTURE CONSIDERATIONS

12

Youth work and inequality

In this chapter I reflect on some personal experiences of youth violence overseas and in Britain, and argue that youth work intervention is effective even in the most acute situations with gangs. I go on to discuss the benefits of youth work in relation to migration into Britain and increasing social inequality.

I got caught up in a gun fight in Brazil in 2007. Young people from the barrios (slum areas) were shooting at each other in the stylish streets of Ipanema while my friends and I ducked in a taxi as bullets flew overhead. My action wasn't that of a skilful youth worker – I was definitely avoiding the street conflict!

One of my first casework issues as a national official of the CYWU union in 1987 was to deal with the trauma suffered by a member in London who had been locked in a youth centre by a 10-year-old, who had been high on cocaine, wielding a loaded pistol.

At one level youth violence is neither new, nor confined to Britain's 1,300 worst estates. But at another level it is a worsening part of urban life in increasingly unequal societies. The conditions of the most disenfranchised young people embody the accumulated neglect caused by 30 years of deindustrialisation and economic liberalism and totally inadequate youth policies. For the first time since the reforming zeal of the late 19th century, the next generation is being abandoned.

Yob rulers

Curious about my overseas taxi experience in Brazil, I watched the film *City of God*, about street children in the Brazilian slums who knew nothing except gang membership and the callous disregard for life that goes with it. I reflected how this environment was a matter of degree away from the 'dangerous places' in Britain observed by Bea Campbell in her 1993 book *Goliath* (Campbell, 1993). I also thought of Francis Gilbert's work *Yob nation* (Gilbert, 2006), where he shows how yobbish behaviour has become more and more woven into the fabric of our institutions. It has cascaded through various subcultures, like the bullying workplace, and has moved from the state to the streets.

I have asked dozens of union members, skilled youth workers, working with street gangs and the most vulnerable and disadvantaged young people in Britain, what causes such irrational gang-related violence. They are all of one mind, whether in London, Birmingham or Liverpool: 'It's the economy stupid,' they say.

Inequality, as Richard Wilkinson and Kate Pickett pointed out in their recent studies, is literally the killer (Wilkinson and Pickett, 2009). The gap between rich and poor is now at its widest for 40 years; Danny Dorling has also shown clearly how it has been reproduced over the years (see Dorling, 2010). The alienation and frustration of not being a part of established social relations compels those who are segregated and isolated to separate themselves further into micro 'gang' units where they are able to find forms of respect and esteem and money that is unavailable elsewhere in society.

Economic and social circumstances pile up on young people and so alienate them that they end up shooting each other in gang-related conflict. Respect for their own lives is so lacking that they subsequently lack respect for others.

The young perpetrators of violence are drawn almost exclusively from what is referred to as the NEET group; there are 1.2 million young people in this category and the figure is rising. Despite expensive initiatives to reduce this figure, and pilot schemes to provide financial incentives to ease the transition into education or work, the numbers keep rising. In 1994 about 5 per cent of young people were classified as NEET. Now in 2012 it has more than doubled, to 11 per cent. There are regional variations and complex reasons and circumstances associated with these statistics, but the persistence of the core problem is leading to more severe behavioural responses.

Quiet riots

The 1980s witnessed frustrated, but nevertheless collectivised, rioting. Now there is what appears to me to be individualistic, fatal lashing out against each other. The market, and its values, whether for guns or drugs, rules.

One lesson from a study (Pitts, 2007a) of recent initiatives with vulnerable young people and those in gangs is that professional youth workers make an astounding difference. The nature of the relationship between youth workers and young people, unlike any other professional intervention, is purely voluntary – the young person can walk away at any time. This fact lays the basis for trust between the two. In most cases when dealing with this group the youth worker is the first professional, and possibly the first adult, that the young person will have trusted. The quality of this relationship will determine the success of the re-engagement and development that the young person then experiences. It comes with time, persistence and tolerance and exemplifies a non-judgemental approach based on believing that the young person, however temporarily brutalised, has something good to offer.

Being able to establish a constructive rapport with young people who have no positive rapport with anyone except their own 'little tribe' of gang members is a skill developed through sophisticated youth work training.

Key to successful youth work is also the active involvement of the young person in the process, curriculum or project that they are creating. When such involvement is missing, other interventions fail.

Young people who have no part in the design of their engagement will misunderstand or reject what is 'being *done* to them'. Through effective youth work, the measure of control over the process of what is happening to the young person is appealing and unique, and encourages positive responses, often for the first time. It is the idea of the youth worker's equality with the young person that may appear so alien to other professions.

Control

The equality of the relationship is critical because the psychological disorders that stem from the stress of feeling totally out of control, of feeling a victim of hostile social forces and punitive authorities, are at the root causes not just of ill health among those who are poor, but of most anti-social behaviour. Youth work plays a vital socially integrative role, with youth workers frequently the most accessible point of contact between an individual young person and society.

John Pitts (2007a, 2007b, 2007c) assessed youth work projects with gangs and found an over 70 per cent success rate in terms of diverting young people from criminal activity and reintegrating them with effective education and employment. No other intervention has been as effective. It remains to be seen whether any government will fully appreciate this.

It is now widely recognised that young people develop a sense of their own identities when they can explore them safely through fun activities in safe environments with friends, but the geography of urban landscapes offers few such safe places. It is in youth centres, where young people feel respected, that rights and responsibilities are most often internalised and they can begin to control their own lives and make choices. Literally thousands of youth centres have been closed down since May 2010. The impact of this should not be underestimated. One young person took their own life very near to their recently closed youth centre where they used to go regularly for support.

Key policy initiatives for funding youth centres would transform this situation, replacing neglect with a caring attitude. Give all 1.5 million 16- to 17-year-olds the vote so that they can have responsibility for having their needs met with effective policies. Employ 4,000 more youth workers to meet the staffing ratios agreed for the sector, and give youth workers key worker status with a professional license to practice and protection of title. Make the Youth Service statutory. Quadruple the new youth centre building budget introduced by New Labour. Ensure local labour market strategies are developed in every neighbourhood and that all movement of capital is subject to scrutiny and youth 'proofing'. End the lower minimum wage for young workers.

In dealing with such a systemic and structural problem, these modest starting points would make a radical difference.

The benefit of youth work to migrant communities is also easy to underestimate. The role of youth work in anti-oppressive, anti-racist practice is vital.

> Nobody who pretends to sense or decency, thinks any longer, that a difference of colour in human beings implies inequality of rights, or that because we find men ignorant we ought to make them wretched. (Leigh Hunt)

This quotation is relevant not just because of its sentiment, but for the date when it was written, in 1811, 201 years ago, by Leigh Hunt writing in *The Examiner* following the abolition of slavery.

Joining us

Much of youth work in relation to immigrant communities has been to make the bonds of human contact and respect, to assist people 'settling in' and becoming valued parts of a community. Much has been about promoting the voices of immigrants and preserving their experiences. For example, youth work lecturer, the late Caroline

Adams, wrote *Across the seven seas and thirteen rivers*, a beautiful example of this, telling us of the lives of the pioneer Sylheti settlers in Britain through their own words (Adams, 1987). Youth work has an immensely proud history in ensuring that migrant communities are made welcome and are able to flourish (DES, 1967).

I believe that philosophy is not to describe or interpret the world, but to change it (see also Marx, 1969 [1873]; Ash, 2007). It is more like an axe than an axiom. In the late 1930s Bertholt Brecht asked, 'In the dark times/Will there also be singing?' and answered 'Yes, there will also be singing/About the dark times' (Brecht, 1976). I believe that the politics of hope, as bell hooks points out, plays a vitally subversive role again today (hooks, 2003).

Too many young minds have been formed in the pervasive culture of commodity fetishism and alienation (Eagleton, 1997). We should, perhaps, consider in this regard the works of the great trade unionist, educationalist and socialist, Paulo Freire, that youth work and community work proper are pedagogies of the oppressed (Freire 1989, 1996, 2001, 2004a, 2004b, 2005, 2006). They are emancipatory practices.

Youth and community workers teach in order that others may, with them, transgress. Their status is to challenge the status quo alongside all others who are oppressed.

In its latest statute, the government has formally redesignated youth work as 'positive activities for young people' (Education and Inspections Act, 2006), but this is limited in its appeal and meaning. Youth workers, on the other hand, reassert the importance of youth work as an educational space for resistance. Only in this sense is it positive, part of the struggle for democracy (Smith, 1994); it is humanist and liberating. Freire talks of the false generosity of a system that deliberately creates loveless poverty and oppression and then pretends, through charity or state intervention, to relieve it. It gives people no property rights, not even to sell their own labour power, then feigns pity. As William Blake once wrote: 'Poverty would be no more/If we did not *make* somebody poor.'

Against the grain

Youth work is not philanthropy – it is for social change, challenging, going against the grain. Young people need youth work to assist them in taking uncomfortable or difficult choices. Without youth and community workers in many areas of Britain division and racism would have been more prevalent.

Youth workers who are unionised have also made a powerful contribution, whether through the successful struggle to organise low-paid workers who clean offices in the City of London, or through fighting for the rights of Gate Gourmet workers, for example, who were suddenly threatened by the company's use of cheaper Eastern European labour. And recent delegations of youth workers to Venezuela have been impressed by the effective work there to achieve government power for the first time for women, and indigenous tribal leaders (Taylor and Mathieson, 2011). What has also been impressive is the way natural resources have been used to benefit the country's people, whether through the country's oil paying for the immigration of 30,000 Cuban doctors to bring healthcare to the slum dwellers for the first time in their history, or paying for free education and literacy for all (VPMCI, 2005; VIC 2007).

Global solidarity

The union believes that Cuba gives a clear alternative to capitalist globalisation (Lambie, 2010). Its international efforts are not greatly known about outside the trade unions, but it was Cuban medical staff, people who had never seen snow, who penetrated furthest into the remote and freezing regions of Pakistan following the earthquake there, to bring aid to the injured and destitute (CSC, 2007). Cuba provided free, no strings attached international aid (Armstrong et al, 1991; Glyn, 2006).

Such movements of people to work overseas are motivated by humane values and contrast with the real causes of the huge waves of migration throughout the world today – war, famine, disease, natural disaster and poverty remain the greatest causes of people moving to 'pastures new'. Marx's late 19th-century essay on *Enforced migration* and Engel's study of the Irish in Britain are worth reading (Engels, 1975 [1845]) – the notion of economic migrants masks the reality that most are forced to migrate by intensely bad social pressures in their own countries.

Ireland has still not entirely reached its pre-famine population levels of 1845-1852. Forty-five million North Americans claim Irish decent. Now Ireland, dominated by the EU economically and politically, is home to some of the most diverse communities itself. It will become no doubt a battleground in the rising conflict between the US and the EU. Its most oppressed have found their eloquent voice in the greatest comic and tragic novels of our time (Doyle, 1993, 1997, 2007).

Many African and now Eastern European countries are complaining of the skills drain that emigration has caused them, making their own development and independence slower and more difficult. I believe that this sustains uneven capitalist development so essential for the constant relocation of capital that provides gluts in one place and, crudely, then moves onto another. The building of community and a respected, permanent place for young people in those communities is a key role for youth workers.

Nomads

Norman Tebbit, the Conservative politician, was unpopular when he said at a time of high unemployment, "[My father] got on his bike and looked for work, and he kept looking 'til he found it." Now we take it as the norm that millions will catch planes or take boats or be crammed into lorries to search for work and a better life abroad. The grass is rarely greener in the 'promised land', however, unless you are, for example, a Russian or Saudi Arabian billionaire, settling in Knightsbridge, helping to make West London one of the world's grandest and guarded ghettos of the super-rich (Cahill, 2001; Sampson, 2004; Lansley, 2006; Williams, 2006), while on the other side of London, there are Bangladeshi communities with many earning less than £3 an hour in the fast food industry (TUC, 2006).

Workers should not be forced to take such desperate measures in their search for work. Stable, settled communities have power, control, decency and respect (Sennett, 1999, 2003, 2006), the greatest expression of which is the self-determining and independent nation. It is commitment to this that gives the most progressive identity to youth workers (Nicholls, 2005).

The union was very proud to move the unanimously supported motion at the TUC on behalf of youth workers opposing the Iraq war. And let's not be liberal about it, it is that barbaric act and illegal war, killing and maiming now over a million young people, children and women, that remains the most tragic legacy of our lack of power and democracy in Britain (Kampfner, 2003; Curtis, 2003, 2004). The crusade for oil dominates the world (Harvey, 2005). Youth workers have a renewed role in being advocates of peaceful coexistence between nations.

Gangs with power

With no sense of irony, the former New Labour Blair government imported a concept from the EU called 'social exclusion'. Professionals then had to create integrated services to 'socially include' people. Gangland developments arose from that other hidden and deliberately neglected world of impoverished opportunities, segregated, dangerous places where those surplus to current market requirements are 'dumped' (Campbell, 1993).

Historians of youth crime and gangs have evidenced the presence of both going back many years (Duckworth, 2002). As a youth worker in the early 1980s I worked with the 'Hillfields Posse', for example. The worst they did under my nose, but while I was blissfully unaware, was to steal three miniature penguins from a zoo. I also worked in an African Caribbean community during the period of Blacks Britannica and the Brixton and Toxteth riots (1980s). Indeed, a causal factor in the formation of the Albemarle Committee, that responded to trade union and voluntary sector demand to create a Youth Service, was the Notting Hill riots in 1958. Perhaps without the moral panic they created there would be no Youth Service today.

A new social exclusion

These days, however, even the group collectivity of earlier rioting against 'Babylon', as many Rastafarian young people described the state, has disappeared. Young people from the same groups are now injuring or killing each other. Respect within communities has turned to a new callous hatred. As Terry Eagleton (2005) observes in relation to extremist violence in *Holy terror*, 'The less the orthodox political sphere seems responsive to the demands of those it excludes, the more those demands can assume a pathological form, blowing apart the very public arena in which they had previously sought a hearing.' The trouble with inter-community violence is that it is a form of terrorism generated by those with no experience of the public sphere and no public space, or territory, to claim other than their bit of turf, or street.

Margaret Thatcher in the 1980s paved the way for this new situation – she said to remove exchange controls on capital, to support financial speculation and the war on inflation, to destroy domestic energy supply and manufacturing. Then she signed the Single European Act, followed in later years by Tony Blair and Gordon Brown signing the EU Constitution (TUAEUC, 2005, 2007; Denny and Katz, 2010). While Thatcher smashed mining, Blair smashed public services (Craig, 2006). Economic demolition has been followed by super-structural changes as unelected bankers and commissioners in Europe and those unelected in quangos at home have taken over. Even job titles change – youth workers are called 'business unit managers', with the appropriate acronym.

The 'f' word

Instead of skill and the power over work and the workplace that goes with it, instead of job insecurity, we get the 'f' word, 'flexibility', and as Richard Sennett has so well described, the decline and fall of public man (Sennett, 2003). Civil society and consciousness have become atomised like the market itself. This provides a material reality that postmodernist thinking slavishly reflects (Eagleton, 1996).

Just as the removal of coal supplies and a coherent national railway network split the nation, so education has been radically broken up and marketised. Education is not offered to develop critical thinking and the mastery of nature and technique and enlightenment, but marketed for the segmented task management of various routine processes. Above all, as Pat Ainley has consistently pointed out, education has been distorted to teach subservience within a fiercer labour market (Ainley, 1988, 1991, 1993a, 1993b, 2007; Ainley and Allen, 2010).

There is no longer any pretence at redistributive social democracy. Thirty seven per cent pay and pensions increases in 2007 for the multi-millionaire chief executives, 2.475 per cent for youth and community workers who were, like all public sector workers, capped by state-controlled pay restraint. In 2009 this was 1 per cent, in 2010 0 per cent, in 2011 0 per cent and in 2012 1 per cent and a radically reduced pension and more to pay for it as well.

Inequality considered

Three leading academics have recently undertaken some important work on inequality in Britain. Danny Dorling has demonstrated that it is economic inequalities that shape our landscape and politics and that we are divided by class lines and economic factors, not racial ones. Bethan Thomas and Danny Dorling's *Identity in Britain: A cradle to grave atlas*, is extremely useful, as is Dorling's separate work on the human geography of Britain (Dorling, 2005, 2007; Thomas and Dorling, 2007). These provide excellent human maps on which youth workers are able to chart the demographics and politics of their communities. Dorling's recent work amplifies previous research and seeks to demonstrate how structural inequalities are maintained and engrained in our social and geographic structures (Dorling, 2010).

Related research by Ludi Simpson has also clearly shown that the fear of racial segregation is exaggerated (Simpson, 2004). We are not 'sleepwalking' towards greater segregation. For example, the number of, as it were, racially mixed neighbourhoods, increased during 1991 to 2001 from 964 to 1,070, and this trend is continuing. The number of mixed households rose in the same period by 20 per cent; again, this trend is accelerating and there are four times more mixed ethnic children than adults. The human trend is towards integration despite the attempts of social forces to divide.

Richard Wilkinson, in his studies of the effects of inequality, has clearly demonstrated that it is inequality, not poverty per se, that generates higher levels of gang and gun crime and, of course, disease and death (Wilkinson, 2006; Wilkinson and Pickett, 2006). The narrower the wealth gap in the US, and any country in the world for that matter, the less likelihood of social breakdown and anti-social activity.

Some forms of racial inequality and discrimination worsened for a period under the benign sounding theory of 'multiculturalism'. This was always based on a reactionary theoretical flaw – it took us backwards to a pre-scientific set of ideas about difference. The Enlightenment, as touched on in Chapter 2, gave us the important virtues of secular rationalism. Human beings are united and indivisible because of their shared capacity to reason. The chains of custom and prejudice and superstition were broken. Crudely, whatever our dissimilarities, we share grey matter and red blood. Dialogue and enquiry between us is universally possible. Not even the extreme difference of speaking a different language, or being deaf, is enough to divide us.

All so different

Multiculturalism alternatively offered a reversal of this. It said: 'I am what I am therefore I am right.' Translating this, it assumed, 'Because of my identity, I am untouchably different and my difference from you gives me my rights, separate and possibly greater than yours.' Universal human rights and working-class rights were replaced by small group rights.

Multiculturalist thinking led to division and the ghettoisation of immigrant communities. As Batsleer says, in youth work we require a position that 'moves the thinking about diversity out of a static multiculturalism and into a sense of the transformative power of challenging injustice and working with a sense of movement and creativity in cultures which embrace difference rather than commodify it' (Batsleer, 2008). Humanity was shattered into irreducible, fixed differences in the forms of multicultural thinking. One could not understand the predicament of another because they were so unlike. There was no commonality if we could not understand each other because of genetic or impenetrable cultural differences. Renaissance universalism was replaced by endless variety. Extreme localism replaced other more generous identities.

Interestingly, political forms of multiculturalism coincided with a time of one of the greatest acts of public scientific discovery and generosity when the human genome project proved beyond doubt the oneness of the human race. This project put the material, objective nail in the coffin to what we had known all along: humankind is one race and man's greatest myth is the fallacy of race. Ashley Montagu pointed this out in 1942 at the height of fascism in Europe in his book exploding the myth of 'race' (Montagu, 1997).

One human race

We should also reflect here on Hannah Arendt's analysis that imperialism required the theory of inferior races in the 19th century to justify its piracy (Arendt, 1968). If that was true, then, what is true now when mass migration in a range of forms, throughout the world, is so necessary to accommodate profit as the flux of profitable capitalist zones shifts around the globe? Something similar is happening today with the designation of young people as 'demons' and therefore inferior and requiring containment in jail or positive activities.

Multiculturalism reflected the competition inherent to capitalism. Groups compete separately for political attention, rights and resources. Feudal cultural traditions have to be maintained among some to prevent migrant communities from organising politically, as workers had done in their host countries.

What has happened has been a resurgence of capitalist power. David Harvey and Henry Giroux, in the *Terror of neoliberalism*, write well about this (Giroux, 2004; Harvey, 2006a). And as Susan George has also pointed out:

> In 1945 or 1950, if you had seriously proposed any of the ideas and policies in today's standard neo-liberal tool kit, you would have been laughed off the stage or sent off to the insane asylum....The idea that the market should be allowed to make major social and political decisions; the idea that the State should voluntarily reduce its role in the economy, or that corporations should be given total freedom, that trade unions should be curbed and citizens given much less rather than more social protection – such ideas were utterly foreign to the spirit of the time. (George, 1999, p 2)

Neoliberal ideology pushes for the privatisation of all uncommercialised public spheres and the upward distribution of wealth. It supports policies that increasingly militarise facets of public space in order to secure the privileges and benefits of the corporate elite and ultra-rich. It breeds a politics of fear which is dramatised in a thousand popular cultural forms, usually North American in origin, in which the end of the world is nigh and one disaster or another is about to destroy the planet and civilisation as we know it.

False freedoms

Neoliberalism does not merely produce economic inequality, iniquitous power relations and a corrupt political system; it also promotes rigid exclusions from national citizenship and civic participation. It suppresses dissent in a new way and fosters intolerant fundamentalisms, whether perversions of Christianity or Islam. The relentless pursuit of personal interest and profit outweighs all others (Bauman, 2001b).

The EU is built on treaties enshrining four of the most significant freedoms of neoliberalism: the free movement of labour, capital, goods and services (McGiffen, 2005; Nicholls, 2005; Denny and Katz, 2010). With the accession of the Eastern European states following the dismemberment of Yugoslavia, capital flowed East, and labour flowed West.

Harvey shows how following the defeat of the US in Vietnam in 1975 the neoconservatives planned their new crusade for world 'freedom' under the 'Stars and Stripes' banner. He also shows how the gargantuan and revolutionary drive of capital to accumulate plunders the world in ever more dangerous rivalries for markets and resources, and shows how capital concentrates in new ways. Instead of the old world of rival imperialisms based on individual countries and empires, the new world order of dominant blocs, around the dollar, the euro, the yen and, of course, the supersonic rise of China (Harvey, 2006a). Naomi Klein has shown how capitalism thrives off natural disaster and the doctrine of shock tactics and wars (Klein, 2001, 2008). It relishes chaos and destruction for the profits it can make from them.

Empires

Power blocs like the EU serve neoliberalism well by cutting the moorings of moral, material and regulatory controls embodied in democratically elected national parliaments. Markets cross all borders. Competition and the ability to accumulate capital must not, in any way, be hindered.

Political parties must be reduced to squabbling irrelevances arguing about technical matters, but agreeing on the four freedoms that underpin the EU and the system. As the laws of the market take precedence over the laws of the state as guardians of the public good, the government offers increasingly little help in mediating the interface between the advance of capital and its rapacious commercial interests. It rejects non-commodified interests and non-market spheres that create the political, economic and social spaces and discursive conditions vital for critical citizenship and democratic public life.

The liberal democratic dialect of rights, entitlements, social provisions, community, social responsibility, a living wage, job security, equality and justice seems oddly out of place in a country where the promise of democracy has been replaced by casino capitalism, a winner takes all philosophy suited to lottery players and traders in the stock market's bear pit alike.

As the prevailing discourse of neoliberalism seizes the public imagination, there is a diminished vocabulary for progressive social change, democratically inspired visions, or critical notions of social agency to expand the meaning and purpose of communal production and life. As Giroux puts it:

> Against the reality of low-wage jobs, the erosion of social provisions for a growing number of people, and the expanding war against young people of color at home and empire building abroad, the market driven juggernaut of neoliberalism continues to mobilize desires in the interest of producing market identities and market

relationships and ultimately sever the link between education and social change while reducing the agency to the obligations of consumerism. (Giroux, 2008, p 7)

Equally important is its role in undermining the critical functions of a viable democracy by undercutting the ability of individuals to engage in the continuous interchange between public and private considerations. Independent informal education played a particularly important part in counteracting this, in re-engaging the expression of the private in the context of the public.

In this environment 'freedom' offers few opportunities for people to translate private worries into public concerns and collective struggle. The voluntary sector once thrived on this kind of spontaneous independence. Now it, too, is being marketised – to resource a public need you must compete with others for funding. The dream of a social order, culture and social relationships creating personal identities totally dominated by commercial interests has come about.

Mind-forged manacles

In such a context, with such potent changes to make and decisions to take, the role of youth workers as educators and trade unionists is now more important than ever before. Progressive education, particularly in youth and community work and adult education, have become all the more significant. As bell hooks says, 'Dominator culture has tried to keep us all afraid, to make us choose safety instead of risk' (hooks, 1994).

We need a new powerful community to emerge, a community of international independent nations, cooperating through peace and fair trade. But fears remain. I therefore end this chapter with Brecht singing in his darkest times, in a poem called 'Difficulty of governing':

> Ministers are always telling the people
> How difficult it is to govern. Without the ministers
> Corn would grow into the ground, not upward.
> Not a lump of coal would leave the mine if
> The Chancellor weren't so clever. Without the Minister of Propaganda
> No girl would ever agree to get pregnant. Without the
> Minister of War
> There'd never be a war. Indeed, whether the sun would rise in the morning
> Without the Fuhrer's permission
> Is very doubtful, and if it did, it would be
> In the wrong place.
>
> It's just as difficult so they tell us
> To run a factory. Without the owner
> The walls would fall in and the machine rust, so they say.
> Even if a plough could get made somewhere
> It would never reach a field without the
> Cunning words the factory owner writes the peasants: who
> Could otherwise tell them that ploughs exist? And what
> Would become of an estate without a landlord? Surely
> They'd be sowing rye where they had set potatoes.

If governing were easy
There'd be no need for such inspired minds as
the Fuhrer's.
If the worker knew how to run his machine and
The peasant could tell his field from a pastryboard
There'd be no need of factory owner or landlord.
It's only because they are all so stupid
That a few are needed who are so clever.

Or could it be that

Governing is so difficult only
Because swindling and exploitation take some
learning?

13

Youth in a suspect society

This chapter takes the form of an extended review of the book published in 2010 by Henry Giroux called *Youth in a suspect society, democracy or disposability?* Giroux's work, while looking at the extreme circumstances of the US, concentrates on how neoliberalism deliberately targets the young as its main victims. This chapter seeks to remind us that youth workers have new more urgent forces to deal with. The inequality that neoliberalism demands is a new danger for young people. Social circumstances have never been worse for the young; there is a new urgency, therefore, to youth work.

Young people are being locked up in great numbers for 'crimes' committed as a result of being locked out of meaningful social engagement and the wealth of society. Giroux's powerful book argues that society and educationalists should lock progressive policies for young people securely into the heart of social and economic policy. It argues, from a completely different national experience, for significant social investment in informal radical education, known in Britain as youth work, and an end to the politics and economics of the insane marketplace.

Youth and community workers have long been alert to the hypocrisy of a class-divided society which claims young people are the demonic source of problems, which says crime is the result of warped minds and unemployment the product of laziness. Youth workers have been keen to point out that the periodic demonisation of young people only serves a punitive state, that punishment is always more costly than prevention, and far less effective emotionally and behaviourally. Young people offer no threat to society. Society, on the other hand, poses a great threat to them.

Young demons

The inhumanity of making young people suffer and bear the brunt of the political and economic mistakes of others has long been the concern of youth workers. Youth workers say it is society that is at fault, not young people, while uniquely, they also recognise their role in working with young people to enable them to overcome society's stereotypes and pressures. The art of youth and community work has been linked to collective, ethical philosophies, whether socialist or social democratic, secular or religious. It has never been linked to the perpetration of interpersonal violence and exploitation, oppression and repression. Youth workers should oppose and challenge bullying and worse between young people every bit as much as they oppose imperialism.

But have youth workers really got to grips with the full implications of their concern to side with young people and to nurture their voice? Do they really empower anymore? A generation of youth workers in the late 1970s/early 1980s was brought into professional and political practice because of the horror of youth unemployment. Now there appears to be a complacency in the face of greater unemployment and social decay than ever before. Perhaps the problems are too great, youth workers think, and the system is always 'over there', just out of reach. This book shows how the system is wrapped into every fibre of youth workers' being, and understanding their self-image and attitudes, and can therefore be changed.

Consider the problems in the US where youth work has less of a tradition, where inequality is more extreme, public services have never been as developed, there has never been a youth or health service, 28 million people are on food stamps, 45 million have no health insurance and 4 million, including many black young people, are in jails with many thousands awaiting the death penalty. It is a

YOUTH IN A SUSPECT SOCIETY

Blade runner world out, there according to all the statistics. Social breakdown of the kind we are seeing in the neoliberal economies is generating a frightening *Blade runner* reality. And this is the future for Britain, if current trends continue.

Extreme circumstances

How could a study of young people in such acute circumstances be of benefit to youth workers? By studying extreme circumstances it is often possible to get a good idea of what is in store if these trends are allowed to develop in Britain. The trends in US society are without question the trends that are dominant in Britain, although they are not experienced so acutely. In recent discussions these have been called the 'neoliberal agenda'. Spotting trends should make youth workers more able to defend their practice and the position of young people in society. Giroux's book should help youth workers to wake up to a few realities. Many do not realise they have been sleepwalking because the neoliberal economy they are part of has been the only thing that many have known themselves since childhood.

In the tradition of informal education in which the self is used to develop understanding with others, Giroux's work helps youth workers question their most natural assumptions about the world and the way things are.

Giroux charts the criminality of the economic and political processes I have highlighted previously in relation to young people in the US; he gives the facts, but it is the way of seeing and the analysis that is significant. Many of the anecdotes are as unbelievable as they are heart rending. He believes 'young people have become a generation of suspects in a society destroyed by the merging of market fundamentalism, consumerism, and militarism'. He puts the position of young people in a wide cultural and economic context and in doing so gives youth workers in Britain conceptual tools to understand and challenge their own predicament.

Giroux is particularly good at showing how things like, for example, education, television, diet and fashion have all been changed by this underlying shift in political and economic policy. He believes that young people have been the main victims of this new agenda and we should be more concerned about this. In fact, he suggests that the improvement of the condition for young people is the essential policy initiative that must take place. Social policy, institutional mismanagement and changing cultural attitudes have led to young people having to grow up in very different and worse conditions. To reverse this is to reverse the current direction of political travel.

As capital accumulates only through the surplus value created by labour, labour markets must be seriously deregulated. For youth work this means the attempt to have a free market in terms and conditions and associated with this resistance to the notion of licensing workers to practice under a scheme that they define and control. Anyone can do the work, the argument goes, and you don't need a qualification and professional terms and conditions of employment.

Democracy, even in the confines of post-war capitalism, gave minimum guarantees of security; there was a kind of social contract that even the most disadvantaged would not be destitute and mechanisms for re-engagement would be found. This contract has been broken and it is more generally acceptable nowadays to blame the poor, the homeless, those with mental ill health, the unemployed and other disadvantaged groups and individuals for their own problems.

Consumer kids

At the same time, the market as an alternative to the democratic state blends with a new authoritarianism that punishes the most marginalised. Young people are either seen as consumers or as 'dangerous demons'. In relation to the consumerisation of children and young people, Ed Mayo and Agnes Nairn contribute much to our understanding in their work *Consumer kids* (Mayo and Nairn, 2009). They demonstrate how lifestyles and health have been made worse by the corporations, with profit-making corporations more influential in polluting the minds and behaviours of children and young people than parents, teachers and youth workers.

Based on robust international and domestic research on corporation policies and the psychological, social and behavioural effects of children and young people's games, clothes, food, technology and communications 'markets' that are now worth over £99 billion a year in the UK alone, Mayo and Nairn's book shows how corporations have lured and groomed childhood behaviours to maximise profit without any regard to social, physical and psychological consequences.

Mayo and Nairn show first how children have become 'their' market, and how blitz marketing techniques and subtle, incessant advertising campaigns have made a generation of young consumers altered in many ways by the fads, fashions and trends that the voracious capitalist market has unleashed. They also show how an alternative, ethical approach could be developed.

The authors write, 'as the profit motive seeps into all aspects of our lives, the number and nature of the child catchers continues to grow'. No aspect of life is spared. The child's bedroom is transformed into a media bedsit, with fast food, sweets and snacks gobbled unhealthily as violent computer games are played. Instead of socialisation in the playground, on average children spend 5 hours and 18 minutes a day in front of some kind of electronic screen. Every screen advertises something eventually, and subliminal messages of what latest candy or toy to buy are conveyed. Increasingly the private lives of children and young people are invaded by the salespeople who are keen to get personal details and tie children into their brands for life.

Fashion is getting younger and children are being made older at an earlier age, with the age of sexualisation and stereotyping falling all the time. Innocence, in many ways, is being lost earlier and earlier. There are even best-selling scents and perfumes for babies and toddlers, and cosmetics for very young girls. Playboy stationery is one of the most popular lines at WH Smiths for girls. Girls can also now get toy lap dancing kits complete with a pole to help release 'the sex kitten inside'.

On the food front abnormality has become the market norm – you should be concerned about being too fat, or too fat to think. Anorexia and obesity are the gifts of a distorted market. Just as the teenage pregnancy rate and inter-youth violence in Britain are the highest in Europe, so young people's diets are still the worst. Only 27 per cent of British children eat fruit every day compared with 42 per cent in Germany, 38 per cent in Italy and 34 per cent in France. The sweets and fizzy drinks market moves on, and increasingly young people are starting their alcohol dependency at a very young age. Twenty-seven per cent of under 15-year-olds in Britain get drunk regularly compared with 3 per cent in France and 5 per cent in Italy.

Technology has revolutionised children's lives forever, and Mayo and Nairn (2009) examine the dependency of children and young people on various forms of technology. One clear result has been what some call 'nature deficit disorder', a complete physical and mental separation from the natural world and a lack of understanding of its role in production and human fulfilment. Incarcerated at home, the great indoors becomes the kind of safe haven from a violent traffic churning world full of dangers but full of its own.

How these markets and lifestyle changes have altered the mind and 'messed' with the collective experience of growing up is examined in very thought-provoking detail, and the effect of this on young people's politics is also considered. Have young people's values become more individualistic and materialistic? What is the topic of discussion among the 70 per cent of 7- to 16-year-olds who are signed up to social networking sites? Half have created their own spaces and websites. What is the effect of this?

Giroux takes this further and shows the devastating impact of the capitalist market aimed at children and young people in the US and how young people have been targeted as commodities themselves by big business. It is not just selling commodities to young people, but a step further turning young people into commodities or rubbish to be disposed of.

Counter-culture

Youth workers have a good grasp of the marginalisation, criminalisation and demonisation of young people. Giroux takes this recognition further by showing how those young people who are not able to engage in the consumer market become a consciously created disposable section of society. Private prisons profit from their crimes and a punitive state's youth justice policy. If there is nothing else for them to do, drive them into the armed forces to fight for oil – Exxon has just signed strategic oil field agreements in Iraq. And listen to how young US soldiers talk about themselves – they refer to themselves only in the third person, not as 'I' or 'me' but as 'this soldier' or 'this recruit', their dehumanisation complete. As the song said, 'the dole or the army the choices are few, no money for hospitals, schools or for factories, but millions to spend on the red white and blue' (Rogers, 2006).

The public and democratic glue that held previous capitalist social structures together have become unstuck and the consequences are a mindless acceptance of the overriding market powers and a fragmentation of opposition to this reaction. In addition, critical pedagogy, essential to youth and community work, is fast disappearing. Instead of questioning the inequalities and injustices of social power, question the judges of *X Factor*! Instead of questions helping us to understand human value, we get questions of understanding prices within the consumer market. Pay to have your phone-in vote for some superficial matter recorded, miss out on a vote on whether your country should be run by the EU or not, and whether it should go to war.

Theatre of cruelty

Giroux describes the neoliberal society as a 'theatre of cruelty', built on the biggest concentrations of wealth in the fewest hands in recent history. Fewer own more and more do more work for less while even more are marginalised and outcast from sources of solidarity and social cohesion. This applies in particular to children and young people who do not work and have considerable, but ultimately limited, spending power. Young people are the main collateral damage caused by this new aggressive neoliberalism.

The popular demonisation of the young now justifies responses to youth that were unthinkable in the US (and here?) 20 years ago including criminalisation, and imprisonment, the prescription of psychotropic drugs, psychiatric confinement, zero tolerance policies and the profit-laden expansion of both the binge drinking markets and the sexualisation of fashion and youth culture. CCTV cameras reign down on young people's spaces in case they rebel, or act as badly as the market wants them to. The great symbol of this culture for me is the Mosquito electronic device that various retail locations put in place to 'zap' young people hanging around on street corners, putting shoppers off.

If the market is to penetrate everything there can be no tolerance of forces that put the brakes on it, forces that are political, organisational and cultural. In summary, such forces go under the name of democracy. People collectivise to assert common interests. To do this they must debate, decide and act. This is all too cumbersome for the market that must move swiftly, constantly revolutionising technique and consumer gadgets to make money. The market will not allow anything to stand in its way so aims to atomise people as individual consumers. Hence the erosion of civil liberties, the rise of authoritarianism and the necessary development of a predatory culture of fear of anything which may challenge the existing market-based philosophy, economy or property rights.

Part of the importance of Giroux's work is in his cross-disciplinary thinking. He makes connections and links between social currents. Too much thinking about the condition of young people is in separate boxes, the sociology of youth, the impact of youth work, youth crime, youth culture, social policy etc. Giroux interrelates these areas and stimulates a way of thinking that more youth workers should get used to.

He sees the theatre of cruelty as a wide stage reproduced daily through the regime of common sense and a narrow notion of political rationality. Neoliberalism 'reaches from the soul of the subject citizen to educational policy to practices of empire'. In other words you could say there is a 'biopolitics', that is, a personal politics of interpersonal relationships and self-identity, which neoliberalism exploits through its penetration of media and games markets and everyday, alienated experience. People are no longer just controlled by coercive state forces but by technologies of consent produced largely by the gaming and media industries. Of course the young are a particular target in this regard – most computer games are military and aggressive.

The revolution will not be televised

Why is there so much competitiveness on television? Why is every food or talent show or reality television programme or talk show built on rampant competition? Does popular culture reflect the dominant economic imperative instead of people's aspirations for justice? Why are most young people and families in soaps depicted as dysfunctional? Are working-class lives so wretched? Is it really the survival of the richest or fittest?

The attacks on democracy and the notion of human beings as agents of change mean that the basic concept of 'citizen' is increasingly difficult to sustain, especially when you try to put the idea of democratic representation alongside it. It is hardly surprising that within the physical landscape so many communities have become disposable, literally relegated in their living space to the frontier zones, removed from public view and warehoused in boot camp estates and institutions. This fragments into the crazed territorialism of gangs divided by postcode, and threatens authentic experience and human communication and engagement.

All too many are dehumanised unnecessarily in prison. As we well know for those groups considered expendable, redundant and invisible by virtue of their 'race', class and youth, life becomes increasingly precarious. Children are assigned early to the coffins of history. The human waste disposal industry has no time for the rights of those it seeks to dump. This is why youth work is being squeezed in the new integrated services. Social work casework and child protection cannot cope. Only developmental approaches can cure the situation in the longer term, yet they are the first to go. The vicious spiral screws itself downwards.

As another commentator, Zygmunt Bauman (Bauman, 2001a), put it, the relationship between power and politics has been fundamentally altered. 'The result is the gradual separation between the power to act, which now drifts towards markets, and politics, which, though remaining the domain of the state, is progressively stripped of its freedom to manoeuvre and authority to set the rules and be arbiter of the game.'

Youth workers must raise again big questions of power and responsibility if they are to engage meaningfully with young people and empower them. Giroux urges trainers in higher education of future generations of progressive educationalists to reassert their commitments to challenging current trends.

Creative consumers

Serious investment in young people as creators and not consumers is being abandoned; this is the biggest indication of disinvestment in society's future. A symbol of this turning away is the demise of the Youth Service. It never had statutory funding; it had an indicative figure, and now that has even gone. Youth services are funded by a 19th-century array of philanthropic organisations and the virtues of faith, hope and charity. Short-term funding builds welcome and flashy new multipurpose buildings with no on-costs and a distracting leisure agenda. 'Keep 'em off the streets.' The lure of the off license is countered by apparently harmless positive activities. These are intoxicating in their own way as they can lack depth and avoid the engagement of young people in feeling empowered. They numb the mind. I believe that positive activities in the youth work sense include moral and political dialogue and debate, and collective organisation in groups. Youth work inspires and illuminates the mind. It should be more about positive thought and social action than activity.

Historically education has been the battleground for the development of critical ideas and challenges to mindless unquestioned orthodoxy. Historically also, in Britain in particular, youth and community work practice has very much been an additional opportunity within the spectrum of education provision to develop a radical, critical, emancipatory, questioning practice, a form of pedagogy linked to collective aspirations for social justice and equality.

Youth workers seek to educate young people, to turn an upside down world the right way up through communal effort and mutual assistance. It has always been absolutely fundamental to the best youth work practice that education evolves in dialogue with young people on the basis of an understanding of the context of their lives and freely chosen engagement. That context is a social construct and youth workers need to understand it more.

So youth workers find themselves with young people at the centre of the neoliberal target and the critical pedagogy that they represent not far away from it. Young people will suffer more unless youth workers can restore their conviction and practice in a socialist-inspired, radical critique of society and an engagement of young people and communities in collective action for change.

Youth workers have always understood culture as Giroux does, 'as an activity in which young people actually produce the conditions of their own agency through dialogue, community participation, public stories, and political struggle'. It is the defence and reassertion of this culture that is now at stake.

The preciousness of the lives of the young is now matched only by the preciousness of defending progressive youth work practice. The two are intertwined within the British context. Giroux's book clearly shows what is in store if youth workers do not assert their defence of youth work and young people.

14

New youth workers and new youth work

A new form of youth work is needed. Youth workers must assert its progressive nature and reconnect with its origins in an alternative socialist education. In this final chapter I argue that socialist commitment must shape this new practice. Youth work's defensiveness has meant that it has articulated an abstract sense of its value; while it has defended its form it has lost sight of its content. This reflects the huge pressures placed on it by the decline of political liberalism stemming from the Enlightenment and the suppression and transformation of socialist thinking and organisation. The effectiveness of youth work's method needs to be combined with a new consciousness and purpose. This will enable it, through face-to-face relationship building and dialogue with young people, to overcome the alienation culturally and economically inherent in the capitalist system. It points very significantly to a new political and economic future.

It is time to put some content in the forms of how youth work is practised – technique and process on their own are insufficient. Youth workers' successful resistance to a capitalist curriculum for youth work that the Tory government sought to impose in the 1990s should not be a distraction from creating a socialist curriculum. Such a curriculum cannot be simply process-driven. Following the election of the Coalition government in May 2010 things have changed, and previous dispositions and ways of working cannot hold things together.

Youth work has been compelled under recent pressures to defend its processes, values and methods. This has resulted partly in a reliance on abstract nouns rather than active, practical verbs. There is also much contentment with process, and not enough concern for product, or what has been referred to as praxis in the critical pedagogical tradition, meaning a combination of thought, and, I add, feeling and action. The phrases have come close to running out of meaning. There is a danger that these key descriptors become empty formal fetishes, slogans without content and purpose. This has perhaps been understandable in that the emancipatory elements of method have been under attack, but the defence of process without regard for the society and kind of citizenship we are seeking to build becomes a flimsy and potentially irrelevant framework to preserve on its own. It is like trying to defend the values of youth work without preserving its core infrastructure.

Process or socialist product

Process-related descriptions of youth work have become like zombies, staggering around without social objectives. What is built around these methodological structures relating to process? What society do youth workers imagine in the future and will fight for? Is it a socialist one, or a repeat of the current capitalist one? Has history really ended, as various apologists of capitalism have claimed (Fukuyama, 1993)? Has youth work, as a profession, accepted that there is no alternative to the inequality, authoritarianism and warmongering of the empire? Will youth workers be individual consumers forever? Will endless talk of their predicament and its unfairness alter things?

Marx, Freire, Gramsci and Christ, whose writings most influence youth work practice in Britain, were political activists. Youth workers must get more political and this means becoming more involved in the struggle for change. What counts is the potent mix of saying and doing what they say should be done. An emancipatory process in youth work must have an emancipatory objective. Action without thought is blind and thought without action leads nowhere, as the first British socialists in the 17th century rightly observed.

Awkward questions

What is informal education for? What is the purpose of a voluntary relationship with young people? Process is important, but what is the product? Will the oppressed remain oppressed forever? How will they be liberated? What are the economics of an emancipated society? What does reflection on practice seek to do? How will young people understand and interpret these endless new experiences that have opened up? Should young people be shown more to encourage them to spectate, to receive passively, or to criticise, engage and change reality?

Youth work is a craft, highly value-laden, and in whose interest? Active citizenship in what, and why? What is participation for? Empowerment is universally acclaimed, but what power for whom and for what? Youth work needs ethics, but what is ethical? Conversation is essential to youth work, but what is it about? Democracy sounds fine, but who rules and how are current rulers replaced? We should have local democracy and influence, but is this possible in a totalitarian state? Global and environmental awareness are necessary, but what do they change? Critical pedagogy is important, but what are we criticising and why? Where has anti-oppressive practice gone?

Youth work must find a new way forward.

Informally educating a young person through a cookery project in a youth centre that certain fridge temperatures are safer than others, or pricing the results of cooking reasonably so friends can afford the cake are moral courses of action, and are worthwhile exercises in themselves, adding to the fun and learning of life. Talking about food markets and the power of supermarkets might add a twist of real endeavour. It might help to start a political discussion. Surely this must be the direction of travel for discussion led by a youth worker?

Young people's minds should be engaged in thinking critically about the world in which they live.

Partial benefits

Ensuring that a youth centre celebrates International Women's Day is a good thing, and ensuring it celebrates Black History Month is also a must. But where is trade union education for young people? When are young people prepared for employment rights, or their rights as young people? Regularly holding discussions to critique media images is a vital part of informal education so that the power and distortions of the media can be exposed. These social-related subjects are the real business of informal education. Youth workers are truly inspirational in their approach to such matters, but I would argue that not enough is going on. Such work is being marginalised at a time when the media and commercial entertainments are distorting views of reality beyond all recognition.

Once a young person has chosen to relate to a youth worker, should the youth worker be merely satisfied with the rapport that develops, the banter, the camaraderie or humour? This sensitive bedrock of affection is just a start. Where will the youth worker take the relationship? To an ice rink, but dreading yet another risk assessment and parental consent form? What will be talked about on the way? The ice? Or will the youth worker, when uncovering some of the young person's vulnerabilities, prejudices and gaps in understanding, seek to take the relationship in a direction which addresses these issues and seeks to raise the young person's self-esteem, challenge prejudices and widen their knowledge?

If there is a successfully mixing and stable youth group that wants to meet a perceived need that will be strongly opposed by the community, or local authority, how should a youth worker proceed knowing that conflict will ensue? If young people have to be enabled to campaign and fight against a local injustice, will youth workers be sufficiently protected by their union and colleagues to take this on?

What would be the point of the whole campaign if it was lost? Is it really better to have fought and lost than not to have fought at all?

In validating their experiences, instilling hope and confidence and steering oppressed young people towards social action in their own interests is good, but youth workers should think if they will have to repeat the same process in five years' time with another oppressed group; how will they be able to permanently eradicate the source of the young people's distress so they can move on to other things?

If the source of young people's distress in ideological and social policies is recognised beyond the immediate environment and community, how will youth workers link up with others seeking a similar vision of a liberated society?

Youth workers continually try to sharpen their approach through supervision, but reflecting on practice glues them to the here and now and the institutional limits of their paid role. Should reflection not include, then, a challenging of these limits and an effort to relate them to a wider context?

Taking young people on a residential course or overseas trip enriches and widens their experience of the world; it is partly a virtue in itself, but are youth workers travel agents? Not many travel agents succeed in the kind of residential and international work that youth workers at their best have excelled in. Imagine taking rival and opinionated tribal groups of young people with nothing but hate for each other, to Auschwitz, for example, to consider the real historical impact of hatred. Imagine the exceptional enjoyment young people may feel in leaving an estate for the first time and seeing real cows in fields. Imagine the excitement and fun in leaving their area for the first time to visit others in other parts of the world and finding they turn out to be just like them. Residential and international work must surely become more prominent parts of youth work, as its transformative power is immense.

New cultural experiences should be opened for young people – films, plays and paintings – but there should also be an analysis of the function of culture in our lives. Consider these questions: is *Avatar* the film just a 3D spectacle, or does it oppose, or support an empire and capitalist way of thinking? Why would anyone want to read the tabloid press? Is *EastEnders* a depiction of reality? How are young people portrayed in the press? Why do 'soaps' portray people and families as dysfunctional? Why are there so many competitive talent and cookery shows? What does popular music do to people? Does it soothe or silence or invigorate them? Has the televised prime ministerial debate finally made politics like *X Factor*, a form of talent show?

Rights

If young people are to be citizens, what are their rights? Why are they able to join the army at 16, but not allowed to not vote on whether they go to war until they are 18? If a youth council and a youth parliament are set up, will the young people have power and resources to implement their decisions? How will collective, democratic decisions take place? What will power be wielded for? What is crime? Stealing a car, or 'giving' a trillion pounds of taxpayers' money to banks that then hold the nation to ransom and demand cuts in public services?

The youth work method is infused with, indeed built on, questioning, on the development of the active mind that criticises the source of exploitation and oppression and encourages infinite curiosity. It is interested in emotional, intellectual and social intelligence. It has inherited virtuous notions of helping and caring (Smith and Smith, 2008) from both socialist and various religious traditions, although such traditions have now been trodden down and cannot be restored in their previous forms. So youth workers have the additional responsibility of being sufficiently organised themselves to deal with the new totalitarianism that has trampled down these positive traditions. Young people cannot be expected to take this on alone.

If the welfare society has substantially gone and a new individualism has taken over despite people's will, how will youth workers be able to build an enhanced new form of welfare out of such ruins?

This is not a reassertion, but a new assertion of a new role for youth work that, a bringing together of the very best of past thought, practice and action in a concentrated and determined form to enable more radical questioning of the world around us and therefore the potential for transforming it, reclaiming and creating a new democratic platform in a lived, live, authentic public sphere. Youth workers must counteract alienation and individualism, experiencing culture and society as passive consumers.

Alienation

As these two negative aspects of capitalist society have been so destructive, it is worth pursuing further what they mean, in particular alienation, which relates to individualism.

Youth workers are able to recognise, usually through body language, when a young person feels uncomfortably alienated from the experience or group of which they are a part. They feel out of place. There is a disconnection between their feelings and the situation they are in; they do not feel empathetic to the situation; they feel put off by it. Creating empathy, a sense of comfort and participation, is a vital part of youth work. An alienating situation is like a nightmare, when a big bad wolf is standing over you, threatening you; when an object seems so much bigger than you, it can oppress and destroy you. A personally alienating experience is one that demeans you.

This is not, however, what I mean by alienation in this context. It is something more social and economic and at the core of the socialist critique of capitalism. I refer here to the social nightmare experienced by human beings under capitalism that alienates them from themselves and society. The effect of structural alienation does, of course, affect personality and individual feeling and it shapes our behaviour. But the personal and psychological elements of alienation are not the focus here. The political elements are the focus, and politics is interwoven with economics.

Workers generally go to work. At work they apply their minds and bodies, their brains and hands, their thoughts and skills; they apply them to processes which either produce real material things in the case of more factory-based and scientific and technical occupations, or help the circulation of those things. Workers are lorry drivers, or nurses, or teachers. Some make things directly and this is primary. All have a direct and sensuous engagement with production. Workers produce. This is ultimately a material, physical endeavour, transformation of nature in the real world.

When those involved in direct production make something it is often as a single item that turns out to be more expensive than its makers can afford. Think, perhaps, of the manufacturers of luxury cars. Track workers cannot afford to buy the cars they make. Whatever workers produce or contribute towards or perform, its value for those who own it and profit from its sale is greater than anything workers may individually earn. They only get back a proportion of the values they create in production. Their inner lives, creativity, knowledge and dexterity pour out in producing things for sale and distribution, and the things they create then dominate them in the market. Their private lives are externalised in a world of things, which in their totality are unavailable to them.

As Paula Allman summarises, Marx's concept 'of alienation depicts a process by which the results of human labour are not conceived by those who produce them, prior to their production and, once produced, have nothing to do with the actual people who have laboured to make them' (Allman, 1999, 2001). Creations pour away from workers onto the market.

Youth work must engage and wrestle with these ideas more strenuously because it is heavily influenced by ideas about alienation put forward before modern socialism, and notably by the philosopher, Hegel. Hegel thought that people were alienated from their 'species being', their real human consciousness as creative entities, simply because they somehow did not realise that they were the creators of reality and that the social world was a creation of their relationships and self-consciousness. He implied that all people had to do was recognise the connection between their creative consciousness and the real world. If they understood that they were the agents of change, they could overcome their alienation. This is the basis of much youth (and community work) practice and theory. If people could appreciate their ability to change things, they would be less estranged from the world and less alienated; and this seems to be how most youth workers understand the dilemma. The obsession with the idea of creating agents of change leads some to forget what changes are actually needed, however.

Marx posed a much more challenging concept. He did not believe that this human alienation could be overcome by thinking smarter and harder and realising one's active role in the world. This was because alienation was not as a result of thoughts; it was a result of a relationship between thought and practice in the economic and social world. As Allman goes on to explain:

> Human beings objectify their powers and activity in the material world they produce. They produce a world of objects with a separate existence from themselves; however, there is nothing inherently wrong with or alienating about this objectification. The source of alienation lies within the social relations of human practice that allow some people to decide what is to be produced and to control the results of production while others become no more than objects to be used in the production process and dominated by the very powers they have externalised through their labour. (Allman, 2001, p 17)

In order to sustain an underlying significance on the side of young people, youth work must instil a consciousness about overcoming this fundamental form of social alienation.

This entails an uncomfortable challenge to various forms of utopianism within youth work. By utopianism I mean the creation within youth work of various limits to satisfaction, the creation of joyous spaces and experiences of small group happiness and contentment. These commonwealths of interpersonal pleasantness and some sense of mutual compassion and sharing and fun are insufficient in themselves.

'Big Society', big con

Youth work's experiential learning for young people creates a society of learners. Such little societies represent big social commitments. With the election of the Coalition government in May 2010 the definitions of society altered yet again. Whereas a previous Tory administration had denied the existence of society, suddenly the new Tories invented the 'Big Society'. But I believe that this is nothing other than a smokescreen for dismantling the public sector and the traditional public sphere of civil society and voluntary organisations and charities. It was an attempt to reintroduce self-help into social concerns and 'philanthro-capitalism', as they called it, instead of social giving. The welfare state is being replaced by a distorted form of self-help.

One of the pet prime ministerial projects within the 'Big Society' agenda has been to quickly put £13 million aside to pilot a national youth citizen's service alongside increasing cuts in the Youth Service throughout the country, and a plan from the youth minister to ask key stakeholders what would happen if there were no such thing as a local authority youth service.

Britain has had a national youth citizen's service since 1961. Participation in it is voluntary. It operates 365 days a year. For every £1 invested in it, at least £8 worth of voluntary activity is generated. It organises around 500,000 committed adult volunteers to support it, 40,000 trained youth support workers and over 7,000 fully professionally qualified youth workers. Their work generates hundreds of millions of hours of voluntary youth involvement each year.

This service is a partnership between the voluntary sector and local authorities, and it is the one service working with young people that Ofsted have said is consistently improving. Funding agencies have always said youth workers' relationship-building work to provide young people with personal and social education is highly cost-effective.

Without the Youth Service there would be no UK Youth Parliament. There would be no national infrastructure of young people's centres, no supportive detached work contact on the streets, no successful anti-gang work. It is responsible for initiatives as demanding as youth councils to building self-esteem and pride among those who have never experienced them. It is a service that has built tens of thousands of social action groups. It has empowered young people to express dignified civic voices, and it has involved many in creative and responsible community projects, helping heal bitterly divided communities.

Every day youth workers work to nurture hidden talents and make engaging work for 'idle hands'. Through them young people can assert their rights and needs. Learning is provided beyond the classroom as youth workers motivate, challenge, entertain and open doors.

National youth citizen's service

This established national youth service also developed international exchange work as part of the reconciliation of post-war Europe. Youth workers often remain the only organisers of international travel and visits beyond the confines of local estates. Youth work was the first profession to call for interagency working at a local level in teams respecting different specialisms. Hundreds of youth workers are currently overseas with groups of young people who have been fundraising to travel and expand their horizons over the summer months, for example.

For generations, youth work has worked with young people on their own agendas and with their concerns most in mind. This is an expression of the right of all young people to voluntarily engage in the 'Big Society' and to take responsibility. It is a professional skill taught in highly practice-based courses that attract those with years of dedicated local voluntary work behind them, but who recognise that young people deserve trained practitioners working with them.

Youth work is a non-elitist profession with status and standing among those it serves. It combines great care for young people with great motivational skills. This is why a previous Tory government set up pioneering and successful apprenticeship schemes targeted at marginalised individuals to qualify them to become skilled professionals. These professionals informally educate. They work with young people in their leisure time, although I would argue that youth work is not a leisure activity. At heart, through fun and group development and individual attention, youth work creates a sense of self-worth, purpose, community, creativity and an ethical sense of action in a complex world. It connects, challenges and changes. To do this, long-term relationships must be built through a publicly funded, sustained service.

There is a place for recreational and diversionary activities in the summer months, especially in some real hot spot areas, but the problem with the recent announcement of summer citizenship placements is, like the rest of the 'Big Society' agenda, being replaced. The amount spent on the pilots is equivalent to the cuts in the Youth Service in five authorities as of August 2010. Overall, these five authorities cut £200 million from overall social services.

No one remembers short-term government gimmicks, yet everyone who has been involved in the Youth Service remembers its impact. It is there for all young people to enjoy when they want to. Its offer is universal. It offers an infrastructure of support and engagement that can take a young person on a journey from active youth centre member, to volunteer youth worker, to paid part-time worker, to trainee, to full-time professional to senior manager of a service.

But all this is up for demolition. The union has recently worked with Conservative councillors and Liberal Democrats who have given a lifetime of voluntary commitment within the Youth Service and on local youth management committees, and who are now seeing those structures being broken up, commissioned out, cut to pieces.

Because of the severity of the attack, youth workers must connect with their progressive past and sharpen their practice and social relevance in the fight against inequality and exploitation.

History of youth work

A powerful and destructive feature of the media-dominated world in which, like financial transactions on the money markets themselves, wants and desires demand instant gratification and virtual reality games require literally millisecond decisions, is the cult of the immediate, the 'now now now' world that appears to have no history and just started yesterday, when the computer was turned on. People seem locked in a constant present of consumerism and absorption of the latest advert or fad. Youth workers must know more of their own history and the social history of youth work, and relish in particular the fact that they are inhabiting a tradition that stretches back deep into the Middle Ages (Kelly, 1992). Radical education for change has been growing on British soil for more than 500 years. It is time to recall it.

Various strands of thinking about teaching and learning methods and forms of learning have been and are closely linked to the socialist struggle for change. Prior to the industrial period the struggle to ensure that the Bible was translated into English and to get church services conducted in English was part of a progressive reforming movement which sought to inspire 'the poorest plough boy' with the egalitarian interpretations of the scriptures. 'When Adam delves/And Eve span/Who was then the gentleman' was the revolutionary question that the radical peasantry asked. In other words, why did some people have things and others didn't, why did some have power over others? 'Why was there class division' was an underpinning question asked by a radical tradition of opposition to both feudalism and capitalism, and it informed the development of many revolutionary groups.

Among the first of these groups were the Lollards, whose 'leader' was John Wycliffe, an early translator of the Bible. The Lollards formed their own 'schools', rudimentary but counter-cultural meeting places, or 'conventicles' as they were called, which completely undermined the hierarchy of the Catholic church by bringing their participants, artisans, weavers, tailors, turners, servants, men and women into direct contact with the gospels. They were considered highly subversive and heretical and a direct and dangerous challenge to the established order. Emancipatory education in Britain, including youth work, therefore has its origins in such oppositional learning from the 14th century. The tendency to relate youth and community work to that other long established tradition of church preaching and missionary work and of correcting the lives of the wicked to the path of righteousness and salvation is misplaced, however. Youth work belongs to a decidedly radical and old tradition (Aston, 1984; Kelly, 1992).

Radical preachers, young people, community workers and adult educators of their day, inspired a poetry and practice of rebellion and dissent that would travel down the subsequent ages. They, like the once radical theologians in Latin America, were the social educators of their time, seeking to advance the cause of the poor to overcome economic divisions.

The spread of literacy and printing meant that by the time of the 1649 English Revolution radical democratic movements and left-wing religious groupings, and in particular, the Levellers and the Diggers, were able to engage in the struggle of ideas and promote their democratic cause in an eloquent English plain style that found expression in the mass circulation of leaflets and pamphlets. Reading and study and the examination of the value of ideas became established in this early socialist movement.

This continued throughout the pre-industrial period, as E.P. Thompson, the great working-class historian, and others have shown. The progressive learning and thirst for knowledge inspired in the Sunday School movement radicalised many generations, including the early trade unionists (Thompson, 1968). Left-wing religious groups were versed in the humanist traditions of a counter-culture that opposed the church and king and the established order.

It was not surprising that education became essential to the early trade union and socialist movements. Thomas Paine's *The rights of man* sold in hundreds of thousands of copies within a short time of publication, testifying to a highly literate working class. The Tolpuddle Martyrs, early trade unionists imprisoned and transported for forming an organisation to demand more pay, wrote eloquently of their struggle to a wide readership. Songs and later, in the Chartist period, when workers were fighting for the vote and a democratic parliament, for example, radical pamphlets and novels would communicate the news of struggles and class struggle generally from village to village and town to town.

With the creation of mass industry, education for survival and liberation became the order of the day. Philanthropists established a tradition of providing education and community development for the urban poor. Social reformers joined in seeing the need to link training of the mind with questions of morality and behaviour and social direction. The industrial unions began to establish libraries and training courses. Mass left-wing book clubs were established. Socialist study groups developed. Even the first scouting organisation in Britain was a socialist one, established by Robert Blatchford. It sought to spread socialist ideals in the police, army and society generally, and sent young people all over the country to argue for socialism in factories, offices and police stations and army barracks. Perhaps a modern equivalent is needed.

Into the 20th century there were also well-developed socialist and trade union learning programmes. There were artistic forms of mass education, socialist theatre and choir groups, a revived tradition of political song, disciplined study in political parties, a vast new literature of scientific socialism, a network of socialist bookshops, demanding trade union study programmes on the nature of capital and the extraction of surplus value; workers looked at how some amassed wealth and others died early in squalor as a result. The working class was more educated in socialism and more successful in arguing and fighting for positive social reforms.

There was also a strong tradition that drew on the works of many educationalists throughout the world of developing teaching and learning techniques that would engage learners and teachers in new more dynamic ways of learning. These often sought to break down the various forms of bourgeois ideology and manners developed within a hierarchical education system. The curriculum and teaching methods of an education system established to create the reserve army of labour and to reproduce docile labour began to be criticised.

Learning was extended beyond the classroom over the decades by socialist, working-class effort: trade union education, radical adult education, community work, youth work, play work – all developed from the 19th-century socialist impulse to liberate minds and broaden the appeal of collective learning. Socialists continually established additional forms of learning for workers excluded from the full benefits of a state and university education. Trade unions encouraged a love of learning. Many of the self and trade union-educated workers who emerged were without doubt some of the most knowledgeable and learned people in the country and could outpace many who had spent their lives in academia. The age of the self-taught person with an insatiable appetite for learning seems sometimes long gone now. Surely youth workers alongside teachers can inspire again this great thirst for learning among young people.

This rich history, summarised briefly here, is still, in part, evident in many areas of life. But, like everything else of value to workers, it has been attacked by a resurgent capitalism. The state has moved in more and more to redirect trade union education, for example. This has transformed the curriculum from one of understanding the workings of capitalism and organising against it, to learning technical ways of coping with decline. Like youth work, it is liable to focus on abstract techniques and a discussion of symptoms rather than causes.

Person-centred learning

We are not just compelled to restore and reconnect with a radical tradition of education with an explicitly socialist dimension; we should link again with a tradition that has sought to promote the vitality and education of children and young people as a social organising principle. In the modern epoch this has its origins in the Renaissance and in humanism (Cunningham, 2006), ideas developed that saw children and young people as occupying a 'special and exalted place'. In breaking the shackles of an agriculturally based peasant society, where childhood existed in the confines of the working family tending its land, humanism made the education of the young both a social responsibility and imperative. Erasmus, an influential humanist author, believed that a child should 'imbibe, as it were, with the milk that he suckles, the nectar of education ... for he will most certainly turn out to be an unproductive brute unless at once and without delay he is subjected to a process of intensive education'. Erasmus also believed that this education should be mixed with appealing fun and play. Child-centred learning was therefore born very early in history.

A new focus on the importance of children and young people led to a radical shift in conceptions. No longer was the child or young person in some kind of dormant state waiting to ascend into adulthood; the preciousness of the early years themselves were valued, and it was believed that the quality of this childhood experience would help determine the quality of the child's later social life. Growing up was, in fact, seen more like a troublesome decline into less godly conditions – childhood was better than adulthood. The trick therefore was to maintain the attitude and brilliance of childhood throughout life. This is what the Romantic poet William Wordsworth meant when he said: 'The child is father of the man', and it was Rousseau who said: 'Who wants to know me as an adult, has to know me as a child.'

A view of children as being fresh from the hands of God emerged strongly in the 19th century. Children and young people were imagined as existing in a state of heavenly innocence. They were not gnarled by original sin, as in earlier medieval views. This paved the progressive way for the missionary zeal of the Christian philanthropists who focused much of their social effort and, if we consider their great writers like Charles Dickens, much of their literature, on the need to rescue young people from the neglect, abandonment and criminality of society. Social empathy with children and young people developed strongly, and led to the professionalisation of a range of services with them. It was no longer simply a question of the random kindness of strangers or the charitable activities of the churches, for example. A secular social responsibility was adopted. Such work naturally led to the idea of seeking to mould and shape the communities in which children and young people existed; and where they lacked families, or work, or any form of communal existence, alternatives were created. Social unfairness could be changed by community action. There would be no such thing as an orphan from society.

Community work

Community work, which was once linked to collective action against injustice, linking trade unionists in the workplace to community groups in the neighbourhood, is now only funded if it has more modest aims, and trade unions are generally seen to lack interest in the local community (Thomas, 1983; Twelvetrees, 1991; Popple, 1995; Gilchrist 2009). The professional autonomy of teachers and lecturers has been threatened with the mechanistic and fragmented nature of 'competencies' and the fragmentation of learning into modules and marketable units of 'knowledge'.

The education system is now skewed towards the workings of the market. University departments sell bits of information to 'clients' paying exorbitant fees to be part of what is a common free treasury of learning. There is almost a glut of free access to knowledge, a kind of cognitive capitalism, as some commentators call it, where an overproduction of information and poverty and unemployment all go together and in which all of life is paid for and huge digital-based conglomerates force millions to rent their information through patents and licenses (Mason, 2008; Rifkin, 2010).

The cyber sphere

An apparent free explosion of information that is universally accessible rests entirely on a lucrative technological platform created by the world's richest man and 'philanthropist', Bill Gates. He's got the whole world, in his hands, the whole World Wide Web, in his hands. Trillions of infinitesimally charged transactions add up to private fortunes worth billions. The virtual world diffuses human knowledge and sets it in new relationships networked across the planet through cyber intimacies and exchanges replacing real physical proximity and face-to-face cooperation. Exclusive private experiences, whether watching a free lecture from a renowned world leader in their field on YouTube, to enjoying a favourite jazz track, to web-caming with former pen friends in Australia, is available for for minimal cost within the interconnected cyber sphere. Such personalised solidarities proliferate as the world fragments and society falls apart.

People are privately able to consume a wide range of subjective pleasures, and a wider range of information than would have been possible even 20 years ago. Political discourse can be evaporated, or concentrated, depending on your perspective, in a million threads of twittering. Individuals can be world-wide personalities and celebrities for achieving little more than reporting on themselves on a blog spot, or on a video clip. People are able to discover and express themselves more powerfully than ever before, with the whole anonymous world their audience for posterity.

Back to face to face

Education, especially as experienced in face-to-face exchange, has always been a battleground where competing ideas about class interests and the future direction of society have been fought. These struggles may be about curricula matters, forms of teaching and learning, methods of delivery, funding mechanisms or levels of qualification. Such struggles have now become intense, with capitalism seeking to put education in its totality onto the market – new towns, such as those in Cambridgeshire, are planned on the basis that private companies will run all of their schools. Student grants for higher education that enshrined the working-class recognition that education, including knowledge at its highest levels, was a right, not a privilege, have gone. Yet there has never been so much socialist literature freely available via the internet. In this context, the rich seam of radical education that has been developed in Britain should be mined again, renewed and changed, recognising that education is the key to social transformation and human equality.

This tradition has very much been about face-to-face educational engagement, dialogue and exchange, and equal transference of perception and understanding. As McLaren rightly puts it in his introduction to Allman's work:

> Freire and Gramsci share with Marx the idea that our
> human potential is directly linked to human relationships
> in naturally occurring circumstances, that is, in lived
> experiences. (Allman, 1999, p 22)

This is the terrain of youth work, face-to-face lived experiences. Youth workers seek the unmediated moment, the moments in which the youth worker and the young person are most themselves, when one can draw out of the other their very best, in the case of the youth worker their best capacity to empower and enlighten, in the case of the young person their most keenly felt sense of wonderment, enlightenment and understanding, a sense of trust in the other person.

Self and others

In youth work training there is an excellent phrase that describes a training process: 'the use of self and others'. What is critical is the dialectical interchange of the individual and others in the group of which they are a part. It is a non-hierarchical, egalitarian exchange. It is not anarchistic; it is directional – the young person creates the direction, the youth worker then needs skill and experience to enable this and to ensure that the direction is neither dangerous nor harmful.

Unlike a psychotherapist who does not necessarily look into the eyes or face of their 'client', but sits alongside them, or behind them even as they reveal their inner life, youth workers work face to face; eye contact is essential and in this human exchange their inner life is blended with that of the young people they work with. This creates a unique psycho-social space within the public sphere and is linked to a deep rooted sense of democracy and the collective.

But an idea of lived experience can also become a fetish. What the experience is about must be the question. It cannot just be about the nuanced relationship between the youth worker and the young person. It cannot be a little utopia enjoyed by the two. The relationship must share its human openness with others to reorganise other social relationships. A one to one exchange should lead to a change for the better for many others.

Individual humanity

It is not just a question of infusing the interpersonal with a keener sense of the political. It is also a matter of recognising that the best quality of the interpersonal as experienced in direct face-to-face exchange is itself deeply political. What is most human is most political. Our intervention defines politics in a fresh way, but it is beyond the reach of established politicians. It is part of a subterranean lifeworld that must colonise the system. It gives a vision of a more collective social future that must be shared, and it is this that erupts out of the exploitation and oppression of the past.

From the everyday, a beautiful alternative vision is constructed. The challenge remains to achieve a new state power to make this vision a reality. The assumption that the lifeworld is the forgotten world of some helpless underclass is mistaken. As history shows, it is those who are excluded and oppressed who have their constant influential murmur of discontent and genius (Harris, 2001).

Youth workers should oppose the commodification of young people and their world; they are for collective engagement, seeking to overcome alienation in society, to challenge the limits of ideology and to open the doors of perception and new experiences that give powerful feelings of self-worth and above all, agency; and they do so in the full consciousness of a radical history of socialist education and movements, and international solidarity. As empowering workers, however, they cannot profess empowerment unless they are empowered themselves.

The skill of youth work has great significance. It stands for the commonwealth of humanity. Like artists, youth work makes an immanent perception of human worth and makes collectivism a universal reality. But it will remain a utopia if confined to its current limitations that are built on a past social democratic political settlement jettisoned by neoliberalism. We need a neosocialism. Youth work is already part of its flourishing human face.

A commodity crystallises a social substance called labour. A youth worker's labour makes social relationships as crystal-like as possible, not for fashion or profit, but to gain a sparkling glimpse of a new world order. It creates a form of social relationships that may no longer coexist with the old. It creates something that has come to fruition at the interpersonal level, but not at the social and economic. Vulnerable, unpicked fruits like this can drop and decay as if they had never existed. I argue that neoliberalism has destroyed the social democracy that gave rise to youth work in the post-war period. It is time for youth work to fight back but in a new way. If it can assert its importance, be inspired by the recent actions of the young, be confident of its past, then it has a better future ahead. Youth workers will have to fight for this as never before.

References and further reading

Aaronovitch, S. (1961) *The ruling class*, London: Lawrence & Wishart.

Adams, C. (1987) *Across the seven seas and thirteen rivers: Life stories of pioneer Sylhet settlers in Britain*, London: THAP books.

Adamson, G. (2007) *Thinking through craft*, Oxford: Berg.

Ainley, P. (1988) *From school to youth training schemes*, Oxford: Oxford University Press.

Ainley, P. (1991) *Young people leaving home*, London: Cassell Education Series.

Ainley, P. (1993a) *Training turns to enterprise: Vocational education in the market place*, London: Tufnell Press.

Ainley, P. (1993b) *Class and skill: Changing divisions of knowledge and labour*, London: Cassell Education Series.

Ainley, P. (1997) *The business of learning*, London: Continuum International Publishing Group.

Ainley, P. (2007) *Education, makes you fick innit?*, London: Tufnell Press.

Ainley, P. and Allen, M. (2010) *Lost generation? New strategies for youth and education*, London: Continuum.

Alinsky, S. (1969) *Reveille for radicals*, New York: Vintage Press.

Alinsky, S. (1972) *Rules for radicals*, New York: Vintage Press.

Allman, P. (1999) *Revolutionary social transformation, democratic hopes, political responsibilities and critical education*, Westport, CT: Bergin and Garvey.

Allman, P. (2001) *Critical education against global capitalism: Karl Marx and revolutionary critical education*, Critical Studies in Education & Culture, Santa Barbara, CA: Greenwood Press.

Arendt, H. (1968) *Imperialism*, New York: Harcourt Brace Janovich.

Armstrong, J. (2002) *Conditions of love, the philosophy of intimacy*, London: Penguin.

Armstrong, P., Glyn, A. and Harrison, J. (1991) *Capitalism since 1945*, Oxford: Blackwell.

Arrighi, A. (1994) *The long twentieth century: Money, power and the origins of our times*, New York: Verso.

Ash, W. (1990) 'Heroes in the evening mist', Unpublished.

Ash, W. (2007) *Workers' politics, the ethics of socialism*, Coventry: Bread Books.

Aston, M. (1984) *Lollards and reformers, images and literacy in late medieval religion*, London: Hambledon Press.

Audit Commission, (2009) *Tired of hanging around*, London: Audit Commission.

Augur, P. (2005) *The greed merchants, how the investment banks played the free market game*, London: Penguin Books.

Badiou, A. (2010) *The communist hypothesis*, London: Verso.

Barnett, W. (1967) 'Presidential address to the conference of the Community and Youth Service Association (former CYWU), CYWU Papers' [quoted in D. Nicholls (2009) *Building rapport: A history of the Community and Youth Workers' Union*, London: Unite the Union].

Batsleer, J.R. (2008) *Informal learning and youth work*, Basingstoke: Sage Publications.

Bauman, Z. (1991) *Modernity and the Holocaust*, Cambridge: Polity Press.

Bauman, Z. (1998) *Globalisation: The human consequences*, Cambridge: Polity Press.

Bauman, Z. (2000) *Liquid modernity*, Cambridge: Polity Press.

Bauman, Z. (2001a) *The individualised society*, Cambridge: Polity Press.

Bauman, Z. (2001b) *Community: Seeking safety in an insecure world*, Cambridge: Polity Press.

Bauman, Z. (2003a) *Liquid love*, Cambridge: Polity Press.

Bauman, Z. (2003b) *Wasted lives: Modernity and its outcasts*, Cambridge: Polity Press.

Bauman, Z. (2004) *Work, consumerism and the new poor*, Cambridge: Polity Press.

Bauman, Z. (2007a) *Liquid times: Living in an age of uncertainty*, Cambridge: Polity Press.

Bauman, Z. (2007b) *Consuming life*, Cambridge: Polity Press.

Bauman, Z. (2008) *The art of life*, Cambridge: Polity Press.

Bauman, Z. (2010) *44 letters from the liquid world*, Cambridge: Polity Press.

Belton, B. (2009) *Developing critical youth work theory: Building professional judgement in the community context*, Rotterdam: Sense Publishers.

Belton, B. (2010) *Radical youth work*, Lyme Regis: Russell House Publishing.

Belton, B. and Frost, S. (2010a) *Differentiated teaching and learning in youth work training*, Rotterdam: Sense Publishers.

Ben-Amos Krausman, I. (1994) *Adolescence in early modern England*, New Haven, CT and London: Yale University Press.

Beresford, P. (2007) *The richest of the rich*, London: Harriman House.

Beveridge, Sir W. (1942) *Social insurance and allied services*, London: HMSO.

Beveridge, Sir W. (1948) *Voluntary action: A report on methods of social advance*, London: George Allen & Unwin.

Blacke, F. (2010) 'The statutory basis of youth work', National Youth Agency circular to local authorities, Leicester: National Youth Agency.

Bodanor, V. (2009) *The new British constitution*, Oxford: Hart Publishing.

Booth, C., Black, L., Dear, G., John, G., Johnson, M., Levy, I., Selvan, F. and Williamson, H. (2008) *The street weapons commission report*, London: Channel 4.

Bowles, S. and Gintis, H. (1976) *Schooling in capitalist America – Educational reform and the contradictions of economic life*, London: Routledge & Kegan Paul.

Braudel, F. (1981) *Civilisation and capitalism 15th-18th century: Structures of everyday life, Vol 1 of Civilisation and capitalism*, London: HarperCollins.

Brecht, B. (1976) *Bertholt Brecht poems, Part two 1929-1938* (edited by John Willett and Ralph Manheim with the cooperation of Erich Fried), London: Eyre Methuen.

Brent, J. (2009) *Searching for community: Representation, power and action on an urban estate*, London: The Policy Press in partnership with CYWU.

Brew, J. Macalister (1940) *Clubs and club making*, London: University of London Press/National Association of Girls' Clubs.

Brew, J. Macalister (1943) *In the service of youth: A practical manual of work among adolescents*, London: Faber.

Brew, J. Macalister (1945) *'Only one living room', 'When should we be treated as grown up?', 'All out for a good time' – dramatic interludes in C. Madge et al, To start you talking: An experiment in broadcasting*, London: Pilot Press.

Brew, J. Macalister (1946) *Informal education, adventures and reflections*, London: Faber.

Brew, J. Macalister (1947) *Girls' interests*, London: National Association of Girls' Clubs and Mixed Clubs.

Brew, J. Macalister (1949) *Hours away from work*, London: National Association of Girls' Clubs and Mixed Clubs.

Brew, J. Macalister (1950) 'With young people', in Bureau of Current Affairs, *Discussion Method*, London: Bureau of Current Affairs.

Brew, J. Macalister (1955) 'Group work with adolescents' in P. Kuenstler (ed) *Social group work in Great Britain*, London: Faber & Faber.

Brew, J. Macalister (1957) *Youth and youth groups*, London: Faber & Faber.

Bruster, D. (1992) *Drama and the market in the age of Shakespeare*, Cambridge: Cambridge University Press.

Bunt, S. and Gargrave, R. (1980) *The politics of youth clubs*, Leicester: National Youth Bureau.

Bunyan, T. (2009) *The shape of things to come*, The EU Future Group, Nottingham: Spokesman Press, for Statewatch.

Cahill, K. (2001) *Who owns Britain? The hidden facts behind land ownership in the UK and Ireland*, Falkirk: Palimpsest.

Callinicos, A. (2010) *Bonfire of illusions: The twin crises of the liberal world*, London: Polity Press.

Calvert, P. (1982) *The concept of class: An historical introduction*, London: Hutchinson.

Campbell, B. (1993) *Goliath, Britain's dangerous places*, London: Methuen.

Cameron, N. (1995) *Dialectical materialism and modern science*, New York: International Publishers.

Caudwell, C. (2008a) *Studies in a dying culture*, London: Kessinger Publishing.

Caudwell, C. (2008b) *Illusion and reality*, London: Lawrence & Wishart.

Cassino, D. and Besen-Cassino, Y. (2009) *Consuming politics, Jon Stewart, branding, and the youth vote in America*, Madison, WI: Fairleigh Dickinson University Press.

Chandiramani, R. (2010) 'Youth work should be in the limelight, editorial', *Children & Young People Now*, 23-29 March, p 15.

Chaucer, G. *The Canterbury tales*.

Chomsky N. (1998) *Profit over people: Neoliberalism and global order*, New York: Seven Stories Press.

Cockburn, C. (1977) *The local state*, London: Pluto.

Cohen, L. (2003) *A consumer's republic: The politics of mass consumption in post-war America*, New York: Alfred A. Knopf.

CYWU (Community and Youth Workers' Union) (2007) www.cywu.org.uk.

Corfield, P.J. (ed) (1991) *Language history and class*, Oxford: Blackwell.

Cornwall, J. (1977) *The revolt of the peasantry 1549*, London: Routledge & Kegan Paul.

Cottrill A. (1984) *Social classes in Marxist theory*, London: RKP.

CPBML (Communist Party of Britain Marxist-Leninist) (1995) *Skill*, London: CPBML Pamphlet.

Craig, D. (2006) *Plundering the public sector: How New Labour are letting consultants run off with £70 billion of our money*, London: Constable.

Craig, D. (2008) *Squandered: how Gordon Brown is wasting over one trillion pounds of our money*, London: Constable.

Craig, G. and Mayo, M. (eds) (1995) *Community empowerment: A reader in participation and development*, London: Zed Books.

Craig, G., Derricourt, N. and Loney, M. (eds) (1982) *Community work and the state: Towards a radical approach*, London: Routledge & Kegan Paul.

CSC (Cuba Solidarity Campaign) (2007) www.csc.org.uk

Cunningham, H. (2006) *The invention of childhood*, London: BBC Books.

Curtis, M. (2003) *Web of deceit: Britain's real role in the modern world*, London: Vintage.

Curtis, M. (2004) *Unpeople: Britain's secret human rights abuses*, London: Vintage.

Darder, A. (2002) *Reinventing Paulo Freire: A pedagogy of love*, Boulder, CO: Westview.

Davidson, A. (1977) *Antonio Gramsci: Towards an intellectual biography*, London: Merlin Press.

Davies, B. (1999) *The history of the Youth Service in England, three volumes*, Leicester: Youth Work Press and National Youth Agency.

Davies, B. (2005) *Youth work: A manifesto for our times*, Leicester: National Youth Agency.

Davis, M. (2000) *Fashioning a new world*, Loughborough: The Woodcraft Folk.

Davis, M. (2006) *Planet of slums*, London: Verso.

DCSF (Department for Children, Schools and Families) (2007) *Reducing the number of young people not in education, employment or training (NEET): The strategy*, London: The Stationery Office (www.dscf.gov.uk/14-19/documents/neet_strategy 0803.pdf).

DCSF (2009) *Raising the participation age: Supporting local areas to deliver*, London: The Stationery Office, December.

DCSF (2010) *Positive activities: Good practice guidance*, London: The Stationery Office.

Dean, J. (2002) *Publicity's secret: How technoculture capitalizes on democracy*, Ithaca, NY: Cornell University Press.

Dean, J. (2009) *Democracy and other neoliberal fantasies, communicative capitalism and Left politics*, Durham, NC and London: Duke University Press.

de Botton, A. (2005) *Status anxiety*, London: Penguin.

Deer-Richardson, L. and Wolfe, M. (2007) *Principles and practice of informal education*, Abingdon: Routledge Falmer.

DENI (Department for Education Northern Ireland) (2005) *Youth Service* (www.deni.org.uk).

Denny, B. and Katz, P. (2010) *N02EU, yes to democracy*, London: Brian Denny.

DES (Department of Education and Science) (1967) *Immigrants and the Youth Service (The Hunt Report)*, London: HMSO.

DfE (Department for Education) (2011a) *Positive for youth* (www.education.gov.uk/positiveforyouth).

DfE (2011b) *Positive for youth: What it means for local authorities*.

DfE (2011c) *Positive for youth: What it means for voluntary organisations*.

DfE (2011d) *Positive for youth: What it means for business*.

DfE (2011e) *Positive for youth: What it means for young people*.

DfES (Department for Education and Skills) (1982) *Experience and participation. Review Group on the Youth Service in England (The Thompson Report)*, London: HMSO.

DfES (2002) *Transforming youth work: Resourcing excellent youth services*, London: The Stationery Office.

DfES (2003) *Every child matters*, Cm 5860, London: The Stationery Office

DfES (2005) *Youth matters*, London: The Stationery Office.

DfES (2006) *Teenage pregnancy: Next steps: Guidelines for local authorities and primary care trusts on effective delivery of local strategies*, London: The Stationery Office.

Dorling, D. (1995) *A new social atlas of Britain*, London: John Wiley and Sons.

Dorling, D. (2005) *Human geography of the UK*, London: Sage.

Dorling, D. (2010) *Injustice: Why social inequality persists*, Bristol: The Policy Press.

Dorling, D. (2011) *So you think you know about Britain?*, London: Constable and Robinson.

Dorling, D. (2012) *The no-nonsense guide to equality*, Oxford: New Internationalist.

Dorling, D. and Thomas, B. (2004) *People and places: A census atlas of the UK*, Bristol: The Policy Press.

Dorling, D. and Thomas, B. and (2007) *Identity in Britain: A cradle-to-grave atlas*, Bristol: The Policy Press.

Dorling, D. and Thomas, B. (2011) *Bankrupt Britain: An atlas of social change*, Bristol: The Policy Press.

Dorling, D., Ford, J., Holmans, A., Sharp, C., Thomas, B. and Wilcox, S. (2005) *The great divide: An analysis of housing inequality*, London: Shelter.

Dorling, D., Rigby, J., Wheeler, B., Ballas, D., Thomas, B., Fahmy, E., Gordon, D. and Lupton, R. (2007) *Poverty, wealth and place in Britain, 1968 to 2005*, Bristol: The Policy Press.

Doyle, R. (1988) *The Barrytown trilogy*, London: Minerva.

Doyle, R. (1993) *Paddy Clarke ha ha ha*, London: Minerva.

Doyle, R. (1997) *The woman who walked into doors*, London: Minerva.

Doyle, R. (2007) *Paula Spencer*, London: Vintage.

Duckworth, J. (2002) *Fagin's children: Criminal children in Victorian England*, London: Hambledon Press.

Eagleton, T. (1996) *The illusions of postmodernism*, Oxford: Blackwell.

Eagleton, T. (1997) *Marx and freedom*, The Great Philosophers Series, London: Phoenix.

Eagleton, T. (2005) *Holy terror*, Oxford: Oxford University Press.

Eagleton, T. (2010) *On evil*, New Haven, CT and London: Yale University Press.

Eagleton, T. (2011) *Why Marx was right*, New Haven, CT and London: Yale University Press.

Elliott, L. and Atkinson, D. (2008) *The gods that failed: How blind faith in the markets has cost us our future*, London: The Bodley Head.

Engels, F. (1975 [1845]) *The condition of the working-class in England from personal observation and authentic sources* [originally published in 1845 in Karl Marx, Friedrick Engels, Collected Works, Volume 4, London: Lawrence & Wishart].

Ewen, J. (1972) *Youth review*, Autumn, Leicester: National Youth Bureau.

Factor, F., Chauhan, V. and Pitts, J. (2001) *The RHP companion to working with young people*, Lyme Regis: Russell House Publishing.

FDYW (Federation for Detached Youth Work) (2007) *Detached youth work: Guidelines*, Leicester: FDYW.

Fine, B. et al (undated) 'Class politics: an answer to its critics', London: Leftover Pamphlets.

Finkielkraut, A. (1988) *The undoing of thought*, London: The Claridge Press.

Finlayson, J.G. (2005) *Habermas: A very short introduction*, Oxford: Oxford University Press.

Fletcher, A. (2008) *Growing up in England: The experience of childhood 1600-1914*, Newhaven, CT: Yale University Press.

Forgacs, D, (ed) (1988) *A Gramsci reader*, London: Lawrence & Wishart.

Freire, P. (1985) *The politics of education, culture, power and liberation*, Westport, CT: Bergin and Garvey.

Freire, P. (1989) *Learning to question: A pedagogy of liberation*, Geneva: World Council of Churches.

Freire, P. (1996) *Pedagogy of the oppressed*, London: Penguin Books.

Freire, P. (2001) *Pedagogy of freedom*, Lanham, MD: Rowman & Littlefield Publishers Inc.

Freire, P. (2004a) *Pedagogy of hope*, New York: Continuum Books.

Freire, P. (2004b) *Pedagogy of imagination*, Boulder, CO: Paradigm Publishers.

Freire, P. (2005) *Education for critical consciousness*, London: Continuum.

Freire, P. (2006) *Pedagogy of the heart*, New York: Continuum International Publishing Group Inc.

Fukuyama, F. (1993) *The end of history and the last man*, London: Penguin.

Furlong, A. (ed) (2009) *Handbook of youth and young adulthood: New perspectives and agenda*, London and New York: Routledge.

Furlong, A. and Cartmel, F. (2006) *Young people and social change: New perspectives*, Buckingham: Open University Press.

George, S. (1999) 'A short history of neo-liberalism: twenty years of elite economics and emerging opportunities for structural', Conference on Economic Sovereignty in a Globalising World, 24-26 March (www.globalexchange.org/campaigns/econ101/neoliberalism.html.pdf).

Gibson, A. and Davies, B. (1967) *The social education of the adolescent*, London: Routledge & Kegan Paul.

Giddens, A. (1973) *Capitalism and modern social theory: An analysis of the writings of Marx, Durkheim and Weber*, Cambridge: Cambridge University Press.

Gilbert, F. (2006) *Yob nation: The truth about Britain's yob culture*, Falkirk: Palimpsest Books.

Gilchrist, A. (2009) *The well-connected community: A networking approach to community development*, Bristol: The Policy Press.

Giroux, H. (1983) *Theory and resistance in education* (Introduction by Paulo Freire), New York: Bergin and Garvey.

Giroux, H. (1991) *Postmodern education: Politics, culture, and social criticism* (co-authored with Stanley Aronowitz), Minesota, WI: University of Minnesota Press.

Giroux, H. (1992) *Border crossings: Cultural workers and the politics of education, New York:* Routledge.

Giroux, H. (1993) *Living dangerously: Multiculturalism and the politics of culture, New York:* P. Lang Publishing.

Giroux, H. (1994) *Education still under siege* (2nd edn) (co-authored with Stanley Aronowitz), New York: Bergin and Garvey Press.

Giroux, H. (1994) *Disturbing pleasures: Learning popular culture*, New York: Routledge Publishing.

Giroux, H. (1996) *Fugitive cultures: Race, violence, and youth*, New York: Routledge.

Giroux, H. (1997) *Pedagogy and the politics of hope: Theory, culture, and schooling*, Boulder, CO: Westview/HarperCollins.

Giroux, H. (1998) *Channel surfing: Racism, the media, and the destruction of today's youth*, London: St Martin's Press and Macmillan.

Giroux, H. (1999) *The mouse that roared: Disney and the end of innocence*, New York: Rowman & Littlefield Press.

Giroux, H. (2001a) *Theory and resistance in education* (revised edn), New York: Bergin and Garvey.

Giroux, H. (2001b) *Stealing innocence: Corporate culture's war on children*, New York: St Martin's Press.

Giroux, H. (2002) *Breaking in to the movies: Film and the culture of politics*, *Oxford:* Basil Blackwell Press.

Giroux, H. (2003a) *The abandoned generation: Democracy beyond the culture of fear*, London: Palgrave.

Giroux, H. (2003b) *Public spaces/private lives: Democracy beyond 9/11*, New York: Rowman & Littlefield.

Giroux, H. (2004) *The terror of neoliberalism, authoritarianism and the eclipse of democracy*, Boulder, CO: Paradigm Publishers.

Giroux, H. (2005a) *Against the new authoritarianism: Politics after Abu Ghraib*, Winnipeg, MB: Arbeiter Ring Publishing.

Giroux, H. (2005b) *Schooling and the struggle for public life* (2nd edn), Boulder, CO: Paradigm Publishers.

Giroux, H. (2005c) *Border crossings: Cultural workers and the politics of education* (2nd edn), London: Routledge Publishing.

Giroux, H. (2006a) *Stormy weather: Katrina and the politics of disposability*, Boulder, CO: Paradigm Publishers.

Giroux, H. (2006b) *Beyond the spectacle of terrorism: Global uncertainty and the challenge of the new media*, Boulder, CO: Paradigm Publishers.

Giroux, H. (2007) *The university in chains: Confronting the military-industrial-academic complex*, Boulder, CO: Paradigm Publishers.

Giroux, H. (2008) *Against the terror of neoliberalism: Politics beyond the age of greed*, Boulder, CO: Paradigm Publishers.

Giroux, H. (2009) *Youth in a suspect society: Democracy or disposability?*, London: Palgrave Macmillan.

Giroux, H. and Searls-Giroux, S. (2004) *Take back higher education: Race, youth, and the crisis of democracy in the post civil rights era*, London: Palgrave.

Glenny, M. (2008) *McMafia, crime without frontiers*, London: Bodley Head.

Glyn, A. (2006) *Capitalism unleashed: Finance, globalisation and welfare*, Oxford: Oxford University Press.

Gould, S.J. (1981) *The mismeasure of man*, London: Pelican.

Gramsci, A. (edited and translated by Q. Hoare and G.N. Smith) (1971) *Selections from prison notebooks*, London: Lawrence & Wishart.

Gramsci, A. (1985) *Selections from cultural writings* (edited by D. Forgacs and G. Nowell-Smith and translated by W. Boelhower), London: Lawrence & Wishart.

Gramsci, A. (1988) *Gramsci's prison letters* (translated and introduced by H. Henderson), London: Zwan.

Gray, A. and Tomkins, A. (2005) *How we should rule ourselves*, Edinburgh: Canongate.

Habermas, J. (1989) *The structural transformation of the public sphere*, Cambridge: Polity Press.

Hadley, F. (2007) 'Introduction', Ofsted-home/News/News-Archive/2007/February/Youth Service (www.ofsted.gov.uk).

Hansard (2006) Column 731 (www.publications.parliament.uk/pa/ld199900/ldhansrd/pdvn/lds06/text/60712-0935.htm#06071250000001).

Hansard (2008) House of Commons written answer 2/06/08 (www.publications.parliament.uk/pa/cm200708/cmhansrd/cm080602/text/80602w0029.htm#08060232000052).

Hardt, M. and Negri, A. (2000) *Empire*, Cambridge, MA: University of Harvard Press.

Hardt, M. and Negri, A. (2005) *Multitude: War and democracy in the age of empire*, London: Penguin Books.

Hardt, M. and Negri, A. (2009) *Commonwealth*, Cambridge, MA: The Belknap Press of the University of Harvard Press.

Harman, C. (2009) *Zombie capitalism, global crisis and the relevance of Marx*, London: Bookmarks Publications.

Harris, T. (2001) *The politics of the excluded, c 1500-1850*, Basingstoke: Palgrave.

Hartmann, M. (2007) *The sociology of elites*, London: Routledge Studies in Social and Political Thought.

Harvey, D. (2005) *A brief history of neoliberalism*, Oxford: Oxford University Press.

Harvey, D. (2006a) *The limits of capital*, London: Verso.

Harvey, D. (2006b) *Spaces of global capitalism: Towards a theory of uneven geographical development*, London: Verso.

Harvey, D. (2010a) *The enigma of capital, and the crises of capitalism*, London: Profile Books.

Harvey, D. (2010b) *A companion to Marx's Capital*, London: Verso.

Hill, D. (2008) *Global neoliberalism and education and its consequences*, Routledge Studies in Education and Neoliberalism, London: Routledge.

HM Treasury (2007) *Aiming high for young people: A ten year strategy for positive activities,* London: HM Treasury/Department for Children, Schools and Families.

Hobbes, T. (2008) *Leviathan*, Oxford: Oxford World Classics.

Honey, P. and Mumford, A. (1982) *The manual of learning styles*, Maidenhead: P. Honey Publications.

hooks, b. (1994) *Teaching to transgress: Education as the practice of freedom*, New York: Routledge.

hooks, b. (2003) *Teaching community: A pedagogy of hope*, New York: Routledge.

House of Commons Education Committee (2011a) *Services for young people: Third Report of Session 2010-1012,* Volume 1, Report, together with formal minutes, HC 744-1, London: The Stationery Office.

House of Commons Education Committee (2011b) *Services for young people: Third report of Session 2010-2012*, Oral and written evidence, Volume II, HC 744-11, London: The Stationery Office.

House of Commons Education Committee (2011c) *Services for young people: Third report of session 2010-2012,* Additional written evidence, Volume III, 744-III, London: The Stationery Office.

House of Commons Education Committee (2011d) *Services for young people: The government's response, Sixth report of Session 2010-12*, HC 1501, London: The Stationery Office.

House of Commons Education Committee (2012) *Services for young people: The government response, Government response to the Committee's Sixth Report of Session 2010-2012*, Tenth report of Session 2010-2012, HC 1736, London: The Stationery Office.

Howker, E. and Shiv, M. (2010) *Jilted generation: How Britain has bankrupted its youth*, London: Icon Books.

Hughes, B. (2001) *Evolutionary playwork and reflective analytic practice*, London: Routledge.

In Defence of Youth Work (2010) http://indefenceofyouthwork. org.uk/wordpress

Irish Statute Book (2001) *Youth Work Act*, Dublin.

Jeffs, T. and Smith, M. (1990) *Young people, inequality and youth work*, London: Macmillan.

Jeffs, T. and Smith, M. (2005) *Informal education: Conversation, democracy, learning*, London: Educational Heretics Press.

JNC Report for Youth and Community Workers (2010) www. cywu.org.uk

JNC Validation Criteria for the endorsement of initial training courses (2010) www.nya.org.uk

Jones, S. (1993) *The language of the genes*, London: Flamingo.

JRF (Joseph Rowntree Foundation) (2004) *The cost of providing street-based youth work in deprived communities*, June, Ref 664, York: JRF (www.jrf.org.uk/knowledge/findings/costings/664.asp).

Kampfner, J. (2003) *Blair's wars*, London: Free Press.

Kashdan, T. (2009) *Curiosity? Discover the missing ingredient to a fulfilling life*, New York: HarperCollins.

Katz, P. (2009) *Thinking hands*, Chichester: John Wiley & Sons.

Kelly, T. (1992) *A history of adult education in Britain*, Liverpool: Liverpool University Press.

Keynes, J.M. (2008) *The general theory of employment, interest and money* (www.bnpublishing.com).

King, J. (2004) *Voices of the English Reformation: A sourcebook*, Philadelphia, PA: University of Pennsylvania Press.

Klein, N. (2001) *No logo: No space. No choice. No jobs*, London: Flamingo.

Klein, N. (2008) *The shock doctrine: The rise of disaster capitalism*, London: Penguin.

Koehn, D. (1994) *The ground of professional ethics*, London: Routledge.

Kolb, D.A. (1984) *Experiential learning: Experience as the source of learning and development*, London: Prentice Hall.

Lambie, G. (2010) *The Cuban revolution in the twenty-first century*, London: Pluto Press.

Lansley, S. (2006) *Rich Britain: The rise and rise of the new super wealthy*, London: Politico's.

Ledgerwood, I. and Kendra, N. (eds) (1997) *The challenge of the future: Towards the new millennium for the Youth Service*, Lyme Regis: Russell House Publishing.

Ledwith, M. (2005) *Community development: A critical approach*, London: BASW/Polity Press.

Levi, G. and Schmitt, J.C. (1997) *A history of young people in the West: Stormy evolution to modern times*, Cambridge, MA: Belknap, Harvard University Press.

Levins, R. and Lewontin, R. (1985) *The dialectical biologist*, Cambridge, MA: Harvard University Press.

Lewis, T., Amini, F. and Lannon, R. (2001) *A general theory of love*, New York: Vintage.

LGA (Local Government Association) (2009a) *Council leader survey on the impact of the economic downturn on local authorities – Full report*, London: LGA.

LGA (2009b) *Hidden talents II: Getting the best out of Britain's young people*, London: LGA.

LGA (2009c) *Hidden talents III: Celebrating achievements, local solutions for engaging young people*, London: LGA, p 3.

LGA (2009d) *The Sustainable Communities Act: Shortlist of proposal made under round one*, London: LGA.

Lifelong Learning UK (2009) *National Occupational Standards for youth work*.

Lipschutz, R.D. (2010) *Political economy, capitalism and popular culture*, Plymouth: Rowman & Littlefield.

Locke, J. (1988) *Two treatises of government*, Cambridge: Cambridge Texts in the History of Political Thought.

Lynam, P. (1999) 'A class act in modern Britain', *Workers*, March, Journal of the Communist Party of Britain (ML), London.

McAlister, S., Scraton, P. and Haydon, D. (2009) *Childhood in transition: Experiencing marginalisation and conflict in Northern Ireland*, Belfast: Queens University Belfast, Save the Children and The Prince's Trust.

McConnell, C. (1996) *The making of an empowering profession*, Edinburgh: Scottish Community Education Council.

McGiffen, S. (2005) The European Union: A critical guide, London: Pluto Press.

McKee, V., Oldfield, C. and Hughes, S. (2010) *The benefits of youth work*, London: Lifelong Learning UK and Unite the Union.

McLaren, P. (1980) *Cries from the corridor: The new suburban ghettos*, London: Methuen Publications.

McLaren, P. (1989) *Life in schools: An introduction to critical pedagogy in the foundations of education*, New York: Longman.

McLaren, P. (with Rhonda Hammer, David Sholle, and Susan Reilly) (1994) *Rethinking media literacy*, New York: P. Lang.

McLaren, P. (1995) *Critical pedagogy and predatory culture: Oppositional politics in a postmodern age*, London and New York: Routledge.

McLaren, P. (1997) *Revolutionary multiculturalism: Pedagogies of dissent for the new millennium*, Boulder, CO: Westview Press.

McLaren, P. (1999) Schooling as a ritual performance (3rd edn), Boulder, CO: Rowman & Littlefield.

McLaren, P. (with Mike Cole, Dave Hill and Glenn Rikowski) (2000a) Red chalk (booklet), London: The Tufnell Press.

McLaren, P. (2000b) *Che Guevara, Paulo Freire, and the pedagogy of revolution*, Boulder, CO: Rowman & Littlefield.

McLaren, P. (with Ramin Farahmandpur) (2005a) *Teaching against global capitalism and the new imperialism: A critical pedagogy*, New York: Rowman & Littlefield.

McLaren, P. (2005b) *Capitalists and conquerors: Critical pedagogy against empire*, New York: Rowman & Littlefield.

McLaren, P. (2005c) *Red seminars: Radical excursions into educational theory, cultural politics, and pedagogy*, New York: Hampton Press.

McLaren, P. (2006) *Rage and hope: Interviews with P. McLaren on war, imperialism and critical pedagogy*, New York: P. Lang Publishers.

McLaren, P. and Jaramillo, N. (2007) *Pedagogy and praxis in the age of empire: Towards a new humanism*, Rotterdam and Tapei: Sense Publishers.

Mandel, E. (1978) *Late capitalism*, London: Verso.

Marazzi, C. (2008) *Capital and language: From the new economy to the war economy*, Los Angeles, CA: Semiotext(e).

Marazzi, C. (2010) *The violence of finance capital*, Los Angeles, CA: Smiotexte.

Marr, A. (2007) *A history of modern Britain*, London: Macmillan.

Marsland, D. (1979) *Coming of age*, Leicester: National Youth Bureau.

Martin, J.W. (1989) *Religious radicals in Tudor England*, London: Hambledon Press.

Marx, K. (1969 [1873]) *Ludwig Feuerbach and the end of classical German philosophy, Marx/Engels selected works*, Volume One, pp 13-15, Moscow: Progress Publishers.

Mason, M. (2008) *The pirate's dilemma: How hackers, punk capitalists and graffiti millionaires are remixing our culture and changing the world*, London: Allen Lane.

Mayo, E. and Nairn, A. (2009) *Consumer kids: How big business is grooming our children for profit*, London: Constable and Robinson.

Mayo, M. (1997) *Imagining tomorrow: Adult education for transformation*, Leicester: NIACE.

Mayo, P. (1999) *Gramsci, Freire and adult education: Possibilities for transformative action*, London: Zed Books.

Meister, R. (1990) *Political identity, thinking through Marx*, Oxford: Blackwell.

Ministerial Conferences Steering Committee (1990) *Towards a core curriculum – The next step*, Report of responses to the Ministerial Conferences Steering Committee Consultation Document, Leicester: National Youth Bureau.

Mitterrauer, M. (1992) *A history of youth*, Oxford: Blackwell.

Morris, W. (1986) *Useful labour versus useless toil*, London: CPBML Reprint pamphlets.

Morton, A.L. (2006) *A people's history of England*, London: Read Books.

Monbiot, G. (2001) *Captive state: The corporate takeover of Britain*, London: Pan Books.

Montagu, A. (1997) *Man's most dangerous myth: The fallacy of race*, Walnut Creek, CA: Altamira Press.

National Assembly for Wales (2001) *Extending entitlement*, Cardiff: National Assembly for Wales.

Negri, A. (1999) *Insurgencies: Constituent power and the modern state*, Minneapolis, WI: University of Minnesota Press.

Nicholls, D. (1995) *Employment practice and policies in youth, community and play work*, Lyme Regis: Russell House Publishing (2nd edn published in 2002).

Nicholls, D. (1997) 'Professionalism, a true reality', in I. Ledgerwood and N. Kendra (eds) *The challenge of the future: Towards the new millennium for the Youth Service*, Lyme Regis: Russell House Publishing.

Nicholls, D. (2005) *The EU: Bad for Britain: A trade union view*, Coventry: Bread Books.

Nicholls, D. (2007) 'Our press ganged street gangs', *Rapport*, CYWU Journal, November.

Nicholls, D. (2009) *Building rapport: A history of the Community and Youth Workers' Union*, London: Unite the union.

Nicholls, D. (2010) 'Our national Youth Service', *Tribune*, 11 August.

Nicholls, D. and More, W. (1998) *Managing violence and aggression at work*, Birmingham: Pepar Publications.

Norden, L. (2007) *Sarah Sze*, New York: Harry N. Abrams, Inc.

Norton, R. (ed) (1994) *National Vocational Qualifications and their irrelevance to youth and community work*, Birmingham: CYWU Publications

NYA (National Youth Agency) (1993) *The core of youth and community work training, The report of the working group to define the distinctive elements with form the core of all Youth and Community Work training*, Leicester: NYA.

Ofsted (2006) *Building on the best: Overview of local authority youth services 2005/06*, London: Ofsted.

Ofsted (2008) *Engaging young people: Local authority youth work 2005-08*, London: Ofsted.

Ofsted (2010) *Supporting young people: An evaluation of recent reforms to youth support services in 11 local areas*, London: Ofsted.

OPSI (Office of Public Sector Information) (1986) *The UK Law Statute Law Database, The Education and Libraries (Northern Ireland) Order 1986* (No 594 [NI3]).

OPSI (1989) *The UK Law Statute Law Database, The Youth Service (Northern Ireland) Order 1989* (No 2413 [NI22]).

Ord, J. (2007) *Youth work process, product and practice: Creating an authentic curriculum in work with young people*, Lyme Regis: Russell House Publishing.

Packham, C. (2008) *Active citizenship and community learning*, Exeter: Learning Matters (www.learningmatters.co.uk).

Paul, L. (1980) *The early days of the Woodcraft Folk*, London.

Palser, R. (2004) '"Learn by doing, teach by being": the children of 1968 and the Woodcraft Folk', *Socialist History, 26, Youth Culture and Policies*, London: Rivers Oram Press.

Paxman, J. (1990) *Friends in high places: Who runs Britain?*, London: Michael Joseph.

Peston, R. (2008) *Who runs Britain? And who's to blame for the economic mess we're in*, London: Hodder & Stoughton.

Pilger, J. (2002) *The new rulers of the world*, London: Verso.

Pitts, J. (2007a) 'Who cares what works', *Youth and Policy*, no 95, Spring.

Pitts J. (2007b) 'Action on gang crime: recent developments', *Community Safety Journal*, vol 7, issue 1, February.

Pitts J. (2007c) 'Describing and defining youth gangs', *Community Safety Journal*, vol 7, issue 1, February.

Play Wale, (2001) *First claim*, Cardiff: Play Wales.

Popple, K. (1995) *Analysing community work: Its theory and practice*, Buckingham: Open University Press.

QAA (Quality Assurance Agency for Higher Education) (2009) *Subject benchmark statement, youth and community work* (www.qaa.ac.uk).

Race, P. (2010) *Making learning happen: A guide for post-compulsory education*, London: Sage Publications.

Ranciere, J. (1991) *The ignorant schoolmaster: Five lessons in intellectual emancipation*, Stanford, CA: Stanford University Press.

Ranciere, J. (2006) *Hatred of democracy*, London: Verso.

Ranciere, J. (2009) *The emancipated spectator*, London: Verso.

Rand, A. (1964) *The virtue of selfishness: A new concept of egoism*, New York: Dutton/Signet.

Rapport (2010) 'The private finance initiative: draining public finances'.

RESET (Resettlement, Education, Support, Employment and Training programme) (2007) The costs and benefits of effective resettlement (www.reset.uk.net/graphics/portfolio/6188.doc).

Rifkin, J. (2010) *The emphatic civilisation: The race to global consciousness in a world in crisis*, London: Polity Press.

Rikowski, G. (2008) *Renewing dialogues in Marxism and education*, London: Palgrave Macmillan.

Robertson, S. (2005) *Youth clubs: Association, participation, friendship and fun*, Lyme Regis: Russell House Publishing.

Rogers, D. (2005) *Singing the changes: The songs of Dave Rogers for Banner Theatre*, Coventry: Bread Books.

Rose, S., Kamin, L.J. and Lewontin, R.C. (1984) *Not in our genes: Biology, ideology and human nature*, London: Penguin.

Rutter, M. (1997) *Psychosocial disturbances in young people: Challenges for prevention*, The Jacobs Foundation Series in Adolescence, Cambridge: Cambridge University Press.

Sagan, C. and Druyan, A. (1992) *Shadows of forgotten ancestors*, London: Arrow.

Sampson, A. (2004) *Who runs this place? The anatomy of Britain in the 21st century*, London: John Murray.

Sapin, K. (2009) *Essential skills for youth work practice*, London: Sage Publications.

Schon, D.A. (1991) *The reflective practitioner: How professionals think in action*, London: Ashgate.

Scottish Executive (2007) *Moving forward: A strategy for improving young people's chances through youth work*, Edinburgh: Scottish Executive.

Scottish Office Education Department (1991) *Youth Work in Scotland*, A report by HM Inspectors of Schools, Edinburgh: HMSO.

Sennett, R. (1999) *The corrosion of character*, New York: Norton.

Sennett, R. (2003) *The fall of public man*, London: Penguin.

Sennett, R. (2004) *Respect: The formation of character in an age of inequality*, London: Penguin.

Sennett, R. (2006) *The culture of the new capitalism*, New Haven, CT: Yale University Press.

Sennett, R. (2008) *The craftsman*, London: Penguin.

Sercombe, H. (2010) *Youth work ethics*, London: Sage Publications.

Shagan, E.H. (2003) *Popular politics and the English Reformation*, Cambridge: Cambridge University Press.

Shor, I. (1993) 'Education is politics: Paulo Freire's critical pedagogy', in P. Mclaren and P. Leonard (eds) *Paulo Freire: A critical encounter*, London: Routledge.

Shukra, K. (1998) *A history of black organisations in Britain*, London: Pluto.

Simpson, L. (2004) 'Statistics of racial segregation: measures, evidence and policy', *Journal of Urban Studies*, vol 41, no 3, pp 661-81, March (www.tandf.co.uk/journals/titles/00420980.asp).

Singh, R. (2006) *Crisis of socialism: Notes in defence of a commitment*, Delhi: Anjanta Books.

Smith, A. (1776) *The wealth of nations*.

Smith, M. (1994) *Local education: Community, conversation, praxis*, Oxford: Oxford University Press.

Smith, H. and Smith, M.K, (2008) *The art of helping others, being around, being there, being wise*, London: Jessica Kingsley Publishers.

Sohn-Rethel, A. (1978) *Intellectual and manual labour: A critique of epistemology*, Atlantic Highlands, NJ: Humanities Press.

Stoneman, R. (2008) *Chavez: The revolution will not be televised*, London and New York: Wallflower Press.

Sunday Times, The (2010) *Rich list*, London: Times Newspapers.

Taylor, C. (1992) *Sources of the self: The making of modern identity*, Cambridge: Cambridge University Press.

Temple, J. (2008) *Living off the state: A critical guide to royal finance*, London: Progress Books.

Thomas, D. (1983) *The making of community work*, London: George Allen & Unwin.

Thompson, E.P. (1968) *The making of the English working class*, London: Penguin.

Tomkins, A. (2005) *Our republican constitution*, Oxford: Hart Publishing.

TUAEUC (Trade Unionists Against the European Union Constitution) (2005) *Trade Unionists say NO to the EU Constitution*, London: TUAEUC (www.tuaeuc.org.uk).

TUAEUC (2007) *The Big EU con trick: Why trade unionists should demand a referendum on the EU's renamed Constitution*, London: TUAEUC.

TUC (Trades Union Congress) (2006) *Poverty, exclusion and British people of Pakistani and Bangladeshi origin*, London: TUC.

Tudge, C. (1995) *The day before yesterday, five million years of human history*, London: Jonathan Cape.

Twelvetrees, A. (1991) *Community work* (2nd edn), London: Macmillan.

Unite (2011) Unite's comments on Positive for Youth discussion papers (www.cywu.org.uk/assets/content_pages/1769297431_Unite_response_to_positive_for_youth_consultation_.pdf).

VIC (Venezuela Information Centre) (2007) (www.vic.org.uk) now known as the Venezuela Solidarity Campaign.

Virno, P. (2004) *A grammar of the multitude*, Los Angeles, CA: Semitotext(e)

Virno, P. (2008a) *Multitude, between innovation and negation*, Los Angeles, CA: Semiotext(e).

Virno, P. (2008b) *The porcelain workshop: For a new grammar of politics*, Los Angeles, CA: Semiotext(e).

Vogel, L. (1983) *Marxism and the oppression of women: Toward a unitary theory*, New York: Rutgers.

VPMCI (Venezuelan People's Ministry of Communication and Information) (2005) *Venezuela: Conquering social inclusion*, Caracas (see also www.mci.gob.ve).

WAG (Welsh Assembly Government) (2007) *Young people, youth work, Youth Service, National Youth Service Strategy for Wales*, Cardiff: WAG.

Westergaard, J. and Resler, H. (1975) *Class in a capitalist society: A study of contemporary Britain*, London: Pelican.

Winter, R., Sobiechowska, P. and Buck, A. (eds) (1999) *Professional experience and the investigative imagination: The art of reflective writing*, London: Routledge.

Williams, N.M. (1998) *Ideology and utopia in the poetry of William Blake*, Cambridge: Cambridge University Press.

Wilkinson, R. (2006) *The impact of inequality: How to make sick societies healthier*, London: The New Press.

Wilkinson, R. and Pickett, K.E. (2006) 'Income inequality and population health: a review and explanation of the evidence', *Social Science & Medicine*, vol 62, pp 1768-84.

Wilkinson, R. and Pickett, K.E. (2009) *The spirit level: Why more equal societies almost always do better*, London: Allen Lane.

Williams, H. (2006) *Britain's power elites: The rebirth of a ruling class*, London: Constable.

Williamson, H. (ed) (1995) *Social action for young people: Accounts of SCF youth work practice*, Lyme Regis: Russell House Publishing.

Williamson, H. (1997) *Youth and policy: Contexts and consequences – Young men, transition and social exclusion*, Aldershot: Ashgate.

Williamson, H. (2004) *The Milltown boys revisited*, Oxford: Berg.

Williamson, H. (2008) *Supporting young people in Europe* (Volume 2), Strasbourg: Council of Europe Publishing.

Williamson, H. and Williamson, P. (1981) *Five years*, Leicester: National Youth Bureau.

Winter, R. (1991) *Outline of a general theory of professional competence*, The Anglia/Essex 'Asset' Programme.

WLGA (Welsh Local Government Association) (2010) *The Youth Service in Wales* (www.wlga.gov.uk).

Wood, A. (2007) *The 1549 rebellions and the making of modern England*, Cambridge: Cambridge University Press.

Wuthnow, R. (1989) *Communities of discourse, ideology and social structure in the reformation, the Enlightenment, and European socialism*, Cambridge, MA: Harvard University Press.

Young, K. (2006) *The art of youth work*, Lyme Regis: Russell House publishing.

NYA (National Youth Agency) (2010) 'The statutory basis of youth work', Leicester: NYA (www.nya.org.uk/)

Zizek, S. (2009a) *Violence: Six sideways reflections*, Big Ideas, London: Profile Books.

Zizek, S. (2009b) *The ticklish subject: The sublime object of ideology*, London: Verso.

Zizek, S. (2010a) *First as tragedy, then as farce*, London: Verso.

Zizek, S. (2010b) *Living in the end times*, London: Verso.

Zizek, S. (2010c) *The idea of communism*, London: Verso.

INDEX

A

Aiming high for young people, 35
Aaronovitch, S., 121, 134
accountability: youth workers, 88, 148, 159
accountability, democratic, 34, 49, 51, 73
accreditation: youth work, 116, 142
Across the seven seas and thirteen rivers, 187-88
Adams, Caroline, 187-88
Ainley, Pat, 14, 193
Albemarle Committee, 113-14, 191-92
alcohol, 208
alienation, 62, 66, 99, 126, 184, 188, 221-24, 236
Alinsky, Saul, 160-61
Allen, M., 14, 193
Allman, Paula, 222, 223, 234
anti-racism, 187
apathy, 62, 67
Arendt, Hannah, 195-96
armed forces welfare services, 153
arms trade, 66
Armstrong, P., 189
Arrighi, A., 54
Ash, William, 97, 188
Aspect, 88
Association of Teachers and Lecturers, 88
Aston, M., 228
Atkinson, D., 77
Audit Commission, 35

authoritarianism, 66-67, 68, 137, 138, 158, 206, 210

B

Badiou, Alain, 2
banks, 52, 72, 74, 76, 77-78, 79, 80, 81
  Royal Bank of Scotland, 70
Barnett, Bill, 31
Batsleer, Janet, 12, 40, 119, 195
Bauman, Zygmunt, 19, 21, 50, 52, 58, 197, 212
behaviour, negative and positive, 167
belief systems, 54-55
Belton, Brian, 6, 84
Beresford, P., 129
Besen-Cassino, Y., 61-62, 63
Beveridge, William, 56, 130-31
Beveridge Report, 56
'Big Society', 224, 226
black activists, 94
Blacke, F., 26
Blair, Tony, 192
Blatchford, Robert, 229
Bogdanor, Vernon, 134
Botton, Alain de, 92
Boyson, Rhodes, 158
Braudel, F., 55
Brecht, Bertholt, 188, 199-201
Brent, Jeremy, 40, 159
Brew, Josephine Macalister, 12, 119
Brown, Gordon, 192
Bruster, D., 59
Budget, Emergency (June 2011), 5

Building rapport, 111
bullying, 204
 workplace, 74, 184
Bunt, Sidney, 158
Bunyan, T., 19

C

Cahill, K., 190
Callinicos, Alex, 49, 77
Calvert, P., 91
Cameron, David, 6
Campbell, Bea, 184, 191
capitalism, 48-49, 55-58, 60,
 99, 121, 128-29, 164, 216; *see
 also* neoliberalism
 alienation, 221-24
 challenges to, 5, 100, 126,
  131-32, 189, 227
 democracy and, 2, 206
 education and, 30, 230, 232,
  234
 migration and, 190, 195-96
 social inclusion versus, 2
 state, the, and, 133-34, 136-37,
  138-39
capitalist society, work in, 15,
 83, 95-96, 125, 222-23
Cassino, D., 61-62, 63
casualisation, 75
Caudwell, C., 59
CCTV, 65, 210
Centre for Social Justice, 32-33
Chandiramani, Ravi, 32
change,
 constancy of, 165
 education and, 12, 171, 175,
  197-98, 213, 227-29
charities: forced to compete,
 137
childhood, views on, 231-32
Children & young people now, 32

Children's and Young People's
 Workforce Development
 Partnership, 149
Children's plan, The, 35
Children's Workforce
 Development Council, 3, 31,
 149, 150, 159
China: public investment,
 76-77
'choice', 52, 61
Choose Youth campaign, 3, 42
CHYPS, 153
City of God, 184
civil liberties, erosion of, 210
class: misconceptions, 90-92
Coalition Government
 attack on public sector, 3-6,
  224
 youth policies, 1, 7-8, 29, 41,
  215-16, 226-27
Cockburn, C., 143
Codorcet, Marquis de, 55
coercion: the state, 133
Cohen, L., 61
collective bargaining, 32, 112,
 113-14; *see also* JNC
collective engagement, 56, 57,
 59, 64, 66, 68, 199, 210
collectivism, 95, 121-22
 democracy and accountability,
  123, 126, 235
 education, 213, 230
 riots, 185, 192
 work, 109, 121, 122
 youth work, 19, 41, 52, 89,
  171, 174-75, 178-79, 212-
  13, 236
 self-organisation, 84, 106
commodification, 63, 68, 143,
 173, 195, 198, 208, 236
commodities, 95, 164, 188, 236

communication, 15, 52-53, 110, 123-24, 131-32, 141-42, 211

communications technologies, 52-54, 58, 59, 79, 208, 211, 232-33

communism, 55

Communist Party of Britain Marxist-Leninist, 109-10

community, 109, 123, 125-31
 meaning of, 59
 cohesion, 52, 126-27
 development, 33
 work, radical, 128

community-based provision, 36, 163

competences, definition of, 21-22

competition
 capitalist theories, 48, 55, 79
 multiculturalism, 196
 neoliberalism, 61, 79, 198
  violence, 67, 68
 public services, 71

computer games, 15, 207, 211, 227

Confederation of Heads of Young People's Services, 153

Connexions, 35, 52

consent, state's role in making, 133

Conservative Party: youth policies, 3, 158

constituent and constituted power, 131

consultants, freelance: in public services, 73, 127

Consumer kids, 206-8

consumerism, 47, 58, 60, 62-63, 166, 198-99, 205, 206-7, 210, 227; see also market, the

consumption, 60, 61

conversation, 131-32, 141-42; see also communication

Corfield, P. J., 91

costs of youth work, 35-36

Cottrill, A., 91

counter-culture, 126

Coventry, 152

CPBML, 109-10

craftspeople, youth workers as, 107-9

Craig, David, 71, 192

crime, 74, 129, 139, 140, 186, 191, 203, 209
 attitudes to, 64-65, 76, 220

criminal justice system, 140, 209
 costs of, 35

criminality, 65-66, 139

criminals, youth viewed as, 65, 158

crisis management, 76

Critical notes on 'The King of Prussia and social reform', 100-1

Cuba, 189

Cunningham, H., 231

curiosity, 161, 163, 220

Curtis, M., 191

'customers', service users as, 73

cuts: unjustified, 6, 75-76, 82

CWDC, 3, 31, 149, 150, 159

CYWU
 code of professional conduct, 104
 cuts, campaigns against, 6-7, 29, 112-13, 149, 151, 152, 154
 international campaigns, 79, 83, 117-18, 189, 191
 pay and conditions campaigns, 111-12, 113-17, 118-19
 youth categorisation, campaign against, 99

Youth Matters, response to, 39-40, 41
youth work values and standards, 25-26, 118-19, 149

D

Daily Show, The, 63
Davies, Bernard, 12, 40, 119
Davis, M., 66, 126
DCSF, 28, 159
Dean, J., 53, 59-60, 65, 93-94
debt, encouragement of, 72, 74, 81, 137
decision making: youth involvement, 28, 30, 37-38, 185-86
democracy, 123, 217, 228
 capitalism versus, 2
 neoliberalism, 57, 61, 62, 81, 198-99, 206, 209, 210, 211, 236
 attacks on public services, 71, 73, 75
 cyberspace and, 53-54
 lack of, 191, 193, 206
democracy
 lifeworld, 126, 131
 local, 34, 217
democratic accountability, 34, 49, 51, 73, 123, 137, 158
democratic education, 30
democratic engagement
 loss of, 3
 unions, 101-2, 124
democratic youth work, 37-38, 40, 52, 98, 127, 138, 188, 221, 235
 humour, 144
DENI, 19-20
DES, 188
Denny, Brian, 192, 197

Department for Children, Schools and Families, 28, 159
Department for Education and Skills, 35, 39, 41, 83
Department of Education and Science, 188
Department of Education Northern Ireland, 19-20
de-skilling, 142
DfES, 35, 39, 41, 83
dialogue: youth work, 42, 52, 63-64, 69, 131, 141-42, 166, 212-13
Dickens, Charles, 65
diet, 208
dissent, political, 131, 133, 141, 197, 228
diversity: youth service provision, 17, 18, 20
diversity, social, 18, 20, 25, 38
Don Quixote, 54-55
Dorling, Danny, 75, 184, 193-94
Doyle, Roddy, 190
Duckworth, J., 65, 191
Durkheim, Emile, 92

E

Eagleton, Terry, 188, 192, 193
Economic and philosophical manuscripts (Marx), 100
economic context of youth work, 70
Education Act 1944, 29
Education Act 1996, 27, 29
Education and Inspections Act 2006, 29, 148, 157, 188
Education and Libraries (Northern Ireland) Order 1986, 20
Education and Training Standards Committees, 153
education,

attack on, 5, 51, 68, 71
marketisation, 29, 193, 232-33
informal, 13, 39, 107, 153, 199, 205, 218, 226
reflective practice, 169, 170-75
radical, 227-30, 233-34, 236
Education Select Committee, 155
educational leisure-time, 27
educational theory:
Enlightenment, 55
educators, youth workers as, 11-43, 69-70, 101, 144, 159-62, 166, 188, 213, 225, 234-35
elections, young people and, 61-62
elite, the, 134
Elliott, L., 77
emancipatory youth work, 11, 12, 29-30, 37, 69, 150, 153, 188, 216, 228
empiricism, 172-73
employment, 14-15
empowerment: youth workers, 83-84
Enforced migration, 190
Engels, Friedrich, 190
England, 24-29, 41
enjoyability, 21, 24, 30-31
Enlightenment, The, 55, 58, 93, 194
equalities campaigns: union, 114-17
Erasmus, Desiderius, 231
'Establishment, the', 139
ethics: youth work, 41, 88, 106, 108-9, 175, 204
European Commission, 79
European Union, 50, 73, 79, 82-83, 133, 138, 192, 197, 198

Every Child Matters, 35
Evolutionary playwork and reflective analytic practice, 173
Ewen, John, 160
Examiner, The, 187
exploitation, 15, 95-96, 98, 105
Extending entitlement, 14, 15-19, 37

F

Factor, F., 39, 40-41
false consciousness, 60, 163
fashion, 207
fear, culture of, 65, 67, 138, 196-97, 199, 210
Federation of Detached Youth Workers, 6
feminism, radical, 94
feudalism, 91, 196
finance capital, deregulation of, 52, 76
finance capitalists, domination of, 72, 81, 133, 134
financial crisis, global, 77-78, 80
financial transactions tax, 82
Fine, B., 91
Finkielkraut, Alain, 91, 93
Finlayson, J. G., 123
First claim, 173
Fletcher Report, 112
flexibility, 193
Foundation learning, 28
fragmentation, social, 59
free enterprise', 48, 50
free speech, 141
free trade, 48, 50, 65, 136
Freire, Paulo, 12, 60, 131, 167, 172, 188, 216, 234
friendship, 42, 100
front-line services: artificially distinguished, 72-73
Fukuyama, Francis, 216

funding: youth service, 36, 76, 113, 130, 147-49, 154, 186-87, 212, 224, 226
fundraising, 36
Furlong, A., 19

G

gangs, 66, 127, 129, 184, 186, 191, 211, 225
Gargrave, Ron, 158
Gates, Bill, 233
George, Susan, 196
Germany: public investment, 76-77
Giddens, Anthony, 92
Gilbert, Francis, 67, 184
Gilchrist, A., 232
Giorgi, Shelley, 1, 6, 7
Giroux, Henry, 68, 196, 198-99, 203, 205-6, 208, 209-10, 212, 213
Glass-Steagall Act, 79
Glenny, M., 64, 129
globalisation, economic, 49, 80
Glyn, A., 189
Goliath, 184
Gramsci, Antonio, 12, 167, 234
Gray, A., 134
Gross Domestic Product, 76-77
group work, 161

H

Habermas, Jürgen, 123, 125, 126-27, 131
Hadley, F., 34
Hansard, 35
Hardt, Michael, 58, 121, 122
Harris, T., 126, 235-36
Hartmann, M., 134
Harvey, David, 50, 164, 191, 196, 197

health and safety at work, 51
healthcare, attack on, 5, 51, 68, 71
Hegel, G. W. F., 162, 222-23
Heroes in the evening mist, 97
Hidden talents III, 33
higher education
  attack on, 5
  privatisation, 74
  youth work qualifications, 30
Hobbes, Thomas, 60
Holy terror, 192
Honey, P., 171
hooks, bell, 188, 199
Howker, E., 64
Hudson, L., 171
Hughes, Beverley, 149
Hughes, Bob, 173-74
human genome project, 195
human nature, understandings of, 55
humanism, 231
humour, 141, 144
Hunt, Leigh, 187

I

idealism, 162, 166
identity, nature of, 54, 58, 59-61, 62, 91
Identity in Britain, 193
identity politics, 89, 93, 94
ideology, 163-64, 167, 236
immigrant communities, 187-88, 195
imperialism and racism, 195-96
In Defence of Youth Work statement, 26, 37-38
inclusivity, 19, 25
individualism, 48, 52, 59, 94-95, 137, 185, 220-21
  youth workers, 88-90

industry, British: run down, 70, 72, 77, 80, 137, 192
inequality, 75, 92-93, 193-94, 209-10
inequality and violence, 51, 184
information marketplace, 232-33
information technology, *see* communications technologies
innocence, loss of, 207
institutions under neoliberalism, 58-59
Integrated Youth Support Services, 11, 31, 59, 149, 151, 158
internationalism: CYWU, 117-18
Iraq, war on, 191
Ireland, Republic of, 13, 21, 190
crisis, 77
Irish Statute Book, 21
IYSS, 11, 31, 59, 149, 151, 158

J

Jackson Report, 112
Jeffs, T., 40-41
JNC, 3, 32, 39, 113-14, 115-17, 153
qualifications, 39, 91, 98
job security, 36, 80
jobs, 14-15, 80
Joint Negotiating Committee for Youth and Community Workers (JNC), 3, 32, 39, 113-14, 115-17, 153
Joseph Rowntree Foundation, 35

K

Kampfner, J., 191
Kashdan, T., 161
Katz, P., 91, 192, 197
Kelly, T., 2, 227, 228
Keynes, John Maynard, 56
King, J., 2
Klein, Naomi, 2, 197
Koehn, D., 106
Kolb, D. A., 171, 173

L

labour market, 14-15, 125, 164, 187, 193
deregulation, 51-52, 205
Labour, New: marketisation policies, 29
Lambie, G., 189
Lancashire, 151
language: youth, 141-42
Lansley, S., 190
law, rule of, 140, 141
leadership: youth work, 177-79
learning
radical tradition, 227-31
child-centred, 231
lifelong, 17-18, 24, 42, 126, 163
learning processes, 171-72, 227
legal system: unjust, 140
legislation, state, and youth work, 13, 30
leisure activity: youth work, 29, 35, 110, 130, 143, 154, 158, 160-61, 212, 226
LGA, 32-34
liberalisation', 71
liberalism, 48
liberation, 167
lifelong learning, 17-18, 24, 42, 126, 163

Lifelong Learning UK, 22, 24–25, 35, 135, 150, 152, 153
lifestyle experimentation, 59–60
lifeworld, 123–24, 125, 126, 127, 129, 130, 131, 134, 235
Lisbon Treaty, 133
local authorities: statutory duties, 26, 27–29
Local Government Act (Northern Ireland, 1972), 20
Local Government Association, 32–34
Locke, John, 55, 60
Lollards, 228
Lynam, P., 92

M

managerialism, new, 74–75
Manchester Girls' Clubs Workers' Union, 117
Mandel, Ernest, 133
marginalised groups: disposability concept, 58, 68, 143
market, the, *see also* consumerism; neoliberalism
consumerism, 47, 58, 222
children as consumers, 206–8
crime, 64
false consciousness, 60–61, 94–95, 127, 185, 209
globalisation myth, 80
historical development, 48, 49, 55, 56, 79, 81
people as commodities, 68
war, 68
democracy versus, 59, 126–27, 196, 198–99, 206, 210, 212
marketisation, *see also* privatisation
domestic properties, 137
everything, 49, 50–51, 58, 59

public services, 5, 49, 71
education, 5, 29, 193, 232–33
voluntary sector, 199
youth work, 29, 38, 148–49, 151–52, 157
Marr, Andrew, 7
Martin, J. W., 122
Marx, Karl, 100–101, 109, 162, 163, 188, 190, 216, 222, 223, 234
Mason, M., 54, 232–33
materialism, 162–63
Mayo, Ed, 206–8
McAlister, S., 20
McConnell, C., 41
McGiffen, S., 197
McKee, V., 35, 39
McLaren, Peter, 167, 234
media, 62, 63, 78, 207, 211, 218, 219–20, 227; *see also* television
attitude to working class, 124
attitude to youth, 12–13, 41
violence, 67
Meister, R., 91
Members of Parliament: for sale, 74
middle class
myth, 105
youth workers' self-perception, 88, 92
migration, 189–91, 195–96
Ministerial Conferences Steering Committee, 41
Monbiot, George, 74
money and wealth, 164
Montagu, Ashley, 195
moral purpose: youth work, 98, 106, 108–9; *see also* ethics: youth work
Morris, William, 15
multiagency/multidisciplinary teams, 36, 142–43, 149, 225

'multiculturalism', 194–95, 196
Mumford, A., 171

N

NAFTA, 50
Nairn, Agnes, 206–8
naive consciousness, 60
National Assembly for Wales, 14, 15–19
National Association of Youth and Community Education Officers, 88, 114, 116
National Council for Voluntary Youth Services, 153
national debt, 6, 72, 76, 82–83
National Health Service, 72, 136
  attack on, 5, 71
National Occupational Standards, 24
National Vocational Qualifications, 22, 106–7, 116, 150
National Youth Agency, 26, 27–28, 35, 106–7, 151, 152
nation-states
  nature of, 56–57
  origin of, 56
nationalisation, 42, 48, 56, 75, 79, 136–37
nature, separation from, 208
NAYCEO, 88, 114, 116
NCVYS, 153
NEET: social group, 23, 166–67, 184–85
Negri, Antonio, 58, 121, 122, 131, 133
neoliberalism, 29, 43, 47–84, 88–89, 128, 137, 196–99, 205–6, 209–11, 236; see also capitalism; market, the
  intolerant of resistance, 67, 210

managerial tools, 169
political nature, 47–48, 68
'positive activities', 157
New Labour
  marketisation policies, 29
  widened inequality, 75
Nicholls, Doug, 26, 32, 103, 111, 114, 191, 197
North American Free Trade Agreement, 50
Northamptonshire, 151
Northern Ireland, 19–21, 153
Norton, Rod, 22
NVQs, 22, 106–7, 116, 150
NYA, 26, 27–28, 35, 106–7, 151, 152

O

occupational standards, 22, 24
Ofsted, 34–35, 154, 224–25
oppression, 96
  notions of, 93–94
Ord, J., 159
organisation, political, and skill, 96
Osborne, George, 5
outsourcing: theft, 74
Oxfordshire, 155

P

Paine, Thomas, 229
Parliamentary Constituencies Bill, 5
Parliamentary Education Select Committee, 3, 13, 41
part-time youth workers, 114–17
participation-based youth work, 18, 19, 24, 27, 30, 33, 221
parties, political: as brands, 63
Paul, Leslie, 126

Paxman, Jeremy, 66, 134
pay, 72, 81–82, 149, 193; *see also*
 youth workers: pay
pensions, attack on, 50
Peston, Robert, 66
Pickett, Kate, 184, 194
Pilger, John, 66
Pinochet, General, 49
piracy: cyberspace, 54
Pitts, John, 21, 39, 40–41, 185,
 186
planning, economic, 48
Play Wales, 173
police, 139–40
political education, 160–62,
 170, 188, 217–18
political parties, 57, 63–64, 139,
 198
politicisation
 of youth, 5, 6
 of youth workers, 6, 43
politics: constrained, 212
politics, young people and,
 61–64
Popple, K., 232
'positive activities', 29, 35, 148,
 157, 159, 162, 165–68, 188,
 196, 212
Positive for Youth, 1, 41
power, constituted and
 constituent, 131
praxis, 167, 216
prices, 50–51
 PricewaterhouseCoopers,
 148–49, 152
pride, professional, 104–5
principal youth officers, 151
prisons, 137–38, 209, 211
private finance initiatives, 73
privatisation, 6, 50, 51, 70–71,
 88, 121, 137, 196; *see also*
 marketisation

youth service, 148–49, 151–52,
 157
professional associations, 26, 88
professional autonomy: youth
 workers, 148
professionalism, 88, 103
 definition, 104, 110
 youth workers, 103–10
profit, private, imperative 49,
 59, 125, 197
profit, rate of, 48
public sector investment,
 71–72
public sector workers,
 scapegoating of, 71, 78
public services, attack on, 3–6,
 71, 73–75, 78, 88, 149, 192
public spending: need to
 increase, 75–77
PYOs, 151

Q

Quality Assurance Agency
 (QAA), 30, 135, 152
quality supervision, 119

R

Race, Phil, 172
racial segregation, 194
racism, 127, 189, 194–95
radical youth work, 128
railway privatisation, 70
RAMPs, 116
Rand, Ayn, 48
Rapport, 73, 118
Reagan, Ronald, 49
recession, economic, youth
 work in, 32
recreational activity: youth
 work, 27, 29, 35, 110, 130,
 143, 154, 158, 160–61, 226
reflective practice, 169–75, 219

reflective analytical practice, 173-75
regional accreditation and moderation panels, 116
regulation, reduction of, 51, 52
relationships, social, 42, 121, 162-63, 164, 166, 167, 199, 235, 236
RESET, 35
resistance to neoliberalism, 68-69
Resler, H., 91, 92-93
respect, 17, 19, 20-21, 22, 24-25, 39, 67, 106, 184, 192
revolution, 100-1
Revolution, English (1649), 228
Rifkin, J., 54, 232-33
Rights of man, The, 229
rights-based definition of youth work, 17-19
riots, 185, 191-92
Rogers, Dave, 209
Rutter, M., 66

S

Sampson, Anthony, 66, 121, 190
Sapin, Kate, 12, 40-41
savings, 81
Schon, D. A., 173
Scotland, 22-23, 153
Scottish Executive, 22-23
scouts, 98, 229
Searching for community, 159
Second World War: postwar reconciliation, 117-18
self, nature of the, 54, 58, 59-61, 62, 91
self-esteem, 106, 218, 225, 236
self-help, 224

Sennett, Richard, 21, 49, 50, 52, 67, 107, 108, 109, 191, 193
Sercombe, Howard, 40-41, 106
Shiv, M., 64
shock doctrine, 197
Shor, I., 161
Shukra, K., 94
Simpson, Ludi, 194
skill, 107-9, 109-10, 169, 171, 175, 236
  political organisation and, 96
Smith, Adam, 48, 55, 81
Smith, H., 220
Smith, Mark K., 12, 40-41, 131, 188, 220
snobbery: youth workers, 89, 90
social breakdown, 75, 127, 130, 140, 194, 205
social categorisation, 92, 166-67
social change: youth workers' role, 12
social cleansing, 58
'social exclusion', 191
social inclusion versus capitalism, 2
social networking, 52-54, 59
social relationships, 42, 121, 162-63, 164, 166, 167, 199, 235, 236
socialism, 55, 96, 100-1, 121-32, 229-31, 236
socialist society, work in a, 15
socialist youth work, 215, 216
Sohn-Rethel, A., 91
solidarity, 49, 66, 83, 98, 100, 124
Somerset Youth Service, 76
speculation, financial, 47-48, 50, 53, 72, 77, 80-81, 82
standards of youth work, 34-35

state, the, 133-44
 changing nature, 50, 51,
  136-38
 responsibility for citizens, 58
status, 92-93, 103
statutory duties: local
  authorities, 26, 27-29
Stendhal, 67
Stewart, Jon, 63
subjects, nature of, 54, 58, 60
subversion, 101, 143-44, 188,
  228
suffrage, universal, 56
Sunday Times, The, 75
support: role of youth work,
  16-17, 22, 23, 28, 37, 52
Surrey CYWU, 112
surveillance, 66
Sustainable Communities Act,
  34
'symbolic' world, 57, 59

Thompson, E. P., 228
Tolpuddle Martyrs, 229
Tomkins, A., 134
trade unions, *see* unions
trade
 balance of, 72
 restrictions on, 50
Trades Union Congress, 82,
  116, 190-91
training of youth workers, 98,
  106-7, 109, 113, 116
*Transforming youth work:
 Resourcing excellent youth
 services*, 29, 39, 83
Transport and General
 Workers' Union, 149
Treasury, HM, 35
trust: youth work relationship.
  42, 185, 234
TUC 82, 116, 190-91
Twelvetrees, A., 232

T

targets, work related, 52, 74,
  142, 151, 154, 159
taxation, 6, 35, 51, 56, 76, 79
taxes, unpaid, 82
Taylor, C., 54
Tebbit, Norman, 190
television, 67, 126, 205-6, 211
Temple, J., 134
tendering process, 71
terms and conditions: youth
  workers, 51, 111-12, 113-17,
  147-48, 151, 206
Terror of neoliberalism, The, 196
Thatcher, Margaret, 192
 attack on unions, 4
 attack on youth, 114
 neoliberalism, 49
Thomas, Bethan, 193
Thomas, D., 232
Thompson Report, 41

U

ultra-left; views on youth
  work, 130, 142
unemployment, 14-15, 51, 70,
  76, 137, 204
unions, 96, 110, 124, 137
 educational role, 228-30
 policies on youth work, 3,
  6-7, 25-26
 youth work, 88, 101-2, 111-
  19, 128, 155-56, 189; *see also*
  CYWU; Unite
 Northern Ireland, 20
Unite, 3, 25-26, 35, 41, 83, 149,
  152, 153, 154, 159
United States: neoliberalism,
  204-6, 208
universities: current role, 5, 232
utilities, privatisation of, 51
utopianism. 223-24

V

value, working class, 94
Venezuela, 189
victim, cult of the, 93-94
violence, 51, 66, 67, 68, 69, 155, 183-85, 192, 204, 211
Vogel, L., 94
Voltaire, 55
voluntary nature of participation, 20, 21, 30-31, 32, 37, 38-39, 41, 166, 185
voluntary sector, marketisation of, 199
voluntary youth sector, 16-17, 112-13, 130-31, 147, 224
voting rights, 187
VPMCI, 189

W

wages, 51
Wakefield, 151
Wales, 13-14, 15-19, 30, 37, 153
 TUC, 153
Walsall: part-time youth workers agreement, 116
wars, 66, 68, 209
Warwickshire Court Case, 29
Wealth of nations, The, 48
wealth, 164
Weber, Max, 92
welfare, social: welfare economy 48-49
welfare state, 64, 75, 79, 101, 136-37
 destruction of, 51, 56, 224
Welsh Local Government Association, 13-14
Westergaard, J., 91, 92-93
Westminster Hall Debate (November 2010), 3, 155
What we stand for, 37-38

Wilkinson, Richard, 75, 184, 194
Williamson, Howard, 14, 40-41, 119
Winter, Richard, 110
WLGA, 13-14
women youth workers, 94
Wood, A., 122
Woodcraft Folk, 125-26
work, preparation for, 125
workers, interdependence of, 71-72
working class, 64, 105, 121-22, 124
 misconceptions, 91
 youth workers, 87-102, 106-7
working patterns, 36
World Trade Organization, 79
Wuthnow, R., 91
Wycliffe, John, 228

Y

Yob nation, 184
young people, *see* youth
Young, K., 40-41, 108-9
youth
 demonisation, 17, 42, 52, 65, 128, 137, 196, 203-4, 206, 210
 emancipation, 99-100
 other professions working with, 142-43
 policies, 187
 politicisation, 5, 6
 rights, 220
 threats to, 2-3, 6, 203-4
 treated as disposable, 58, 68, 143, 208-9, 211-12
 victims of neoliberalism, 68, 128
 viewed as criminals, 65, 158, 210
youth centres, 186-87, 225

youth clubs, 127-28, 158, 160
Youth Council (Northern Ireland), 20
Youth in a suspect society, 203-6, 208-13
Youth matters, 39
Youth Parliament, UK, 30, 225
youth professional status, 150
youth service
  funding, 36, 76, 113, 130, 147-49, 154, 186-87, 212, 224, 226
  plot to demolish, 41, 155, 226-27
  privatisation, 148-49, 151-52
Youth Service (Northern Ireland) Order 1989, 20
youth work
against neoliberalism, 61, 68-69
assessment, 3, 150, 154, 169-70, 173, 174
attacks on, 68, 70, 137
competences, 21-22, 106-7, 152
complexity, 31
costs, 35-36
definitions, 11-43, 104, 135
deprofessionalisation, 148, 149-50
dialogue, 42, 52, 63-64, 69, 131, 141-42, 166, 212-13
economic context, 70
emancipatory, 11, 12, 29-30, 37, 69, 150, 153, 188, 216, 228
equality of relationships, 186
historical foundations, 227-32
leisure, 29, 35, 110, 130, 143, 154, 158, 160-61, 212, 226
power, 2, 42
process versus product, 216-17

public funding, 147, 148
qualifications, 30, 31
standards, 34-35, 154
international, 219, 225
residential, 219
Youth Work Act (Republic of Ireland, 2001), 13, 21
Youth Work Curriculum Statement for Wales, 30
Youth Work Week, 26
youth workers
accountability, 88, 148
class consciousness, 87-102
communities of interest, 83
craftspeople, 107-9
educators, 11-43, 69-70, 101, 144, 159-62, 166, 188, 213, 225, 234-35
leaders, 177-79
levels of awareness, 138-39
pay, 32, 51, 96, 103, 111-12, 147-48, 152, 193
politicisation, 6, 43
professional autonomy, 148
professional validation, 135, 151
professionals, 103-10
self-organisation, 83-84
shortage, 113, 155
Shylock, 140
terms and conditions, 51, 111-12, 113-17, 147-48, 151, 206
trade unionism, 7
training, 98, 106-7, 113, 116, 153, 154, 225-26
victims, 26
working class, 87-102, 106-7
working for the state, 134
part-time, 114-17

Z

Zizek, Slavoj, 2, 57, 66, 70